D1407017

"The Mentally Sound Dog

How to Shape, Train & Change Canine Behavior))

Gail I. Clark, Ph.D
William N. Boyer, Ph.D

Alpine
Blue Ribbon Books

Alpine Publications, Inc., Loveland, Colorado

THE MENTALLY SOUND DOG
How to Shape, Train & Change Behavior

Cataloging in Publication

Clark, Gail I., 1950–
    The mentally sound dog: how to shape, train & change canine behavior / Gail I. Clark, William N. Boyer.
    280 p.   cm.
    Includes bibliographical references (p. 2) and index.
    ISBN 0-931866-67-7
    1. Dogs—Training. 2. Dogs—Behavior. 3. Dogs—Psychology.
    I. Boyer, William N., 1937–   . II. Title.
    SF431.C513   1995
    636.7'0887—dc20   95-15516
                                                               CIP

This book is available at special quantity discounts for breeders and for club promotions, premiums, or educational use. Write for details.

Disclaimer: Throughout this book, the dog is referred to as "he" for the sole purpose of brevity and clarity for the reader, and not to be construed as a preference for one sex over another.

Front Cover Photo: Copyright Wendy Senger, Photos Plus

All Other Photos: Copyright Kent Dannen, unless otherwise indicated.

Illustrations: Martha Lageschulte.

1 2 3 4 5 6 7 8 9 10

Printed in the United States of America.

Table of Contents

To
all the people and dogs
I have had the pleasure of working with over the years,
and to all those who helped make this book a reality.
And to my patient family and loving companion animals.

Acknowledgements

Contributions and support for this book came from many people and although not everyone is mentioned individually by name, their work and patience is greatly appreciated and remembered. We are very grateful to the handlers and owners who took part in the photo shoots. Their patience and cooperation produced some very memorable pictures. Many special thanks go to Kent and Donna Dannen and Melvin Tucker for their ideas and quality photo production. We are grateful for the exceptional talent of Martha Lageschulte who created the wonderful illustrations. A special thanks to John Mulnix, D.V.M., for his interest in reading the manuscript and for his expert advice on the issues which overlapped medical and behavioral fields. Thanks to Mary Hughes whose hunger to get this book's unique and practical material out to the public chained me to the computer. To Kathy Heun, fellow trainer and long-time friend, thanks for patiently reading every draft of everything I've ever written. Your support and excitement for my achievements has always been a source of inspiration. Finally, this book could not have been possible without my soul mate of 23 years, Richard Clark, who was my man-Friday when things needed to be done.

Gail I. Clark, Ph.D.
William N. Boyer, Ph.D.

Preface

Our goal was to write a book that was straightforward, yet above all, relevant to the interests of dog owners and trainers. The book was designed to provide basic canine learning principles that relate to many meaningful everyday examples rather than list technical findings and theory. To meet this objective, we describe in a simple and clear fashion, numerous obedience training and behavior problem circumstances that dog owners and trainers typically experience and can easily identify with.

Besides offering many practical training techniques, which readers can easily master themselves, the book also includes a wealth of practical information to help readers understand the developmental nature of dogs and promote responsible dog ownership as well.

Finally, throughout the book we have inserted a number of engaging photographs. While some authors may use such items for digression purposes, perhaps to reinforce page turning or make books appear a little shorter, our hope was that our photos would not only make our subject matter more realistic, but also give it more impact.

Foreword

Drs. Clark and Boyer have written an excellent book on the multiple aspects of dog ownership. Dr. Clark's skill and knowledge as an animal trainer, dog breeder, behaviorist, and owner of many fine pets and animal companions shows through in this book. The authors have skillfully covered a wide array of questions and subjects that have confronted all dog owners at one time or another. This book covers training and behavioral concerns from the time the puppy arrives home with his new owner to that very painful and final good-bye that we all face sooner or later. Having worked with all of Gail's dogs as a veterinarian over the past 10 years, I can honestly say that she has never presented a "bad" dog. What a pleasure the life of a veterinarian would be if all our clients could earnestly apply what the authors teach in this book.

John A. Mulnix, D.V.M.
1995

Introduction

Over the last two decades, dog training has undergone tremendous change. Today's obedience consumer wants to know more than just how to teach the dog to sit, down, and stay. Average pet owners not only want their dogs to sit, they want to know how to prevent and fix behavior problems, and why their dogs behave as they do. Most contemporary pet owners also have an idea of how they wish to accomplish this training. The average pet owner is much more educated than in years past and therefore demands that the trainer explain and defend why and how a training method works. The modern pet owner is looking for positive educational methods rather than the forced training so popular twenty years ago. In order to keep up with the demand from the general public for these newer training methods, trainers have sought higher education about canine behavior through classes, seminars, and books that address the behavior of the domestic dog. The successful instructor must now understand more than the mechanical aspects of training; he or she must demonstrate a conceptual understanding of canine behavior, learning, and problem solving and communicate that information clearly to the pet owner. As a trainer for the general public for the last eighteen years, my own class material has gone through a drastic evolution. When I first started teaching, my classes were described as obedience classes, and my class material, like that of all the other trainers in my area, consisted only of come, sit, down, heel, and stay. Over the years, by demand of the pet owner, the focus of the class has become behavior. Instead of being an obedience class, the class is now a behavioral course that teaches obedience to channel behavior. Similarly, the material in this book is for trainers who wish to give their clients more than just an obedience class and for pet owners who want to go beyond basic obedience training. Lay readers can easily grasp and apply the learning theories and problem-solving methods presented, and professional trainers will find much of value to incorporate in their own training programs. They also will be able to extrapolate from the concepts fresh ideas for working out behavior problems and teaching more complex tasks. The trainer who understands motivation, successive approximation, reinforcement versus punishment, reinforcement schedules, and the difference between a bribery and reward system can effectively teach a dog to complete any task, whether for basic control or for a precision performance in a competition trial.

Once the basic theories of canine learning and behavior are mastered, all readers can creatively use them to train and happily live with any age, size, or temperament of the domestic dog.

1

The Domestic Dog and His Behavior

The domestic dog is an animal that has lived under the roof and protection of humans for centuries and is not a wolf. He is as far removed from the den as humans are from the cave.

Although some canine behaviors may parallel the behavior of the wolf, the domestic dog has developed many unique adaptive behaviors as a result of his cohabitation, companion relationship, and interaction with humans. Consequently, training techniques extrapolated from wolf behavior are not necessarily effective with the domesticated dog. For example, the she wolf is said to pick up the misbehaving pup by his scruff, shake him, drop him to the ground, and pin him there. The wolf's behavior is interpreted as a correction to the pup that demonstrates the mother's dominance. Theoretically, if the trainer or pet owner imitates this correction, it should demonstrate to the dog undisputed dominance and control. While the wolf pup may understand such language, the domestic dog may not. There is little evidence to indicate that

The wolf in his natural habitat.

The domestic dog. Although a few breeds of dog may look similar to the wolf, the domestic dog is very different in behavior.

domestic bitches shake their puppies by the scruff or use the alpha rollover as a correction. In addition, even if bitches did correct their puppies in this manner, domestic puppies, unlike their wolf counterparts, are usually removed from the litter long before there is an opportunity to experience such discipline. And, even if the puppy does understand the correction, the method needs to be adapted after the dog reaches his adult size and weight to be effective. These are only a few of the factors that preclude correcting the dog in a manner designed for wolf puppies; therefore, trainers and pet owners would benefit greatly in understanding dog behavior as opposed to wolf behavior.

A Different Species: The Domestic Dog

In order to understand dog behavior, the trainer and pet owner must first consider the effects of the human contact that occurs from the day the domestic pup is born until the end of the animal's life. These interactions are strong catalysts that add to the inherent differences between the wolf and dog. Whereas the dog easily weaves into the family and social structure of humans, the wolf has failed to do so. The integration of the dog into the human environment is so comfortable and complete that many people even refer to their dogs as their children. This reference is not an accident. The analogy comes to mind for many people because the canine is often adopted as a family member and fits the child's role easily and naturally. To create the most rewarding human-canine relationship, the unique qualities of the domestic dog must be considered by themselves rather than from the standpoint of the wolf.

The dog, like the human child, seeks affection and approval, and has the ability to learn. Like children, dogs are playful, affectionate, curious, adaptable, innocent, and basically happy-go-lucky creatures. Depending upon the home environment, and many other factors, the dog, like the child, can be an angel or a delinquent.

DELINQUENT DOGS
Few dogs go through life without acquiring some behaviors an owner finds annoying or even intolerable. Intolerable behavior can be the result of either genetics, caused by unknowledgeable breeders indiscriminately breeding poor-tempered dogs, or the environment, in

4

which the dog has been raised without proper training and guidance. Like children, if dogs are not disciplined and taught manners, they can become out of control and a problem to themselves and everyone in the community. These problem dogs all too often wind up at animal shelters waiting on death row for an unnecessary demise. If the owner is willing to endure the undesirable behaviors, the problem dog may receive a lifetime sentence to the backyard with very little human contact. The jail sentence to the yard only exacerbates the problem behavior, and often turns the dog into an incessant barker, chewer, digger, or aggressor. Fortunately, behavior modification through obedience training is very effective in repairing problem behavior.

Prevention and Solutions for the Problem Dog

A comprehensive obedience and behavioral course can teach owners how to prevent and resolve behavior problems. The ideal purpose of obedience training is to channel appropriate behavior and discourage problem behavior. The majority of dogs, regardless of their age, can be rehabilitated. Problem behavior can be redirected into appropriate behavior with consistent, persistent, and clear communication from the dog owner through obedience training. Obedience training communicates concrete rules which provide the dog with predictable outcomes via reinforcement and consequences. Obedience training with competent instruction teaches the owner the essential skills for raising a well-mannered, well-adjusted canine by using principles of consistency, persistency, and reinforcement for good and inappropriate behavior.

Thus, the purpose of the following material is to give the reader a practical working knowledge of how to modify the dog's behavior through obedience training and offer methods to prevent and resolve problem behavior. The material provides an excellent knowledge base about dogs and their behavior, from puppyhood to adulthood, to compliment any level or quality of training program available.

Photo by Richard Piliero

2

The Companion Dog

The human-canine bond is a powerful relationship. One need only glance at humankind's art and literature over the past thousand years to grasp the impact the domestic canine has had on our lives. The famous phrase, "man's best friend" is only one of many attempts to describe the quality and significance of the enduring and affectionate attachment between a person and a dog. For many people, the attachment is so strong that the dog is often described and treated as a family member or a surrogate child. Whether the dog is considered a best friend or something more like a blood relative, the attraction between canine and human has endured over centuries and is an integral part of our civilization. By understanding the importance of this bond, the trainer and pet owner may be motivated to put forth an ardent effort to improve the relationship.

Benefits

Researchers investigating the benefits associated with the human companion animal bond have linked the interaction between humans and companion animals to improved health. These studies suggest that people who pet friendly dogs exhibit a decrease in blood pressure and reductions in cardiovascular, behavioral, and psychological indicators of anxiety. In addition, the nurturing of an animal seems to have positive consequences on intimate human interactions. The nurturing behaviors involved in caring for pets may have positive psychological and emotional health effects that may also assist the pet owner in finding solace in a busy world.

However, there is no evidence that blood pressure decreases in the presence of a disobedient animal. On the contrary, the unruly canine may cause enough stress in a household to damage relationships between family members. An extreme case was a couple who was contemplating divorce as a result of heated arguments about the dog. The couple owned three dogs and described their dogs as their children. Two dogs were designated as the wife's dogs, and the third, a young hyperactive dog, was considered the husband's dog. The husband traveled

The human-canine bond is a powerful, enduring and affectionate attachment.

We share every aspect of our lives with our dogs.

extensively, which left the wife home all day with the dogs. The wife had spent much effort training her two dogs; however, she did not want to interfere with the bond between her husband and his dog and did not train the third dog. In spite of this woman's devoted love for dogs, the husband's dog was so out of control that she confessed to her psychologist that she was developing an immense dislike for the dog and that this was the root of the arguments between her and her husband. The psychologist contracted with the couple to seek professional advice about the animal's behavior. The wife was assured that her training the dog would not interfere with the relationship between her husband and the dog. She attended training classes with the dog, and the dog was brought under control. The arguments and additional stress in their lives caused by the dog ceased, as did thoughts of divorce. As naturally as the benefits that accompany a good companion relationship with a dog strengthen intimate relationships and family interactions, so may stressful interactions with a dog permeate and undermine relationships.

Owners and Dog Behavior Problems

Clearly, the quality of behavior the dog exhibits directly affects the owner's satisfaction with the relationship. An owner chooses a companion animal for the animal's expected behavior, and most people who acquire dogs have expectations about how their ideal dog should behave. Owners often have grandiose visions of their new puppy developing into the perfectly behaved canine citizen. When the puppy turns out to be a delinquent without the proper intervention and supervision to direct his behavior, particularly during the 3-9 month old stage, disappointment and disillusionment may breed a stressed relationship.

Dogs who exhibit behavior problems run a particularly high risk of being rejected by their owners. Even pet owners who have a very strong commitment to and love for their dogs find embracing and showering their animals with affection difficult after entering the house and having to wade through a puddle of urine and recline on a shredded sofa. The mere anticipation of returning home every night after a hard day's work to a house that looks like the Roman ruins would be enough to alienate any normal pet owner from the cute ball of teeth and fur. While the puppy consumes the carpet, the owner endures a daily diet of stress.

Returning home to canine Roman ruins.

A pragmatic understanding of canine behavior is essential to rehabilitate the delinquent canine and foster a healthy, happy companion relationship. A basic understanding of canine behavior will help resolve and prevent inappropriate behaviors that detract from a quality human-canine bond and produce stress, tension, and anxiety for the owner. Owners who seek professional behavior counseling and training to channel their dogs' behavior will have more satisfying relationships with their dogs. A dog's obedience performance may even increase the owner's pride and self-esteem.

Building a Relationship through Obedience

Obedience training develops a consistent, common language between human and dog in which both parties may trust and rely upon the information transmitted. Obedience training as a communication tool informs the dog of the owner's expectations, rules, and how to earn reward and avoid punishment. Training also promotes a meaningful, consistent, vocabulary which assists the dog in interpreting the owner's words and associated body language. The language communicates specific rules to the dog, which encourages the dog to feel secure about his environment. The obedience trained dog learns which behaviors are acceptable, and subsequently, feels more secure and confident about the surroundings and how the humans will react. Consistent rules replace uncertainty, and thus reduce fear and stress for the dog. Obedience training also offers a wonderful opportunity for the astute trainer to observe and gain an understanding of the dog's body language, and to interpret the messages sent. A dog and owner who can successfully communicate their needs, desires, and expectations will naturally develop a stronger bond and a closer relationship through positive interactions.

Good Expectations Foster A Positive Relationship

Optimistic puppy owners usually envision their dog ignoring the passing cat and lovingly coming to them every time they call. But, without obedience training, returning on every call even when there is no passing cat, may be very unrealistic. When an owner teaches obedience to a dog, he or she knows what behaviors to expect from the dog at different levels of training. Owners with realistic expectations about their dogs' behavior will avoid the stress of giving commands their dogs do not understand or cannot perform correctly. The dog's stress is also greatly reduced and negative interactions are eliminated when the dog knows how to earn praise and respond correctly to the owner's commands.

POSITIVE VERSUS NEGATIVE INTERACTIONS

Positive interactions promote a secure companion relationship, whereas severe punishment and negative interactions increase insecure behavior and may prevent mutual trust. A good example of a negative interaction and its consequences is shown in the following typical scenario about the dog that runs off from the owner. Against all reason, the owner who has never taught the dog to reliably return on command when off lead, takes off the lead in the park to allow the dog to run loose. The dog charges away from the owner at lightning speed for a free two hour frolic around the neighborhood. The owner can be seen and heard screaming unmentionable words as the dog circles for the twentieth time. The dog's obnoxious behavior clears the park of all humans, and he finally tires of playing "catch me if you can." Just as he begins to return, envisioning the food dish and cool water waiting at home, the infuriated owner screams, with obvious frustration, one final command for the dog to return. The dog finally saunters over to the owner, since there is nothing more interesting going on, only to be grabbed by the skin and punished for running off. The dog immediately associates being grabbed and punished with the act of obeying the call to return to the owner, and not with running off. The owner precipitated a negative interaction in several ways that could easily have been avoided. First, the dog should not have been let off lead in an uncontrolled environment and given the opportunity to disobey a command until trained. Second, punishing the dog instead of rewarding the dog for returning on command taught the dog that returning to the owner was unrewarding. And last, harsh, painful, or abusive corrections such as grabbing the dog by the skin are very aversive and only teach the dog to mistrust the owner's hands and to avoid close contact.

Trust and close contact must not be abused if strong emotional bonds are to be developed between human and dog. Trust can be established only through consistent communication, humane discipline, and positive interactions all of which can be achieved through proper obedience training and environmental management.

Owner erroneously teaching the dog the game, "Catch me if you can!"

3

Fostering Good Behavior

The puppy owner's preconceived notion that the dog will be a naturally well-behaved, devoted companion generally stems from the tendency to store mostly the good memories about childhood pets. One client who scheduled a consultation to discuss a very long list of dog behavior problems was very frustrated with his new puppy after recalling the dogs he grew up with. All of the puppies he remembered while growing up were perfectly well-behaved, and he could not understand why his present dog was so badly behaved. When I asked him how much training he had done with his dog, he indignantly commented, "Oh, none. We never had to train our puppies at home; they always knew what to do." Intrigued by the idea of puppies that were perfectly behaved without training, I asked this gentleman to tell me more about his childhood pets. During the course of the discussion he admitted that these dogs were never let in the house. When pushed to remember more things about his dogs, he recalled that maybe they were kept outside because they had accidents in the house, and yes, there might have been a couple of bushes eaten and a few holes in place of the planted flower beds. Even if this client's childhood pets were truly perfectly behaved animals, he needed to accept the concept that no two puppies are the same, and each puppy comes equipped with his own set of individual behaviors and responses. Pet owners who only retain the fond memories of past dogs are quickly disillusioned by the time their new puppy reaches 4 1/2 months of age and displays destructive and independent behavior. Older dogs acquired from other homes may also harbor some serious surprises for the new owners. Nonetheless, people often wrongly enter the pet companion relationship with unrealistic expectations about the animal's behavior, and consequently, rarely dog-proof the environment or plan to address problem behaviors as they arise.

The Dog's Environment

Many problem behaviors can be directly tied to environmental factors, and can often be prevented or controlled by changing the dog's surroundings. For example, a dog who spends most of the day sharing a chain link fence with the canine next door that barks all day and chases butterflies along the fence, would have to be deaf and ill not to be tempted to join in on the merriment. Likewise, the fence that separates the 2-year-old male from the neighbor bitch who just came into season better not be scalable, or made of smooth steel to keep the dog from fathering a litter and effectively learning fence jumping in the process. A yard that offers a dog no shade is another example of the environment encouraging inappropriate behavior; the dog may learn to dig down to the cool earth for some relief from the heat. Some dogs can spend many unsupervised hours at a time in the backyard without developing behavior problems, while some dogs cannot stay in the yard for two minutes without barking, digging, chewing, or escaping. Whether the dog's habitat simply needs modification or he is in need of serious behavior therapy and environment changes, depends upon his problem behavior and the underlying causes.

Communication Problems

Dog behavior problems are frequently the result of unclear communication. The owner may not even be aware that the messages he is sending to the dog are confusing. The owner of a well-trained Standard Poodle was unaware of her confusing messages during an epic long session of grooming. The Poodle tired and attempted to sit. The owner, wanting the dog to remain standing, yelled "Don't sit." The dog stood for a few seconds in a crouched position, and, confused about what the word "don't" meant, tried to sit again. Totally perplexed, he was trying very hard to comply with what he thought was his owner's request. Good communication is comprised of clear, consistent, distinct messages. A dog cannot possibly respond correctly if the vocabulary or the rules change at whim from day to day. Another example of inconsistent, mixed messages is demonstrated by the owner who allows a behavior occasionally, punishes the dog for it at other times, and does not use distinct cues to inform the dog when the conduct is not acceptable. A dog who is petted for jumping up when the owner arrives home from softball practice is going to be encouraged, to the owner's

Avoid mixed messages.
Commands should be clear and consistent.

dismay and anger, to jump up when the owner comes home from a party all dressed up. Unfortunately, few dogs are able to distinguish between the owner's softball jump up clothes and the owner's party stay off clothes. Consequently, without any distinct warning, the dog may receive a swat for jumping up on the wrong clothes. The dog learns that jumping up will sometimes be rewarded by petting and other times, for no apparent reason, will elicit a smack. The only lesson a dog may learn from inconsistent messages is that the rules are unstable. Clear and consistent communication requires that an owner teach a command for each desired and undesired behavior to inform the dog about acceptable behavior. For example, you can teach a jump up command that tells the dog jumping up is acceptable, and another command such as, "off," that instructs him not to jump up. When messages are confusing, the dog can neither establish a pattern to earn the owner's approval, nor predict the owner's reactions. The dog who cannot establish a way to earn his owner's approval gives up trying to please. The dog who does not know how to predict his owner's reactions becomes fearful, mistrusting, and avoidant.

Dogs also become fearful when the correction is too abusive. For a correction to be effective and convey accurate information to the dog, it must fit the transgression. A puppy that is teething and nips does not need, and will not understand, a correction fit for the dog who has just bitten someone because the person's hand touched his food dish. Unnecessarily abusive corrections will inhibit the dog from developing an outgoing, joyous, companion personality. The owner who finds a day-old pile of feces left by the 10-week old puppy and reacts by beating the puppy until he cowers has only taught the animal to be very fearful and mistrusting in his owner's presence when feces are on the floor. Beatings and physical abuse only produce fear and mistrust. Abusive treatment of any living entity is inhumane, cruel, and not to be tolerated for any reason. If any canine behavior, perhaps other than a deliberate act of aggression, can elicit enough anger in a pet owner to result in a severe beating, then ownership of a dog should be seriously reevaluated and professional advice sought. A trusting relationship cannot develop or flourish in an abusive atmosphere.

Furthermore, a dog may also learn to mistrust an owner who delivers untimely corrections or discipline. Specifically, a correction must occur immediately following the behavior or during the enactment of an undesirable behavior. The dog will not connect a correction with the undesirable behavior if the correction occurs several minutes after the event. The puppy who was beaten after the owner came home to a dried up mess on the floor associated the punishment with the owner coming home rather than the accident on the floor. The dog associates punishment, and praise for that matter, with the last event or action that occurred prior to the consequence. A correction must occur during or immediately following the behavior for the dog to connect the punishment with the undesirable action. On the other hand, if the owner should unintentionally lose control of his or her temper once or twice in the relationship, a dog is a very forgiving animal. Depending upon how traumatic the temper tantrum was, the dog may eventually forget and forgive.

Communication problems also develop when the owner credits the dog with too much ability to comprehend messages. Such an owner expects the dog, frequently without the dog receiving formal training, to automatically know what or what not to do. When the dog does not respond as expected, the owner becomes angry and punishes the dog. The owner who truly believes the dog inherently knows which behaviors are wrong neglects to teach the dog right from wrong. The dog, who in spite of the owner's claims cannot read minds, does not know what behaviors deserve the punishment or how to avoid a reprimand, and therefore becomes mistrustful and confused. Quite often, faulty expectations are associated with house soiling. A good many people who have dogs that soil the house really believe that the dog knows not to eliminate in the house. These people often claim that the dog is urinating or defecating in the house out of spite. These owners may not realize that a couple of dry nights or days does not necessarily mean the dog is thoroughly housebroken. Even if the dog has been maintaining clean standards for months, there are many reasons why dogs may regress in their elimination habits, and spiteful behavior would be the least likely factor. A typical incident of regression may take place when the puppy owner has a schedule change and cannot let the dog outside to eliminate at the same time of day, and does not think to change the dog's feeding schedule. The dog, either not used to or incapable of holding the matter with the change in schedule, soils the carpet. The owner is gone and no one is around to communicate to the dog that soiling the carpet is improper behavior. Thus, the dog, who was supposedly house trained, learned that when his owner is not home, soiling is acceptable. Unfortunately, making matters worse, the dog was also richly reinforced for soiling when the bladder and sphincter muscles were relieved of pressure. Unless the dog is corrected during or immediately after the act, he cannot possibly know what is expected, and thus, should not be accused of deliberate spiteful behavior. Owners who believe their dogs hold grudges and purposefully retaliate with spiteful behaviors will brew unwarranted feelings of guilt, frustration, and anger. Such feelings will surely and wrongly poison the companion relationship.

Unintentional Messages

An open line of communication between owner and dog does not always ensure that the messages sent will be received correctly. A common instance in which unintentional messages are sent to a dog is during a fearful episode. The dog encounters a frightening object, event, or person and displays a variety of fear reactions, which may include shaking, barking, and backing away. The owner then sends out messages to comfort and assure the dog that there is no reason to be fearful. These messages are highly potent as the owner lovingly strokes the dog and commiserates with a cross between baby talk and sincere empathy, "It's okay, no one will hurt you." The message the owner intends to send to the dog is the information that the situation is not threatening. The message the dog receives through the stroking and baby talk is that acting and being fearful is rewarding and pleasing to the owner. Being consoled and stroked overshadows any information the dog could receive from the environment should he be allowed to remain in the situation without any intervention. Furthermore, the dog is reinforced for exhibiting fearful behavior by the pleasure of being stroked and consoled. Avoid the strong temptation to lovingly comfort the fearful dog lest he learn to act frightened for subsequent reinforcement.

Observing the Dog's Behavior

As easily as fearful conduct can be reinforced unknowingly and unintentionally, other undesirable behaviors may become part of the dog's repertoire simply by not being discouraged. Frequently, the average pet owner misses cues that signal forthcoming behavior, particularly cues associated with aggression. The dog that stops eating when someone passes the food bowl does not draw much attention from the passerby, yet this action is a warning sign that the dog is learning to protect the

The first signs of aggression may be subtle and the cues may be missed by inexperienced pet owners.

food dish. While protecting a food dish sounds harmless enough (after all, few people are in the market for a used dirty old dog bowl), the dog can easily escalate the protective behavior with little or no provocation, to growling and even biting when an unsuspecting victim enters the room. Generally, the first hints of aggression are very subtle, and a pet owner may easily miss the signals. If the cues are ignored and the dog continues without a correction, or "attitude adjustment," he learns the response is acceptable. Consequently, the behavior will intensify and most likely generalize so that anyone walking near the food bowl will be in jeopardy. To prevent undesirable behaviors from being reinforced unintentionally, monitor the dog's reactions closely to quickly discourage inappropriate behaviors before they become part of his behavior pattern.

Climbing the household social ladder.

GOOD BEHAVIOR VS. CHAOS

Inappropriate behavior such as aggression is not a sign that the dog does not love his owner. It simply reflects the dog's natural desire to establish a social order. The canine is a social animal. To avoid anarchy, any society, including the canine society, needs a leader. Since leaders enjoy certain benefits not available to the followers, few dogs miss applying for the position if the opportunity arises. Unfortunately, if these attempts to climb the social ladder go unchecked, the dog may become demanding and aggressive. A grumble that is not corrected when the dog is physically removed from the couch may intensify to tomorrow's snap. Each time an aggressive or dominant act goes unchecked, the dog becomes more confident to continue and persist in attempts to elevate up the social ladder. A dominant animal that feels threatened or challenged will bite in defense, and a dog who is allowed to exhibit dominance over his owner is a dangerous, uncontrolled dog. Serious ambition needs to be curtailed; negotiation for top position is unacceptable. Although the pet owner buys the dog food, and therefore, deserves the dominant position, the canine will persist in taking advantage of any opportunity to climb the social ladder. These attempts at promotion must be snuffed out if human and dog are to live safely and harmoniously in the same household.

20

PERSISTENCY MUST PREVAIL

Plainly, the dog who persists in taking opportunities to be leader will also take advantage of the owner's lack of persistency. Should you give in, the dog learns very quickly that his own persistence will be rewarded. For example, the excitable dog has an enormous amount of energy, which makes enforcing the stay command very difficult. The dog is told to stay, and within three seconds pops up. The owner walks over and places the dog in position again, and again, and again, at which point the owner finally tires and gives up. Instead of the owner being more persistent and tiring the dog out, and teaching the dog that there is no other option than to stay, the dog is rewarded by the owner for popping up and not giving in to the battle first. Consequently, when the next battle occurs, the dog will endure even longer because he has already learned that persistence is the way to obtain reinforcement. Conversely, the stubborn owner who refuses to give in until the dog obeys will be richly rewarded when the dog concedes to authority. If the owner is not persistent and does not enforce commands, the dog will generalize and take advantage of this weakness in other situations as well.

Clearly, both persistency and consistency are critical elements in a good line of communication. A good communication system conveys precise and reliable information that is essential in developing and maintaining a well-mannered and properly behaved companion dog.

4

Causes of Behavior Problems

Evidence of problem behavior is fairly easy to recognize: the chewed shoe, the backyard that looks like an excavation site, the canceled checks for paid barking fines. However, these problems may stem from a variety of conditions that are not always obvious or identifiable to the owner. Although identifying a problem's cause does not guarantee a cure, understanding the motivation behind it can be very useful in resolving the problem behavior. A behavior known to originate from loneliness may be quickly and easily cured by leaving a radio on when no one is home. The teething puppy's energy can be miraculously redirected from the sofa to a tasty knuckle bone. Insight into the possible root of a problem behavior can allow you to predict and even prevent certain behaviors from becoming difficult, frustrating, and incurable problems for the household.

Breed Differences

Behaviors that are the result of characteristics bred into the dog often manifest themselves as problems, particularly if the animal is no longer used for the role he was bred to fill. For instance, the Rottweiler was bred as a guard or police dog and is not easily intimidated as a pet; therefore, he may exhibit aggressive behavior toward people and other dogs. The Border Collie, bred to herd and keep intense watch over sheep, may fixate on and herd the first woolly human foot in motion. The Greyhound, a coursing animal, may not let a furry critter or cat pass without a good run for its money and remaining cat lives. Dogs who have been bred for a strong purpose and wind up as sedentary pets may be driven to vent working urges. Creative channeling of energy, may be the answer for the unemployed canine. Perhaps the terrier whose life goal is to burrow holes through land and carpet to chase vermin can be satisfied with furry toys hidden in a private sandbox. The sandbox can be contained within a pen and lined on the bottom with chicken wire to prevent damage to the yard. If the animal's energy is

In following his herding instincts, this Bearded Collie is doing
what he is bred to do.

spent in the pen, the yard and house may be the chosen spot for the dog to relax rather than dig. Considering the characteristic traits and temperaments of the dog's breed or combination of breeds may be the key to finding ways to channel pent up urges or energy that would otherwise manifest as problem behavior.

Nature Versus Nurture

A dog's innate temperament is another large factor in behavior problems. A variety of temperaments that predispose dogs to certain behaviors can be passed from the dam to the puppies, either genetically or through the dam's behavior toward the pups. A dam's overly assertive interactions are learned and imitated by the puppies. In addition, the dam's emotions in reaction to events in the environment cause hormonal and chemical changes. These hormones and chemicals travel through the pregnant bitch's bloodstream and undoubtedly have a profound affect on the fetuses' system, and consequently, their temperament. An aggressive dam is much more likely to produce aggressive puppies than is a nonaggressive dam. Aggression may also be passed to the puppies from the sire's genes which may contain coding for inordinate amounts of hormones such as testosterone which influence aggressive behavior. Nervousness, another undesirable trait in a dog, may be passed through genetic material. The environment or events are often blamed for the nervous or fearful dog, and therefore many breeders feel justified in breeding these fearful animals based on the premise that the temperament is independent of the animal's genetic makeup. Even if a temperament problem were environmentally produced, the nervous animal, like the aggressive one, interacts with the pups. A nervous mother teaches the offspring to be nervous. Furthermore, a nervous organism produces increased hormonal and chemical reactions which may be passed to the offspring. The safest and best solution for preventing the propagation of aggression or other undesirable temperaments is to neuter dogs who possess problem temperaments. Breeding good temperaments is much safer and easier than attempting to improve poor temperaments.

Sex Differences

Differences in behavior and some behavioral changes can be attributed to hormonal or sex differences. For example, physiological changes involving decreases and increases of hormones can have a profound affect on behavior. Roaming and aggression in the unneutered male dog are attributed to sex hormones. The intact male roams for sexual opportunity and should the animal "get lucky" he better be prepared to battle and defeat other interested males with his aggressive behavior produced by the hormones. The most confident, aggressive dog will be the animal who is allowed to breed the bitch in heat. Unfortunately, the male dog, whether bred or not, may be so affected by hormones that aggressive behavior is fairly constant and misdirected at other animals or people.

Also, the hormonal and resulting behavioral changes of the intact bitch during anestrus to proestrus are extremely drastic. Bitches may become irritable, fearful, and/or aggressive. Many bitches experience moody behaviors from lethargy to false pregnancy. The behaviors associated with the false pregnancy are very similar to the behaviors of a bitch whelping a litter. The bitch may begin to dig, which is a nesting behavior associated with labor and delivery of puppies. The bitch experiencing false pregnancy very often projects maternal emotions onto a stuffed toy. These bitches will carry and protect these toys as if they are live puppies, and are very reluctant to even leave the house without the toy. Irritable and/or fearful behavior can be unpredictable and may cause problems for other animals or people around the bitch. Like the intact male dog, any aggressive, fearful, or irritable behavior may be redirected or displaced toward people. In many cases, neutering, and thus reducing hormonal levels, will abate many if not all of these behaviors, and you will have a much calmer, more enjoyable pet. This is especially true if it is done at a young age.

Development

Some problem puppy behaviors are indicative of the period of development or age of the animal. Generally, the puppy with proper supervision and management will grow out of developmental behaviors such as chewing and house soiling. The puppy under 9 months old that is teething will mouth and chew everything. If the chewing is not redirected or prevented and is allowed to continue past the normal

The typical 5-month-old puppy will eat anything
that does not eat him first.

teething stage, the behavior will become a permanent habit. Similarly, the 7-week-old puppy that is mistakenly considered reliably house-broken and is left alone too soon will learn to soil in the house when he sneaks off in a corner to relieve his bladder. If the mess is not found immediately and the puppy is not properly taught good toilet habits, the animal will continue to soil the house throughout adulthood. Misdirected puppy behaviors do run the risk of becoming ingrained as full-fledged adult behavior problems if left without correction.

Dominance and Territorial Behavior

Today's violent society has motivated many a pet owner to seek out and acquire the guarding breeds for personal and property safety. These animals are typically brave, confident animals who are not bashful about chasing off strangers, human or other, from their per-ceived boundary or territory. Although dominant behavior is more

prevalent in the guarding breeds, any dog may possess dominant behavior and exhibit strong protectiveness or overprotectiveness toward
family members and/or property. The overly ambitious canine may not
feel limited to protecting the house from strangers, and may become
aggressive toward his owner for touching favored toys or food. If not
promptly curtailed, such unsolicited protectiveness may end in serious
damage from a tragic bite. The person who desires to own a dominant
or guard breed must gain and always maintain control through obedience. The owner's vigilance in monitoring and ensuring that protective
behavior is appropriate for the situation must be relentless.

Health Problems

A dog's general health is another element in behavior. For example, my Standard Poodle had a daily habit of stealing the cloth napkins from the dining room table and hiding them around the house.
Each night before dinner I would notice the napkins gone and proceed
to search the house. I was sure she derived great pleasure and personal
entertainment in following me from room to room in search of the napkins. One day I noticed she had stopped stealing the napkins. Her
health check was coming due soon, so I decided to make an early appointment. When the veterinarian asked how she was feeling, I commented that I didn't think she was feeling up to par. I honestly hoped
he wouldn't ask me why, but he did. I knew I risked all future credibility
with this man when I told him I didn't think she was feeling well because she wasn't stealing napkins from the table. I was impressed with
the man's constraint in not telling me I was crazy as he reviewed her
history, which showed she had lost a couple of pounds and had a few
too many bouts with diarrhea. Subsequent blood tests, although not
textbook numbers, did not reveal any problems. He instructed me to
watch her weight closely. A week later she became severely ill, and we
discovered that she had Addison's disease. In this case the behavioral
change was subtle, but such changes may well be caused by failing
health. In a multiple-dog household, the older or ill dog may lose
status among the pack. The sign may be very subtle, perhaps a bump
by the underdog goes by without admonishment or a bone is taken
without retaliation. Changes in the dynamics of pack behavior can be
a very important indicator that a dog's health is failing.

Behavioral problems may also develop when the hurt or ill dog becomes irritated when touched or worked. He may first withdraw, then even begin to react aggressively toward other animals or handlers. A 4-year-old canine that has always adored children may begin snapping at the neighborhood children because of an insidious disorder such as a skin irritation or a thyroid imbalance. Geriatric dogs can also display behavioral changes. The old dog that was house trained suddenly becomes incontinent, or the slow onset of arthritis causes lower thresholds of tolerance toward puppies, children, or general handling. Eye disorders that impair vision often precipitate fear reactions and biting. When the environment appears unfamiliar to the dog because of poor eyesight, he feels severely threatened and may defend himself by fear biting. Any physical condition, such as mats in the coat, sores, dental pain, injuries, structural problem, or general poor health can manifest in irritability or snapping.

Problem behaviors can develop for a variety of reasons other than health problems, and an examination by a veterinarian should be the first step to rule out physical reasons. Antibiotics or a diet change can be a much simpler, less frustrating fix than unnecessary behavior therapy. A dog that habitually exhibits a stable behavior and suddenly behaves in an opposite or disruptive manner deserves a visit to the veterinarian to rule out illness. The trip to the veterinarian may save unnecessary or even cruel corrections or punishments. For instance, the dog that has lost control of his sphincter muscle and cannot prevent from defecating in the house would be horribly abused if his owner kept correcting or punishing him for a behavior beyond his power. Only if the animal has received a clean bill of health should the next step be to formulate a training remedy or contact a professional behavior consultant.

Hyperactivity and Anxiety

Hyperactivity, anxiety, or nervous energy that is not properly channeled may manifest itself in destructive problem behavior. Rescue Greyhounds are notorious for chewing and destructive behavior as a result of either close confinement or separation anxiety. People chew their fingernails or pencils to reduce feelings of anxiety, and dogs chew objects or dig holes to release nervous energy and reduce anxiety. Dogs have been reported to be destructive to themselves. They may lick and chew on themselves to such an extent that lesions and deep sores develop. In either the case of severe separation anxiety or compulsive licking, the use of drugs along with a behavior modification program may be in order to resolve or reduce destructive behavior. There are a few medical problems such as fleas or allergies that can cause excessive chewing and licking. An owner should consult a veterinarian as soon as he or she notices the behavior. Destructive behavior can be dangerous to the dog if the wrong item is swallowed or the licking and chewing causes sores to become infected.

Any action that expends nervous energy and reduces anxiety is reinforcing for the animal. When anxiety, an uncomfortable feeling, is reduced, the act that lowered the anxiety (chewing, in this case) becomes rewarding, and thus, is reinforced.

In addition, boredom and neglect often produce anxiety in the dog, and as a result, he attempts to entertain himself to counteract these emotions. Chewing, barking, or any activity that releases energy and relieves boredom or frustration becomes rewarding. These so-called self-reinforcing behaviors need to be discouraged and the energy redirected appropriately to prevent the undesirable behaviors from becoming maladjusted habits. Again, this is where training, games, and supervised free exercise play an important role.

5

Body Language and Communication

The puppy's first experience with the art of communication is within the litter. The social structure of the litter exposes the pup to the most critical and influential lessons of communication in his life. The infrastructure of the litter becomes observable around 7-8 weeks of age when subordinate and dominant roles are formed. The social hierarchy of the litter and interaction with the dam teach the pups how to use and interpret body language associated with behaviors such as aggression, play, and sex. The outcome of these relationships and interactions affects all future social relationships. The puppy that earned the position of litter leader will not be willing or pleased to relinquish this prime position to his owner. Unfortunately, the owner who fails to gain control of such a dog creates at the least a community nuisance, and at worst, an extremely dangerous community hazard. The dog owner who recognizes the early, subtle cues given by the dog that is running for household tyrant, or the dog that is fearful of children and may bite, can intervene before the situation gets out of control. The

31

canine's body language is the best source of these subtle cues. Dog owners who wish to remain in control of the relationship with their dogs must first understand canine body language; second, frequently observe and evaluate the messages sent; and third, intervene if the dog's body language indicates a need for an attitude adjustment.

Dominance

During the litter experience, the first level of communication between the puppies is usually based on size and strength. The largest and strongest puppy is usually the most dominant of the litter. The dominant pup is the one who gets the best teat and gets to lie on the top of the heap when the puppies huddle in a pile. The dominant dog is often called the top dog because during play, sex, aggression, or feeding, he is either on top or first in line. Position within any social structure changes constantly, and for the canine, social position remains an issue throughout life. The most sought after position in a social order is usually that of the leader, and this position is very frequently challenged in the social order of canines. The leader, in order to maintain leadership and reap the benefits of the position, must continue to display strength through size, and hide any signs of weakness. A display of strength is a critical element of the canine social structure, and naturally transfers to the social structure of the human-canine relationship. The owner who is taller, stronger, and happens to outweigh the dog by 50 or more pounds will have a lot less trouble convincing the dog to take a lower rung on the social ladder than the person who lives with a 200 pound Great Dane. The good news for owners of the giant breeds is that as long as the dog perceives the owner to be bigger and stronger, he will treat his owner as unquestioned leader. The illusion of size to achieve dominance is most frequently demonstrated in the human-equine relationship. Few humans are as strong as the horse, and therefore, the horse's subordinate position to the handler is mostly based on the illusion of strength created by the halter. The halter placed on the young horse gives the handler physical leverage when the animal is still a somewhat manageable size. The horse that experiences the subordinate role early in life rarely challenges the position of the handler after maturity. Likewise, the dog that experiences your dominance early on in the relationship, before he becomes an unmanageable size with large canine teeth, will be less

Observing the body language of your dog is an important clue as to the dog's intention. While these two dogs are playing, many messages are being sent and received about the play limits.

likely to challenge your position of authority later if you maintain it through consistent training and discipline. In the human-canine relationship, the illusion of strength depends on the leash, body stature, tone of voice, eye contact, and body language.

Owner Body Language

The dog owner must maintain appropriate body stature to communicate the dominant position. Body position, human or canine, communicates emotions. The person who stands tall and erect with shoulders straight and head up communicates confidence. This person further communicates confidence by moving with great assurance, as if he or she owns the territory. People who display a confident stature during interactions with their dogs properly communicate dominance and authority. Once you communicate confidence and dominance, other body signals are of secondary importance to the relationship.

EYE CONTACT

The owner who avoids eye contact with the dog during a challenge may unknowingly telegraph weakness as leader. Each challenge may be likened to a rung on a ladder. Every successful challenge by the dog is a step up the ladder for him and a step down for his owner, bringing the dog closer to the top. You need not spend the majority of your time glaring at your dog to establish leadership but you must use direct eye contact to communicate undisputed authority when either challenged by him or engaged in correcting his behavior.

The importance of you earning and maintaining dominance cannot be stressed enough. While the thought of the canine running the household, for instance, having control over the refrigerator can be amusing, it can also be very scary. Commanding the dog to get off the couch and being answered with a snarl is not a laughing matter. Every dog has the potential to challenge his owner, and most dogs do at one time or another. Whether the challenge arises from a dispute over a favorite chair or a discarded chicken carcass, you must be the victor in the confrontation. If not, the challenges will become more frequent and escalate in intensity until someone is physically harmed or the dog must be euthanized for the safety of the community. The content of the communication to the dog is simple. The dog must believe you are stronger and serious about enforcing the rules. The communication from the dog may appear a bit more complex. The dog has a large repertoire of nonverbal signals, and understanding them is crucial to the companion relationship.

Body Language of the Dominant Dog

The confident, dominant dog stands erect and tall trying to appear larger. The dog may even appear to be walking on the tips of his toes in a very deliberate manner as if he owns the place. The body appears to be stiff, with the neck arched and the head held high and straight on to the opponent. In addition, the hackles are raised on the top of the shoulders and rump.

The Dominant dog, tail and ears erect.

Direct eye to eye contact is interpreted as a challenge to a social position or just a threat in general. The first one who glances away communicates submission or backing down from the challenge. A dominant dog will stare unwaveringly into the opponent's eyes.

The aggressive dominant dog holds his tail high and stiff. The end of the tail either quivers or is set in a slow wag. Needless to say, the tail is not the best barometer of emotion in a breed without a tail. A happy dog also wags his tail, but the motion is faster and often circular.

When a dominant dog exposes his teeth, you can be certain the dog is not sending idle threats. The dog's head will be pointed straight at the opponent to show off the big pearly white canines. The teeth, in this situation, are a show of force or strength. Once the dog gets down to heavy teeth-showing and fierce snarling, there is little hope that he will back down if the threat continues, and attack is imminent.

Body Language of the Fearful Dog

Unlike the dominant dog, the fearful one will most frequently try to appear smaller by cowering or slinking close to the ground as if trying to melt into the scenery and become invisible. The ears are held flat and close to the head. Sometimes, the fearful dog will raise his hackles. He may move around or dart in different directions to find an escape route. Rarely will the fearful dog face the object of fear directly.

Generally, the fearful dog avoids staring at an opponent. He will either throw quick glances at the object of his fear or appear to look at

it from the side of his eye. A fearful dog looks past the perceived foe, probably planning an escape route, and is indirectly watching and noting any of the opponent's moves or advances.

The tail is usually held tight and close to the rump, and may even appear to be held tightly between the dog's rear legs.

If the dog does expose his teeth, it is usually because he is not allowed an escape route. Furthermore, the lips will quiver

The Fearful dog, tail tucked, panting, and ears back.

or move up and down, and periodically the tongue may go in and out in a licking motion.

The Fearful-Aggressive Dog

The fearful-aggressive dog will maintain a fairly natural stance, neither trying to appear smaller or larger. The ears are usually quite mobile listening for movement from all directions, particularly the rear. The fearful-aggressive dog may raise his hackles slightly and face the object of fear directly, maintaining some distance.

The fearful-aggressive dog will look directly into his opponent's eyes. The stare is not as cold or as intense as the dominant dog, and the eyes may shift occasionally, revealing the white portion of the eyes. The look is indicative of an animal in conflict, or the

The Fearful-Aggressive dog, crouched, ears back.

fight or flight response animals experience during an undetermined threat.

The tail of the fearful-aggressive dog is down and relaxed, rather than held tight to the body.

The teeth of the fearful-aggressive dog are generally seen after the bite. The dog rarely gives warning by displaying teeth.

Body Language of the Submissive Dog

The submissive dog, like the fearful dog, will try to appear smaller, but will rarely raise his hackles. The submissive dog will either scoot along the ground in a sit position to get closer to the dominant entity or roll over on the ground to expose his belly and genitals, displaying vulnerability to the aggressor. The dog may even urinate during this display. The head of a submissive dog is held in a tipped position and his tongue will dart in and out as he tries very hard to get close to lick the dominant entity's mouth and face area for appeasement. The same licking gesture is observed when a pup approaches his dam. A submissive dog will also lean on the dominant creature, probably as a defense from attack. If the submissive animal leans on the dominant animal, the aggressor has difficulty reaching crucial body parts during an attack. A good analogy to this concept may be the technique used to avoid injury when a horse kicks. The person who steps closer as the horse kicks will usually suffer less bodily damage than the person who is farther away and receives the full force of the strike.

The submissive dog will not initiate eye contact and tries very hard to avoid any visual contact. He will even go so far as to turn his head to avoid meeting the eyes of an opponent. Do not mistake the head turning as inattention to the body language of the dominant adversary, however. The submissive dog always watches body language to determine protocol in each social situation.

The submissive dog will expose his teeth in what can be mistakenly interpreted as snarling. The difference between a submissive show of teeth and an aggressive one is the position of the head and the absence of growling. The submissive dog approaches with teeth exposed and head in a lowered, tipped position. The display of teeth in the submissive dog has been termed smiling, and as a rule, the submissive dog does not growl or make any aggressive sounds when approaching. Behaviorists speculate that the submissive animal exposes his teeth to

37

display his strength or lack thereof. The theory suggests that an adversary gains a serious advantage in battle if the opponent reveals his defensive strength; therefore, the submissive dog is attempting to ward off an attack by showing the perceived adversary the lack of threat by revealing the size of his teeth. In addition, the posture of his head and body, along with the showing of teeth, communicates the infantile greeting gesture. The body language of a submissive dog does not always ward off attack.

Fearful, aggressive, and submissive behaviors can sometimes be confused. The dog owner must make a distinction between these emotions to properly interact with the dog. Should you mistake submissive behavior for aggression and correct the dog, the submissive behavior will only become more intense. Distinguishing between these behaviors may be quite difficult. Not all submissive dogs will display the entire array of classical submissive behaviors. Samoyeds, a very verbal breed, may mix growling sounds with a display of submissive behavior. The puppy that is separated from the litter too early, before 10 weeks, may display a mixture of behaviors that can make interpreting his body language confusing. The puppy that is placed in a new home at six or seven weeks, with very limited experience in body language, may erroneously mix different body postures, and consequently approach an adult dog without an appropriate display of caution. On the other hand, the puppy who remained with the litter and dam long enough to learn social protocol greets new dogs properly with much more restraint. A dog may mix his signals so you must consider them all in evaluating the dog's emotions or intentions. Body language along with the dog's verbal communication may aid in mood evaluation when body language alone appears contradictory or confusing.

Dog's Verbal Communication

The domestic dog often verbalizes with a mixture of growling, barking, whimpering, and whining. Therefore growling often associated with aggressive warnings may be part of dog talk, and may not mean aggression when mixed together with other sounds. Trainers often misinterpret these noises as protests or threats of aggression, and may harshly and unnecessarily correct the dog, which can be very confusing to him. The dog may incorporate growling in his "talk" simply because dogs inherently have a limited number of sounds they can make, and mixtures maximize the verbal repertoire. In some instances, the dog may include growling with other verbalizations if he is experiencing conflicting emotions or confusion over a particular situation and is uncertain about how to respond. As is the case with humans, verbalizations should be evaluated within the context of the situation and the presence of other body cues.

GROWLING

The uninterrupted loud throaty sound the aggressive dog emits is an unmistakable warning. It conveys strong irritability, annoyance, or anger, and the intention to bite. The fearful dog's growl is quieter and intermittent. If a healthy dog growls at another animal or person, it seldom communicates anything other than an intention of serious threat. One exception may be growling during play. Games such as tug-of-war often elicit much verbalization and growling from a dog. This verbalization is usually directed at the object being tugged on and is rarely transferred to the play opponent.

BARKING

Barking behavior in dogs is an intraspecies communication system that conveys more information than we may imagine. For the domestic dog, barking is an alarm system that relays information about intruders. Dogs bark when their perceived territory has been trespassed by animal or human. The observant dog owner may notice that the way the dog barks when a familiar person arrives is different from his bark when a stranger approaches the premises. There are many different sounding barks depending upon what the dog wishes to communicate. For example, there are barks for play, alert, hunger, and loneliness, to name just a few. Most pet owners are very proficient at interpreting their dogs' assorted barks and the meanings these different sounds hold. If these distinct verbalizations are reinforced, they can become even more meaningful, and the dog and owner can establish a consistent form of communication. For instance, if you wish the dog to bark at the back door to go out, you can encourage it by opening the door immediately every time he barks at the door. Reinforced and directed barking is a good example of potential problem behavior being channeled into a useful and appropriate behavior.

YELPING

The yelp is a sharp sound comparable to a human's scream and usually indicates surprise and pain. In many instances, the yelp may be likened to the human "ouch!" Generally, the yelp indicates that the dog is in some sort of peril, as when attacked. The yelp may signify a cry of "uncle" or submission to the attacker. Ironically, the sound of a yelping dog might bring on more attackers if other dogs are in the area. These attackers will gang up on the unfortunate victim. Sometimes dogs yelp when they are extremely excited. The submissive dog that tries hard not to draw attention to himself and may not have the resources to stand up to the dominant attackers is more reluctant to yelp. The sound of a yelp is fairly distinct and draws the attention of other animals or the dog owner.

WHINING OR WHIMPERING

Whining is a high-pitched sound that may be analogous to human crying. The sound projects the notion that the dog is unhappy or uncomfortable. Dogs whimper or whine when they are confined or left alone. They are social animals and are not happy when they are isolated. A dog that is confined in a room or yard all by himself may whine incessantly. In addition, the dog that is tied to a chain or lead, even for short periods of time, may whine out of frustration and unhappiness at being restricted to a small area. Whining is also very common when you leave him with other people or in a strange place. Although he's left with another person and may have the run of the area, he feels confined or restrained from contact with you. Separation from the owner, even though other people are present, may be equivalent to being isolated in an empty room. The dog voices unhappy emotions about isolation with considerable whining. In spite of the owner's comforting promises to return soon, the dog whines incessantly until distracted or the owner returns.

Owner's Verbal Communication

Words do not have meaning for a dog until you associate specific events with them. For example, "cookie" has meaning for the dog only after you repeatedly say "cookie" and give him a snack immediately following the word. The dog learns to associate the word "cookie" with a tasty morsel. You can teach any word in the same manner. You could hold up a cookie and say "poop" or "sun" as you give the dog the treat, and he will associate the word "poop" or "sun" with a tasty morsel. (For dogs that already consider poop a tasty morsel, see Chapter 12.) Although a particular tone of voice may enhance the significance of a command, the command only holds the meaning the pet owner chooses to attach to the word.

TONE OF VOICE

Your tone of voice, like your body language, communicates more information to the dog than any number of words can ever hope to. Tone of voice used properly and carefully associated with distinct behaviors informs the dog of your mood and possible intention. Dogs may also interpret human sounds within their own frame of reference. Therefore, the human scream, similar to the yelp, is correctly interpreted as a signal of surprise and pain. The human low throaty sound, comparable to the growl, may predict that a correction or dominant gesture is forthcoming. Most dogs learn very quickly to run in the opposite direction when the owner yells or screams certain expletives. The low coarse or growling voice backed up with eye contact and a firm correction informs the dog that the owner is not happy and will not tolerate the present behavior. Dogs interpret happy tones of voice as praise and reward, while they hear fear or pain in a screeching voice. Commands sent with the intention to control or correct the dog from biting must not be delivered in a shrill voice. The shrill voice communicates that you are fearful. Likewise, do not praise the dog in the same low, throaty voice that normally communicates dominance. Tone of voice is a powerful communicator and should be used in proper context to help the canine learn.

6

Canine Learning

In order to survive, the newborn puppy is prepared to learn from birth. From birth to approximately 4 weeks of age, the puppy's primary concerns are learning how to find food, keep warm, and walk from one point to another. After 4 weeks the puppy begins to expand his learning to a larger physical environment through developmentally appropriate independence and increased exploratory behavior. The puppy steadily and gradually shows more confidence, curiosity, and willingness to learn. If behavior is not channeled appropriately during this learning phase between the ages of 2 and 6 months, behavior problems will develop. Young puppies, 2–4 months of age, exhibit strong dependence on the new family and usually try to follow everyone around. By 4 1/2–5 months, the imaginary umbilical cord attaching the puppy to the owner is severed. The puppy that has no training and is used to following the owner everywhere without a leash suddenly decides that he needs to go to the owner when called only if nothing else is going on. The 5-month-old is at the height of teething and eats everything that does not eat him first. Contrary to the recommendations of many contemporary trainers, the best time to teach appropriate behavior is before the dog is 6 months old, starting the day the puppy enters the home and before habits become ingrained.

If you acquire an older dog you can speed up the attachment and bonding process by communicating and defining the rules immediately through a positive approach training strategy. Even if you missed the optimal puppy learning period and the dog already has acquired some bad habits, old dogs can indeed be motivated to learn new tricks.

Motivating the dog is a very essential part of training. There are three basic methods to motivate an animal: positive reinforcement, negative reinforcement, and punishment. A mixture of all three methods is very effective for training most canines.

Reinforcement Methods

Reinforcement, which increases the likelihood of a behavior being repeated, can be either positive or negative.

POSITIVE REINFORCERS

Positive reinforcement is a reward or event that the dog perceives as pleasurable. The dog that associates obeying your command with a tasty treat willingly obeys in anticipation of the reinforcement. Food, verbal praise, toys, and physical praise such as petting are all good positive reinforcers, but food is usually the strongest motivator. The list of reinforcers can be very long, and each individual dog may have a custom list of reinforcing stimuli. The value of the reinforcer is dependent upon individual taste. The retriever may perceive a game of Frisbee as being equivalent to the pleasure of eating a one-pound T-bone steak, while the Basset Hound may find the idea of a Frisbee totally disgusting. A good trainer experiments by offering many different stimuli to the dog to find several good reinforcers for training.

QUALITY OF REWARD

Novel treats maintain the highest value for the dog. Varying the type of treat occasionally from meat to cheese keeps the value of the reinforcers high. Dogs are naturally motivated to work hard for a new reward. If the dog receives the same reward every day, the reward becomes routine and loses its ability to motivate. In addition, the quality of the reward must be adjusted according to the complexity of the task. The dog that chases rabbits and does not come when called will require a very high quality reinforcer, steak for instance, to be tempted to turn away from a running hare. No sane dog would turn down a good rabbit chase for a biscuit. Biscuits are low-quality reinforcers because most owners give them out to their dogs just for living and breathing. If the dog routinely receives a biscuit for simply existing he will not consider the biscuit a treat worth any effort.

To be effective, reinforcers should also be quickly consumable and delivered immediately after the appropriate behavior. The owner who has to battle a tight pocket or run to the refrigerator to get the treats will lose valuable reinforcement and training time. If the treat is delivered too late, the dog will not associate the correct behavior with the reinforcer and will not learn how to reliably earn the reinforcer. Also, the dog that chews a biscuit for three hours and licks up the crumbs is distracted from repeating the training task and valuable time is again lost.

SIZE OF REWARD

You can adjust the value of the reinforcer by its amount. A bigger treat or a handful of treats occasionally can add novelty to the reward. For most occasions, the food reward does not need to be a full meal, a small reward will suffice. In fact, if the dog is satiated before the training session ends, he will become lethargic, which will hinder the learning process. The slightly hungry dog is more aroused and alert. The food reward should be soft, tasty, and small. If the reinforcer is a game, the game should not go on until the dog tires and loses interest in learning. For example, one or two tosses of the ball in between training trials as a reinforcer for learning is much more effective than a fifteen-minute game of fetch.

PRAISE AS REWARD

As with any reinforcer, the quality and amount of praise is important. The dog is not going to be very rewarded or motivated to complete the next task if the praise is a monotone "Good dog." On the other hand, if the praise is too long and exuberant, valuable training time is lost between how much time the praise occupies and the time it takes to calm and focus the dog for the next repetition. Praise should be strong enough to motivate the dog without losing control of the dog. Praise should never be used as encouragement during an exercise while the dog is problem solving. While the trainer's intention is to encourage the dog, the praise interrupts his train of thought and ability to figure out the exercise. In fact, the dog may become focused on the praise rather than the task. For example, if a dog is praised while retrieving, he may become excited or distracted and not complete the task of picking up the toy. As the tasks become more complex, so does the timing of reinforcement. Praise should be given only after completion of the task.

NEGATIVE REINFORCERS

While positive reinforcement uses pleasant stimuli to motivate desired behavior, negative reinforcement utilizes aversive stimuli to achieve the same end. We pay taxes by April 15 to avoid penalties and carry an umbrella on cloudy and overcast days to avoid getting wet. A shock collar used on the dog that barks excessively is a similar negative reinforcement. The dog remains quiet to avoid shocks; therefore, the presence of the collar motivates quiet behavior. Another example of negative reinforcement is teaching a dog to sit by pushing on the dog's rump. The aversive stimulus is the pressure on the rump and the dog is motivated to sit to avoid the pressure. The list of negative reinforcers, like positive reinforcers can be long, and the value of each reinforcer varies with the dog. The gun dog may not find a firecracker the least bit disturbing, and in fact, the more the firecracker sounds like a gun, the more excited the dog may become at the prospect of a fallen bird. On the other hand, the shock from the noise of the firecracker may be enough to straighten a Toy Poodle's kinky coat. The quality or force of the negative reinforcer must be adjusted to the temperament of the dog. A shock used on a soft-tempered dog may damage his spirit to such an extent that he may become nervous, fearful, or catatonic. Likewise, a pop on the collar may not be enough force for a hard-tempered dog.

Neither negative nor positive reinforcement alone is sufficient to train a dog to obey all wishes and commands. A proper blend of positive and negative reinforcement, optimally timed to encourage desired behaviors, is necessary to produce a well-behaved, trained dog.

Schedules of Reinforcement

Continuous and intermittent reinforcement are the two most effective schedules for dog training. The continuous (100 percent reinforcement) schedule is most often used for shaping new behaviors.

Each dog reacts differently to noises .

Every time the dog sits on command, he receives a treat and/or verbal praise. The dog is reinforced for every correct response. Once he associates the command with the response approximately 90 percent of the time, you should change the reinforcement schedule to an intermittent, or variable, schedule. Maintaining the dog's behavior on the continuous schedule is discouraged for two reasons. First, he will become satiated more quickly and the training sessions will have to be shorter when a food reward is given for every correct response. Likewise, the dog that is continuously reinforced with a game will tire quickly. Second, the dog that becomes conditioned to receiving a reward 100 percent of the time may become treat dependent, and will quickly cease responding if the owner runs out of treats or if the reinforcement is withheld for a few responses. The dog quickly notices when the treats stop and gives up trying to earn the reward. You should provide treats on a variable schedule of reinforcement to maintain consistent good behavior.

The variable schedule generally consists of randomly reinforcing responses. For instance, using an intermittent reward schedule, the dog's second, seventh, or twentieth correct response may be reinforced with both a treat and praise, while all responses in between are only verbally reinforced. On the following training day, however, you may choose, arbitrarily, to reinforce more or less frequently, and on a totally different response-based schedule of reward. The key to the variable schedule is that from the dog's perspective, the reinforcements are unpredictable. The variable schedule strengthens and maintains trained behaviors because the dog is motivated to respond each time, just in case there might be a treat forthcoming. For this approach to be most effective you should avoid giving the dog any clue about the availability of food, such as wearing a treat/bait bag or fanny pack. The presence or absence of the bag or pack is as obvious a cue as a big neon sign on your body that says, "I HAVE TREATS!" or "I DO NOT HAVE TREATS!" Place the treats in your pocket. To prevent the dog from learning to work only when the bag or pack is present, avoid anything that lets the dog second guess you.

Of the many things that motivate dogs, there are three primary motivators: specifically, food, sex, and water. Of these primary motivators, food is the only one you can carry around and easily deliver. Food or any positive reinforcer may be analogous to receiving a salary. Few people will labor forty hours a week for a pat on the head, and because they love their boss and their boss loves them. Yet most dog owners expect the dog to cease chasing a rabbit for a mere pat on the head. People work for money, or the pleasures that money may afford them, including buying food. They will work only so hard for a survival salary. People need extra motivation to work hard; the salary or motivator needs to be raised. In addition to the salary, many people may receive satisfaction from doing a good job and the recognition they get from their boss and co-workers. The dog prefers to work for a food salary, and if he is expected to stop chasing a rabbit, the salary has to be higher than a few square meals a day. The motivator should include tasty and novel groceries such as liver, cheese, or steak. The pat on the head, approval, and affection from you are secondary reinforcers and an added source of satisfaction just as recognition may be for some people. While, the dog's primary motivator is food, it may be impractical to use it 100% of the time. You should pair praise with all reinforcement so it can assume a secondary reinforcement value and maintain behavior in the absence of primary rewards.

You can frequently substitute secondary reinforcement for high-value primary reinforcers, such as food, on an intermittent schedule to maintain behavior. The secondary reinforcer, praise, will maintain a high value for the dog if you pair it with a primary reinforcer such as food on occasion. Once you have trained the dog, you can interchange food and praise to motivate him to obey.

Food rewards and positive reinforcement fell out of favor with many trainers during the middle of this century. Training with food was considered a mortal sin. Trainers became convinced that training with food caused the dog to work only when food was available or the dog was hungry. Possibly the most influential dog trainer during this period was William Koehler, creator of the "Koehler Method." This method was based on Mr. Koehler's experience with training dogs for the military. The method condemned the use of food, and it involved strict discipline using negative reinforcement and punishment. For example, the trainer taught the dog to sit by commanding "Sit" and simultaneously snapping back on the choke collar hard enough to force the dog's weight backwards into a sit. The dog was motivated to sit on command to avoid the snap. No reward was given, and the trainer may or may not have given verbal praise. Although punishment and negative reinforcement methods are quick and effective, the dog is only motivated to avoid adversity and does not work on a willing basis. In the case of a recall, some trainers used a shock collar to train the dog to return to the handler on command. The handler commanded "Come"; if the dog did not return, he sent a shock to the dog through the collar. The dog was motivated to return to the handler to avoid the shock. When the trainer removed the collar, the motivation was also removed.

A method that uses a mixture of positive reinforcement and punishment teaches the dog in a positive manner and makes him willing to obey. In teaching the sit, you coax the dog into a sit with a treat. The motivation is to get the treat. Most dogs are highly motivated by food and will rarely turn down a gourmet treat even if not hungry. More importantly, you have control over the dog's hunger by manipulating the time of day and the amount you feed him. Once you condition the dog to associate the command with the treat, you should then implement a reward system in which the dog must first obey the command to get the treat. You command him to sit, and if he doesn't, you deliver a correction, such as a tap on the rump. As soon as the dog sits you give him a treat. With this method there are two motivators involved: first, sit to earn the reward; and second, sit to avoid the correction. Even when you cannot correct the dog as in the case of working off leash, the motivation to earn a reward is still present, particularly when you pair it with praise, because the praise is always with the trainer. Dogs trained solely with punishment or negative reinforcement often fail to work for long periods on complex tasks. Complex tasks, such as fetching a ball from a long distance, usually require the dog to work off leash. If the lead is off and the dog has no other motivator to perform than avoiding a correction, he might see no reason to obey.

During the 1980s Mr. Koehler's influence began to wane as trainers delved into the principles behind learning and positive reinforcement to motivate their dogs. Although the stigma associated with food and positive reinforcement remains in some training communities, many myths about these methods have been discredited.

Learning Theory at Work

The concern that dogs only work for food if they are trained with food can be eliminated by understanding the use of secondary reinforcements. When you give a treat and praise at the same moment, through association the praise will take on almost as high a value as the food. Therefore, the dog will work and respond for praise. But, for the praise to maintain this high value, you must continue to pair food and praise occasionally. If you eliminate food totally and never again pair it with praise, the praise will decrease in value for the dog as a motivator. The praise loses value when you begin initial training with food and then eliminate the food after the dog has learned the task, a process many trainers refer to as "weaning" the dog off the food. The process is analogous to having your salary cut after you know your job. Trainers eliminate the food based on the belief that once the dog knows the exercise, he should perform commands for the fun of it and/or devotion to the trainer. Unfortunately, passing up another dog, a good sniff, or a wild coursing beast for the fun of working obedience for a mere pat on the head is unrealistic to expect of even the most devoted canine. To maintain the specific responses and the perceived high value of a secondary reinforcer such as praise, behaviors and secondary reinforcers must be reassociated occasionally with the primary motivator, food.

Another misconception about food, that the dog becomes too distracted by it, can be dispelled after thinking through the principles of learning. Many trainers will not reinforce the stay with food because the stay is a stationary exercise and the trainer does not want the dog to become excited and distracted at the sight of the food, and as a result, move from the stay position. A trained dog should know the exercise under all distractions, with the exception of a stimulus that is physically threatening, causing him to move to avoid injury. If the dog is excited about the food, the food is a good motivator, and if you use the treat properly, you can teach the dog that it's only available if he remains in position. To reinforce a stay with a treat, walk to the dog to give a treat; if he moves, correct him and withhold the treat. Remain in position in front of the dog. When he stays in position, offer the treat quickly right to his mouth so that he doesn't have to move to get it. Repeat giving the dog the treat for staying to reinforce the behavior. Walking in to give him a treat on the stay exercise has several benefits. If he is used to you walking in randomly to deliver reinforcement instead of just correction, he won't be apprehensive when you walk in to correct him. He'll focus on you, wondering when you're going to deliver the next reinforcement. Understanding the principles of reinforcers broadens your ability to use food to your advantage in motivating behavior positively rather than relying only on corrections. If the dog is distracted by the food, the behavior is caused by using the food as a bribe and training him to focus on the food, making it a carrot on a stick. Although the carrot and stick concept is quite effective for shaping canine behavior, once the dog understands the exercise, you should remove the stick and give the dog the reinforcement only after he completes the desired behavior correctly. For instance, to teach the dog to come, you might give the command "Front" and manipulate or guide him to the correct position by using a treat in front of his nose. Ian Dunbar, D.V.M., an excellent dog writer has termed the manipulation or guiding method as "luring" the dog. The dog follows the treat to directly in front of your body and receives the treat and praise, verbal and/or tactile, immediately upon getting into correct position. After several lures and receiving the treat for being in front of the handler, the dog learns an association between the command "Front" and the position the handler desires. Once the dog is conditioned, you switch the focus from the food to the task. You call the dog into position rather than lure him. If he responds correctly, you give him a treat as a reward. If the dog does not respond correctly, you give him a pop on the collar to motivate the desired response. When the dog responds properly, you reinforce him with food and praise. Withholding the treat until he completes the behavior is now considered a reward instead of a lure. The dog's focus is now switched to the task and then the reward. During the lure phase, the dog is focused first on the treat. During the reward stage, the dog must first focus on completing the behavior correctly in order to earn the reward. When he is accurately performing the command and earning the treat 100 percent of the time during the reward stage, you can shift to the intermittent reinforcement schedule discussed above.

Shaping

The process of shaping behavior consists of motivating the dog to act and then reinforcing the desired action and ignoring or not reinforcing the superfluous responses. Teaching the young puppy to sit using a treat is an example of shaping. You hold a treat over his head to motivate him to sit. In order for the puppy to look at the treat, he

A treat is held over the puppy's head to coax him into a sit.

falls back on his haunches into a sit. Initially, the puppy may jump up and bounce around. These responses are not reinforced by withholding the treat. Once the puppy falls back on his haunches into a sit, command, "Sit," verbally praise, and give the puppy the treat to reinforce sitting. The chowhound puppy may be so motivated by the treat that he anticipates the treat before the command and sits whenever you go toward the closet to get the treat. Anticipation means the dog has understood or associated the behavior, sit, with the reinforcement, cookie. Now he has just one more step to learn, which is to wait for the command before performing. You may quickly command, "Sit," and reward the dog when an anticipation occurs. You may also choose only to reinforce those sits the dog performs on command. After several repetitions, the puppy associates the word "Sit" with the action of placing haunches on the ground. Now he is shaped to sit on the command and the action is reinforced by the treat.

An important aspect of shaping is that the dog must be motivated to perform the behavior of his own volition. For instance, the handler who tries to teach the dog to shake hands by lifting his paw and commanding him to shake only teaches the dog that the handler will lift the paw on the word "Shake." Observational learning, in which the dog learns the exercise by watching the handler do the work or another dog perform the exercise is rarely a good option for teaching new behaviors. Although dog owners will testify that their dogs learn bad habits from other dogs, there is little evidence to demonstrate that dogs learn any behaviors simply from observing others, particularly good behavior. Bad behavior that seems to be learned from observing another dog is usually a result of joining in on the action. For the dog to learn to reliably perform a desired behavior on command, you have to motivate him to perform the behavior independently. One way to motivate a dog to lift his paw is to tap his front paw with your foot. The dog will lift his paw out of the way of your foot. Once he connects or associates your foot with the shake command, the dog will lift his paw to avoid the tap. Command "Shake," and then reinforce paw lifting with a treat. The dog learns he can earn a food reward by lifting a paw on the command to "shake". You can shape the dog to lift his paw higher and higher by reinforcing only the higher lifts with a reward or tasty morsel. When you withhold the treat he will become more active and try harder to earn the treat. The dog will be more likely to raise his paw higher, and you can reinforce the new behavior with the treat.

Timing

In developing a good training strategy it is important to remember that the canine learns by temporal association. The temporal learner associates the consequence of every action with the events that occurred during or immediately after a behavior. For instance, a dog may interpret a startling clap of thunder at the wrong moment as a correction. The dog who sniffed a turtle just as the thunder sounded may become leery of going near a turtle again, because he erroneously assumed that the noise was a reaction to sniffing the turtle. There is no way to explain to him that the aversive noise was an independent event and had nothing to do with his greeting the turtle. The only way you might teach him not to fear the turtle would be to get him to sniff it time and time again when there is no thunder, until he finally disassociates thunder with turtle sniffing.

To make the best of temporal association in teaching a specific behavior, good timing of the command and reinforcer is essential. For example, in teaching a dog to sit you need to give the command, "Sit," and just as the dog sits, you must give effective reinforcement immediately after the correct behavior. The longer the gap between the behavior and the reinforcement, the less meaningful the reinforcement will be in relation to the behavior. If you command the dog to sit, and an hour later finally get around to praising him, there will be little or no association between the behavior and the reward. The best reinforcer or reward is one that you present immediately after the behavior. For every second that you delay the reinforcer, the association between behavior and reward becomes weaker. After as few as fifteen seconds, the dog may not make an association at all, particularly if another or several events intervened before reinforcement. When you must delay a reinforcement, you can form a verbal chain to connect the reward with the behavior. For example, if you tell your trained dog to sit from a distance of twenty feet and he obeys, he needs reinforcement for obeying the command. You cannot possibly get to the dog immediately after he has responded, and running up to him to give him a treat can oftentimes be threatening if he doesn't know a treat is in your hand. The dog may think you are running toward him to give a correction. The solution is to form a temporal chain between the response and reward by giving valued verbal praise from twenty feet away and continuing the praise until you get close enough to the dog to give him the food reward. The verbal praise tells him to expect the food reward. This method prevents a break in continuity and creates a chain of events that connects the desired behavior with the ultimate reinforcement.

Length and Location of Sessions

Timing is also important in the length of a training session. Since dogs do have short attention spans, long training sessions are not reinforcing or pleasant. If the sessions are too long or the material too complex, the dog may tire and become distracted. The training sessions should be long enough to provide time for several repetitions of each exercise the dog is currently learning, and short enough so that he doesn't become bored.

The complexity of the training session may also tax the dog's capacity and make the session stressful and unrewarding for him. You can reduce the stress of learning by breaking down the teaching exercises into small and simple forms. For example, you should break the sit-stay exercise into at least two steps. First you teach the dog to sit, and then you teach him to stay. You then break the sit-stay exercise into several more steps, increasing the time the dog stays and the distance between you and the dog. A good trainer does not introduce the next phase of an exercise until the dog demonstrates a good understanding of the exercise by performing it accurately and on command approximately 90 percent of the time.

Once a dog performs an exercise on command most of the time, change the setting where you train and work him. Most dogs do not naturally or easily generalize learned information from one context or setting to another. The dog that was taught to obey the sit-stay command in the living room will not automatically transfer this obedient behavior to the dining room or the front lawn. You must teach him to sit-stay in many different places and contexts before he will begin to generalize the sit-stay to all environments. Fortunately, each lesson the dog learns in a new environment is learned more quickly than the last lesson. Eventually, fewer and fewer lessons are required, and the dog learns that sit-stay means to stay in position in all surroundings and settings. Before a dog can be considered trained, he must be trained in all surroundings. A dog will never learn to be obedient among other dogs if you don't train him around other dogs. Dogs must be exposed to distractions in order for them to perform amid distractions. Training in varied situations is the best way to teach the dog adaptive behavior. A dog that obeys at a dog show of 3,000 dogs is one that will be more likely to obey in a room of two visitors.

Punishment

Dogs are often disciplined with punishment, and it can be an effective training tool if used properly. While negative reinforcement encourages desired behavior, punishment discourages the likelihood of a behavior being repeated. For instance, to teach a dog to heel using negative reinforcement you would hold the lead tight except when the dog is in heel position. Theoretically, the aversive tight lead increases the chances that the dog will heel to avoid the tight lead. When using punishment to teach the dog to heel, you would snap the dog's collar as he leaves heel position, and he will leave heel position less frequently. In dog training, punishment is used much more frequently

This dog was rewarded for getting up on the counter. The correction should be strong enough to override the reward.

than negative reinforcement. Punishment must be adjusted for the transgression. The punishments must be harsh enough to get the message across to the dog that the current behavior is unacceptable without being so harsh as to cause fearful or aggressive reactions from the dog. The dog that is beaten with a stick experiences harsh and abusive punishment, which, understandably, makes him fearful. In retaliation, the dog can become aggressive to protect himself from the abuse. A punishment or correction does not need to be abusive to be effective. The correction should only be more aversive than the pleasure gained from the inappropriate behavior. For example, the correction to discourage stealing food from the kitchen table must be strong enough to override the reward of eating the food. A possible correction might be to attach the food to a metal pan. When the dog pulls the food off the table, the pan will crash to the floor, creating considerable aversive clamor. If you are lucky, the pan might even accidentally pop him on the head on the way to the floor. The noise cues you that he is stealing, and you have the opportunity to run into the room and catch him in the act. Running at the dog adds even more adversity to the situation. Catching him in the act provides the perfect opportunity and timing to meaningfully admonish him for food stealing along with the already traumatic falling pan. For most dogs, the experience would be upsetting enough to negate the pleasure of eating stolen food. Consequently, to avoid the same punishment, the dog refrains in the future from the temptation to steal food.

A combination of reinforcement and punishment teaches the dog a very clear distinction between acceptable and unacceptable behavior. You promote the distinction by offering strong, clear praise or reinforcement to strengthen good behavior and strong reasonable punishments or reprimands to decrease inappropriate behavior. Generally, dogs would rather obey and earn the approval of their human companions than suffer their wrath.

Positive and negative reinforcement conveys to the dog how he can earn approval for proper behavior. Punishment teaches the dog which behaviors elicit your displeasure. Good training strategies teach the dog how to avoid punishment and earn reward. But even the best training strategies can be ruined if the trainer fails to convey consistent messages or to persist in enforcing those messages.

Consistency and Persistency

If the rules change from day to day, the dog becomes confused. He needs to know how to consistently earn reward and avoid punishment or he will give up responding. The good trainer is consistent and always uses the same command for the same behavior. Most dog owners teach the dog that the command "down" means to be in a prone position. Unfortunately, many dog owners use the same command to mean, lie down, remove thyself from the couch or bed, or stop jumping on people. When a command has many different meanings, the word ceases to have an important message. Give each behavior its own command. The command "off" can be used to mean paws on the floor, and "down" may remain to define the prone position. After you decide on consistent commands, the next step is to be persistent in using them.

Dogs are naturally good at persistent behavior, and even better if rewarded for it. Many a dog owner has given up trying to correct the dog that barks all day or jumps on people. Dog owners drop out of obedience classes all the time because they are worn down by their dogs' seemingly persistent behaviors, and they give up trying to teach their dogs new behaviors. The key is that the owners gave up, and the dogs learned that persistency pays off. When an owner gives in, the dog's persistent behavior is strengthened and reinforced. Any determined dog owner can wear the dog down. Therefore, it is extremely important that you be more persistent than the dog about continuing the training process until the dog performs the desired behavior. The dog must learn that the energy he spends engaging in undesirable behavior is not worth the effort, because you will persist. If you correct him for jumping up the first four times and don't correct him for the fifth jump up you simply teach him to jump up five times for the payoff.

Similarly, if you correct the dog for barking at the moon sometimes and not at other times, you teach him that sometimes barking is acceptable and sometimes it is not. The dog will continue to bark to determine when barking is acceptable and when it is not acceptable. Consequently, correcting barking sometimes actually encourages even more barking.

If you don't correct the dog for barking in the backyard because you are not at home, he will learn that barking is acceptable when you're away. If you sneak out of the house so as not to cue him that it is acceptable to bark, he only needs to bark twice with no correction to figure out that you are not at home. A behavior will be extinguished or changed only if you persist in correcting the dog every time he misbehaves. Likewise, a dog will not perform a behavior if you are not persistent in enforcing commands. The dog that is told to sit and ignores the command will continue to ignore commands unless you enforce the sit command each time you give it. If you don't enforce the command to sit, the dog learns that the command means nothing.

Most dog owners do not insist that their dog obey the first command. As a result, they end up commanding the dog to sit three or four times before they wind up screaming and physically forcing him to obey. The dog learns to sit just before his owner reaches the fourth command or the end of his or her rope, whichever the dog judges to be first. The dog thus maintains control by deciding on which command to sit, and does not sit until he absolutely must to avoid bodily harm. The owner is not aware of this unintentional pattern and becomes angry and resorts to yelling. When the dog finally does sit, the owner does not give praise because of the mounted anger at the dog for not sitting on the first three commands. The dog learns that sitting is not rewarding, and the owner learns to yell to get the dog to sit. Furthermore, the dog learns to sit on the fourth command to avoid punishment rather than to sit on the first command and obtain praise.

The dog that learns to obey for approval and praise is usually a

Photo by Janet Yosay

more relaxed and happier animal. A good human-dog relationship is based on positive feelings and motivation rather than adversity and avoidance of punishment. There is no question that dog owners are more content with relationships that are based on positive feelings. If you clearly communicate to the dog the behavior you expect from him and enforce it persistently, a good relationship will be much easier to attain.

Temperament Differences

Although few dogs fit an explicit temperament model, there are similarities of temperament that allow for some general categorization. These models can be used to predict the dog's response to different methods of training and possibly prevent some serious mistakes.

SOFT-TEMPERED DOGS

The soft-tempered, or sensitive, dog may become very despondent with strong or harsh corrections. These dogs very often display submissive behavior. Even everyday household yelling, which may be the normal sound level in a home full of children, can send the soft dog cowering into the corner. If a training method is too harsh for a soft dog, he may become fearful as the stress level increases. Rex was a big dog with a soft temperament, and he liked to pull his owner down the street. Rex was placed on a buckle collar and his owner was taught how to give a proper correction when he pulled. The first time Rex pulled on his owner in obedience class and received a hard correction, he hit the ground as if he'd been shot. Rex's owner quickly discovered that gentle pops were sufficient to teach him to heel. For dogs like Rex, high stress levels hinder the learning process. The dog may even freeze or have the glazed look Rex had when he hit the ground and refused to move. Unfortunately, the sensitive dog does not respond as well to training as the confident dog that is not feeling nervous or stressed. As a result, the owner of a sensitive dog can become very frustrated and make even stronger corrections, compounding the problem. The owner who intensifies the corrections unintentionally supports and reinforces the dog's fear and nervousness. This is not to say that you should never correct the soft-tempered dog. But the correction for the soft-tempered dog should only be strong enough to get your point across. Although sensitive dogs can become fearful if trained by harsh methods, such dogs are not innately fearful. Owners of very soft dogs quickly find out that a stern look and a shake of the finger are usually more than adequate admonishment for any wrongdoing. Depending upon the degree of softness, the primary method of training should be positive reinforcement. Sensitive dogs can be a lot of fun to train because they are usually very invested in pleasing their owner.

HARD-TEMPERED DOGS

Less sensitive or hard-tempered dogs can also be a lot of fun to train, even though they do not appear to concentrate on pleasing their owner as much as the soft-tempered dog. These dogs keep trainers on their toes as the trainers attempt to keep a balance between reinforcement and punishment. The hard-tempered dog can tolerate harsh corrections, and may even require a fairly strong one just to get his undivided attention. Fancy was a very sweet Rottweiler who was big enough to have her way and direction regardless of the apparatus on her neck. She pulled her owner everywhere ignoring the snaps he gave. Fancy just never noticed or cared. One day, Fancy took off chasing another dog while on a long lead. Her clever owner quickly ran around a nearby tree with the end of the lead, wrapping the lead around the tree once. He braced and waited for Fancy to hit the end of the lead just short of the dog she was chasing. One can only guess what went through Fancy's mind as she heard the command "Come" just as she hit the end of the lead with enormous momentum and flipped on the ground. After that very harsh correction, the first correction Fancy ever paid attention to, a pop on the collar and a strong command was all she needed to remind her to come and not to chase. While the soft dog may need positive reinforcement as a primary method of training, the tough dog usually requires a heavier dose of negative reinforcement or punishment.

HYPERACTIVE DOGS

The hyperactive or overly energetic dog requires a trainer who can be firm, consistent, and calm in voice and movement. The excitable trainer must eliminate fast, jerky movements and animated speech, which may only serve to further energize the reactive dog. Slowing down your movements and using calm tones are very effective for gaining tractability and attention from the hyperactive dog. You must try to keep your hands off these dogs, because they are usually hypersensitive to touch, and it excites them even more. A hypersensitive dog can become very reactive with frequent collar corrections. Pepper was a hyperactive dog that drove her owner nuts. Whenever her owner reached for the collar around Pepper's neck, Pepper would start jumping in the air, and the two of them looked like two kangaroos boxing as her owner tried to gain control. Her owner was instructed to slowly run her hand down the leash and take hold of the collar. With collar in hand, she was told to hold on like a statue without talking or fussing until the dog calmed down. Pepper fought the lead and collar for well into five minutes like a Marlin on the end of a hook. After five minutes, she sat panting pitifully. Her owner praised her for sitting and went back to working obedience with her. Thereafter, each frantic episode was shorter, and eventually they became nonexistent.

LETHARGIC DOGS

While the excitable dog needs a trainer with a calm manner, the lethargic dog does better with an excitable owner. The lethargic dog needs to be energized or aroused to a level of awareness that facilitates learning. If the dog is "asleep," he is probably not learning the lesson you intend. Unfortunately, energizing a dog takes a lot of effort using excited and exuberant praise, which has a tendency to wear many owners down. Clyde was a lethargic Clumber Spaniel who lagged during heeling. His owner had to start running to get him to even notice that something was going on. Clyde's owner did not wish to be a sprint runner and was determined to find a different motivator to speed Clyde up. Lagging improved to almost heeling after Clyde's owner shortened the length of the lessons and found the right motivator, a furry little toy rat for Clyde to chase. For best training results, you need to evaluate you dog's energy level and adjust learning methods and motivators to maximize it.

Canine Intelligence

There are many theories about the intelligence of the dog. The majority of dog owners know that their dogs are very bright: these owners can tell any number of stories that demonstrate the animal's high intelligence. In addition to the clever ways in which dogs outwit their owners, canine intelligence shines when dogs are asked to perform the tasks for which they were bred. For instance, the Border Collie is exceptionally quick to learn how to herd a flock of sheep, and only risk appearing stupid when you ask him to scent out a bird. The bird dog who finds the bird naturally, without training, is labeled extremely intelligent. Yet this same genius will look dumb, and probably get trampled, if allowed to mingle with a flock of sheep.

Motivation is a big part of intelligence. One client scheduled an appointment to have her dog evaluated after a discussion with her friend. The client and her friend were convinced that the dog had a learning disability because the friend's Labrador Retriever could open doors with his nose and paw, whereas the client's dog would just sit in front of the door and wait for someone to open it. The idea never occurred to this client that the dog didn't want to go through the door all that badly or that he was smart enough to wait for her to open it instead of expending energy. Another client who owned and trained Border Collies labeled one of her dogs retarded because the dog did not appear to grasp the concept of retrieving as quickly as her other Border Collies. Once the training method was adapted for the dog's particular temperament, which was different from that of the typical Border Collie, she learned and enjoyed retrieving. This same dog would display aggression toward other dogs by growling and curling her lips to show her teeth. The trainers thought the owner was quite effective and consistent in correcting the lip curl until one of the trainers observed that when this "retarded" dog approached another canine, she quietly

This dog has learned to avoid a correction for aggression by curling only one side of her mouth.

curled only one side of her mouth, the side the owner could not see.

Frequently, people believe that bitches are smarter than dogs. However, there is no evidence to date to support the theory of a significant difference in intelligence between the sexes. Those who claim there is a difference may be tainted by their prejudice toward or preference for one sex or the other. Intelligence is more apt to vary individually rather than by the sex of the animal.

Trainers shouldn't assess canine intelligence against human standards. Each individual canine may possess his own unique talent. If the occasion does not arise for the animal to display this talent, it doesn't mean he's dumb. For centuries, behavior experts have been trying to devise a test that measures all aspects of human intelligence and have failed miserably. With this success rate in mind, how can canine experts profess to measure the dog's intelligence when we do not even speak the same language? Labeling a dog dumb can be as unproductive and damaging as labeling humans. If an animal is labeled dumb, the owner usually gives up trying to teach the dog. The label then becomes self-fulfilling because if his owner won't train him, the dog really won't know anything. On the other hand, labeling a dog smart may create unrealistic expectations and disappointment if he doesn't respond as expected. Perhaps all these "dumb" dogs are just clever enough to make their owners think they are dumb to avoid the effort of obeying! A very frustrated Basset Hound owner complained to his instructor that he had spent a month trying to teach his dog to sit on command and the dog just didn't get it. As the owner was explaining his dilemma, the instructor was mindlessly playing with a piece of liver that she had not put away after working with another dog. The Basset noticed the liver and began nudging the instructor. From pure habit, she told the dog to sit. The Basset plopped his rear end down as fast as Bassets do. This is a good demonstration of learning theory proven long ago that a lack of response does not mean that learning is not occurring. This dog was learning, the owner just hadn't found the right motivator to get him to respond.

Perhaps canine intelligence is not measurable, particularly when the criteria for intelligence are measured on another species' yardstick. Fortunately, regardless of breed, the great majority of dogs are intelligent enough to grasp basic obedience commands when training is intelligently presented. A trainer armed with motivating training methods and a good understanding of the principles behind canine learning can shape a dog's behavior into desirable conduct.

Choosing Training Methods

Before choosing a particular training method, carefully examine the technique to ensure that it will communicate proper associations. Certain methods may not communicate what you intend.

A dog-aggressive Akita was enrolled in a training program that his owner thought was reputable. The trainer convinced the owner that the only way to break the Akita of aggression toward other dogs was to let a more dominant dog put him in his place. The trainer's dog displayed dominance toward other dogs, so she placed him in a room with the Akita and left the two dogs to work things out. When the trainer heard a window crashing, she opened the door to find that her dog was injured, and the Akita had been richly rewarded for his aggressive behavior with a nice victory under his collar. If the method does not make sense to you, it probably won't make sense to the dog, either. One trainer sent around a flyer giving free advice to the general public on how to stop dogs from digging. The trainer suggested filling the newly dug hole with water and taking the dog over to the hole by the scruff of the neck to dunk his head in the water filled-hole. The next sentence on this flyer cautioned the owner that the dunking probably would not stop the dog from digging; instead, forcing the dog down to the water by the scruff of the neck was a demonstration of dominance, a root cure-all for problem behavior. The trainer thought through the method far enough to figure out that the water would have no effect on future digging. Unfortunately, he did not explain that the dog would learn to mistrust his owner for trying to drown him. Shortly after this flyer was distributed, another trainer was indicted for animal abuse for employing this very correction technique.

Occasionally, even thinking through a method does not result in a clear understanding of how it works. One day a fellow drove up to class in a pickup with his dog in the back. I explained to him that it was very dangerous to have the dog in the back of an open pickup. I went through the normal lecture on how the dog's nose and eyes could be damaged from debris in the air, the danger of the dog being thrown out of the truck in an accident, the danger to passersby who could be bitten in the face or on the hand if they tried to pet the dog and he decided to become territorial, and last but not least, the danger of the dog jumping out of the truck. The fellow proudly said, "I fixed the dog from jumping out of the truck. He was jumping out and I would throw him back in. We did this for five or six times when I finally got really mad and threw him in the truck for the seventh time and stuffed a piece of horse manure in his mouth for good measure. After that the dog never jumped out again, and the next time he does something bad, I am going to use that manure trick again." It was really hard to determine if the dog stopped jumping out of the truck because he got tired of being thrown back in, or if he was grateful for the gourmet horse manure treat. If you are not sure about exactly how or why a method works, it is probably best to avoid the technique altogether.

Even the most popular methods use techniques that may not be suited for every breed or temperament of dog. A trainer who evaluates each method based on the efficacy of the associations and motivators will be better equipped to match the appropriate obedience method with the canine's individual temperament.

7

Controlling Behavior with Obedience Training

The ideal image of a companion dog is an obedient, loving canine, always at his owner's side ready to serve and ready to defend his owner's life. He's a friend to spend a large majority of time with and look forward to meeting at the door after a hard day at work. In reality, too many people are afraid to go home for fear of what the dog has damaged. The imagined ideal dog winds up in the backyard or at the humane society because of his disobedience and disruptive behavior. If the dog soils the house, chews, bites, jumps, and generally runs amuck, his owner avoids spending time with him. A quiet, relaxing walk with a dog is not possible if he's pulling your arm out of its socket. Conversely, if the dog is obedient, you not only look forward to spending time with him, but may also take pride in him. Obedience training controls and directs the dog's behavior appropriately and effectively in the house, around people, and around other dogs. An obedience trained dog is more pleasant to be with and is welcome in more settings, including the house.

HINTS THAT YOUR DOG NEEDS
OBEDIENCE TRAINING

1. After a walk with the dog, one arm appears to be four inches longer than before the walk.
2. You call your dog to come, you don't know whether the dog is scratching his chin or using sign language.
3. Your command sounds like a loop tape: sit, sit, sit.
4. Invited dinner guests ask before they accept if THAT dog will be there.
5. The veterinarian greets the dog accompanied by two burly technicians.
6. The dog has a vacant stare and glazed over eyes whenever he hears a command.
7. The UPS driver beeps the horn and throws the package from the truck rather than delivering it to the door.
8. The neighbors stopped talking or coming over shortly after the dog arrived.

Any of these coincidences may be a sign that you should seriously consider some obedience training.

Obedience Equipment

A couple of pieces of equipment are necessary to successfully train and control a dog's behavior. The most important piece of equipment is probably the collar.

COLLAR

There are many different styles of collars on the pet market. Most people use choke collars. Choke collars are lengths of either chain or nylon, and have a ring at both ends. You slip the chain or nylon fabric into one of the rings to form a collar, which you then slip over the dog's head. You attach the leash to the live ring, the one that will tighten the collar when you pull on the leash. When you snap or pull the collar, theoretically it chokes off the dog's air. If the collar is too large or incorrectly used, as most are, it will have no effect on the dog. If the collar is too big, it winds up sliding down to the base of the dog's neck, the strongest part of his neck. When the collar is down this far, the dog

Proper way to put on a choke collar. The chain should look like a horizontal "P."

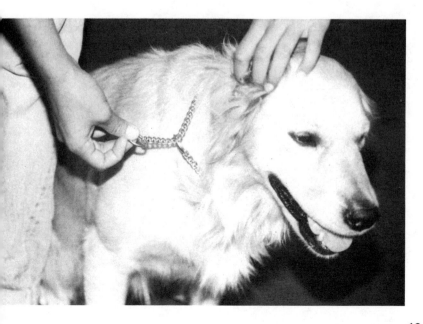

The dog halter provides strong leverage in controlling the dog from pulling.

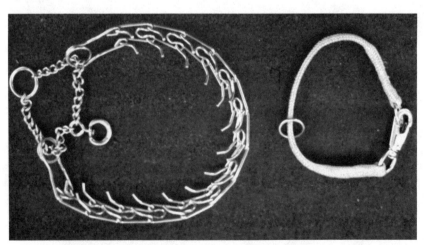

The snap choke is shown on the right, and the prong or pinch collar on the left.

hardly feels it pull and tighten. City streets are peppered with dogs on choke collars pulling their owners down the sidewalk. The dog constantly pulls the owner, the owner pulls back, and in effect, the dog is building more neck and chest muscles to pull even harder. The dog quickly becomes desensitized to the collar and ignores any cues from the collar. To be effective, the collar must remain either high on or in the middle of the dog's neck. Instead of pulling back on the collar, you must give a quick snap on the lead. Immediately after the snap tightens the collar, you should let the lead slack to release the collar.

The principle behind the choke collar is that the tight collar, and resulting loss of air, is a punishment, in this case for pulling. The immediate release and flow of air is the reward for staying close to the handler. When a dog has a choke collar on, the lead should never be tight. If the collar remains tight after the handler snaps the lead, it was placed incorrectly on the dog's neck and needs to be taken off and adjusted.

Keep in mind that you should never leave any form of collar on a dog when he is unsupervised. A collar can get caught and strangle the dog, particularly choke collars. You can replace the collar that you use to carry his identification tags with tattoos or other identifying systems.

The proper use of a well-fitted collar will provide much better control than a loose choke collar. If the dog has been desensitized to a choke collar, you should retrain him with a different type of collar to break any association with pulling and the old collar.

Dogs do not need to be trained on choke collars. The best kind of collar is made of very narrow fabric and can be fitted to remain high on the dog's neck, right below the ears and under the jaw. Fit the collar high on the neck to provide you with maximum leverage against the strength and weight of the dog. A properly sized, thin fabric buckle collar or a product called "Snap Choke," fitted for the upper portion of the neck, works best for training. The Snap Choke collar is placed around the dog's neck and the clasp is attached to the ring at the end of the fabric. The lead is attached to the floating ring between the two ends of the collar. The collar cannot choke the dog when placed around his neck in this manner.

A properly fitted choke chain arranged so that it does not choke also provides good leverage. To keep the collar from choking the dog, attach the lead to the ring closest to the dog's body. If the lead is attached to the non-choking ring, the new sensation will not be associated with the choke collar and pulling. A dog does not have to be choked to learn. In fact, the purpose of the collar is to communicate to the dog, and choking him curtails communication. When the dog is choked, he is more interested in breathing than learning. Once the dog gets a breath after being choked, he gags or gasps for a while, and training time is lost. Learning can occur much faster when the collar is used for leverage and gentle communication rather than torture.

An alternative to collars, which provides maximum leverage and fingertip control, are the head devices patterned after the horse halter. These dog halters are extremely valuable for people who are not strong enough to give powerful corrections or who have physical problems and cannot afford to be pulled around by the dog. However, there are a few drawbacks to these halters. The halter looks like a muzzle to most people which makes them leery of the dog, and the halter can be clumsy to use. The dog must first be desensitized to wearing the halter, and if you want to use a collar later, you will have to retrain the dog with a collar. Fortunately, the retraining process is usually much faster and easier than the initial training process.

Pinch or prong collars, another training alternative, look extremely brutal. These collars consist of prongs evenly spaced which, theoretically, tighten and pinch the dog's skin and neck when you snap the lead. Unfortunately, too many inexperienced trainers and owners put these collars on dogs without first learning how to properly fit or use them. Like choke collars, pinch collars are usually too large for the dog, and the dog becomes desensitized to the collar. A pinch collar that is too large is useless because the collar cannot close properly around the dog's neck. Even if the collar fits properly, people often use the device improperly and inhumanely by pulling back on the collar rather than delivering a quick snap. The pinch collar, when fitted properly, is so effective that one snap usually is sufficient to communicate to the dog to stop pulling. A snap sends an impressive correction, and the dog responds spontaneously by not pulling, whereupon the collar loosens to deliver immediate praise to the dog for not pulling. You can achieve fingertip control with these collars when you fit and use them properly. You should only use these collars after a lesson with a qualified trainer who knows how to use and fit them. The pinch collar is an excellent device for certain dogs and provides marvelous control for people who have physical problems or weigh significantly less than their dogs. A comfortable lead attached to whichever collar is chosen can also make a difference in the effectiveness of the communication between handler and dog.

LEAD

There are numerous types of leads on the market. These include different lengths, colors, widths, and working designs. The optimal lead should only be long enough, normally between four and six feet, to go from the dog's collar to the handler's waist and allow enough slack to keep the clasp pointed toward the ground. Leather or cotton are the gentlest on your hands. The strongest leads are braided and stitched at the clasp and handle ends. As a rule, the strongest and best clasp is made of brass. The width of the lead depends on the size of the dog and your hand. A thick, heavy lead, which gives little advantage over a strong smaller lead, can be very uncomfortable to hold in your hand. However, no matter how large the dog, there should be no reason to have a lead wider than an inch if the lead is braided and has a brass fitting. The more lead there is, the more difficult it and dog become to manipulate. Use a lead to control the dog outside. Indoors, four to six foot leads can get caught up on everything, so use a handle there instead.

HANDLE

The handle is a clasp, preferably brass, with a six to fourteen inch piece of leather or strong cord attached to it. You attach the handle to the dog's collar and leave it on him all the time when he is supervised. If the dog is a chewer, you can spray products that deter chewing, like Tabasco sauce or ammonia, on the handle, or you can substitute a piece of jewelry chain or a slightly heavier chain for the cord or leather. You use the handle to get a grip on the dog in the house, or anywhere he's not wearing a lead. If you need to get physical control of the dog for instance, to prevent him from jumping on a child, you can grab the handle, instead of skin or hair. Skin holds are not very secure to hold on to and can be very aversive for the dog. Grabbing at the dog's body teaches him to stay out of your reach.

Another handy piece of equipment is a squirt bottle that is capable of sending a good hard stream of water. Proper and effective use of the squirt bottle is discussed on pages 101–102.

Training Sessions

Training sessions should be long enough to provide several repetitions of the obedience material, and short enough not to tax the dog

The short lead or handle gives the owner a "handle" on the dog's behavior when the leash is not attached.

and accomplish little more than making him dread his lessons. A competition obedience trainer was very serious in seeking advice as to why a dog just stopped performing and was unwillingly to work after one and a half hours into the daily training session. Effective training sessions should be five to thirty minutes long. The appropriate length of time for each session is dependent upon several factors:

1. *The amount of material the session includes.* If there are a lot of exercises to teach and/or review, the session time will increase. Dogs will

not tolerate many repetitions of the same exercise without becoming bored, so in a long session use a variety of exercises to keep their interest longer. Generally, dogs don't have extremely long attention spans, and you must build this attention gradually. Training long past the dog's attention span will make the lessons unnecessarily laborious for him and he'll learn to hate the sight of his lead. In order to increase the dog's attention span, occasionally extend a session just past his normal attention span with fun and easy exercises that he can perform for reward.

The puppy that is learning to sit, down, and heel will do fine with a ten minute session, whereas the older dog that is learning more exercises may need thirty minutes to fit all of them into a session. If the material requires more than thirty minutes, you should break the training sessions into two separate sessions. If you and your dog are having fun, the sessions can be longer, but if he's bored, cut it short.

2. *How long it takes the dog to correctly perform.* Each session should be long enough to include three correct repetitions of every exercise being taught. If the dog is confused or distracted and has difficulty grasping a particular lesson, you can manipulate the training objective. For instance, you may choose to train only long enough to meet the objective of three successful repetitions for the confusing task, and eliminate all other exercises, or you might lower the objective so the dog only has to successfully perform part of the exercise, and then go on to another task.

Avoid making the session so long that the dog becomes frustrated or bored. If he is having difficulty performing three repetitions correctly, end the session the first time he correctly performs the problem exercise to avoid a negative marathon session. During the next session, you may again require the three repetitions criteria. A good trainer has a flexible agenda and does not dwell on problems. Dwelling on problem areas by repeating the exercises over and over in the same session only serves to embed the problems in the dog's mind. Problem sessions, conflicts, and corrections will remain as strong negative memories for the dog and sour him on these exercises and lessons. Many strong memories that humans or canines harbor are of especially negative experiences or the last event in a particular situation. For instance, the hour-long training session in the backyard during which you yelled at the dog and made him sit 135 times until he sat correctly 5 times in a row, will be an unpleasant memory for a long time. The mere act of placing a lead on the dog and going into the backyard will cue unpleasant emotions in him. When a training problem arises, motivate the dog to perform correctly once, then end the session.

End training sessions on a good note, that is, with the dog performing correctly and being praised, so he'll remember the last event of a training session as positive. Even if a session has been going poorly, end it with a simple exercise the dog can do to earn praise. For instance, you might talk funny and ask him to wag his tail. Your happy voice is usually enough to elicit a wag. Praise the dog for tail wagging, and then end the session. Even if the dog does not understand how or why the session ended happily, he will have a positive memory of the training. Good training strategies include planning easy exercises for the end of the training sessions.

3. *How well the dog knows the material.* Training strategy involves planned exercises and varied session times. Some sessions may involve the review of all known material and the adding of one or two new exercises. You can add another short session for only working on one problem exercise and one old maneuver that the dog finds easy and enjoys performing. Don't overload the sessions with so much new or problem material that the dog has no opportunity to relax and/or earn a reward and praise. Naturally, the amount of time the training sessions take will vary based upon whether the material is new or just review.

4. *Time available for practice.* You can be reasonably sure that a dog understands an exercise when he executes the task on command 90 percent of the time. Even when he demonstrates an understanding of an exercise, practice the lessons occasionally to maintain the behavior. The cliché, "use it, or lose it" applies to dogs as well as people. The more often the dog and trainer practice, the more proficient the team will become. While you may elect to increase practice sessions for the dog who is showing difficulty with an exercise, the routine number of sessions should comfortably fit your schedule so that the sessions are easy for you to maintain. Even one training session a week will train a dog. The training will just take longer than if more sessions were available.

5. *The trainer's frame of mind.* Always keep training sessions upbeat. If you are having a bad day and training does not make you feel better, skip the session. Your attitude travels to the dog through the lead. If you are tense, the lead will be tight and jerky. The dog has no conception that your boss was a jerk that day; he only knows that sometimes training is fun and sometimes it's a drag, and that you are unstable.

6. *The location.* Training should take place in different settings to help keep the sessions new and upbeat. New settings also teach the

dog to be obedient in different places. The location of the training sessions must mimic the environment in which you expect the dog to be obedient. For example, if he's to be obedient around other dogs, you must train him in the presence of other dogs. If the dog is to be trained not to take food off the floor, you must place food on the floor and train him not to take it. The more novel training situations you can set up, the better. Many different places will be much more effective than just a few different locations.

7. *Variety.* When two techniques are available for training the same exercise, practice both methods. Each method has advantages, and the variety will minimize boredom. For example, you can teach the down physically or by the inductive method, using a treat. The physical technique teaches the down and communicates to the dog that you are more powerful, while the inductive method also teaches the down and helps maintain the dog's playful and upbeat attitude.

Obedience Commands

The majority of obedience exercises or commands did not originate solely to entertain or impress people; rather, these commands were conceived to control and direct the dog's behavior appropriately in all situations. The sit command not only impresses visitors when the dog reacts willingly and quickly on the first command, but also keeps him from jumping up, because he can't jump up and sit at the same time. Therefore, you successfully discourage jumping on visitors by reinforcing the sit.

Obedience commands are words you teach the dog and expect him to obey. You shouldn't yell or speak these commands harshly, but give them in a normal voice. The exceptions are the action commands "come" and "heel," which you should deliver in a happy, motivating tone, and the correction commands such as "no" which you should give in a harsh tone.

Use the dog's name before all moving commands, such as "Snoopy, Heel," "Snoopy, Come." Using the dog's name alerts him and allows him to realize that you are addressing him. Don't use the dog's name on the stationary commands "stay" and "wait," when he is expected to remain calmly in position. Using his name stimulates him and encourages activity which is counterproductive when performing the stationary exercises.

A command is meaningless to a dog unless you teach him properly. A command is worthless if you do not require him to obey it. Also, avoid repeating commands after the dog has learned the meaning of them. For instance, if you command him to stay, and he gets up from position, and repeat "stay," he may interpret the second command as a signal that a new exercise has started. The dog may not interpret the second command as the correction it was intended. You should correct the dog that breaks position without a new command. Even if the dog corrects himself by returning to position as you move in to deliver a correction, you must follow through with the correction so that he learns that the only way to avoid the correction is to perform the exercise correctly the first time. If you don't follow through with the correction, he'll learn to correct himself only after you begin to move. He needs to learn to stay in position on the first command, and not to move until you give a release command.

OKAY

Common release commands are "okay" or "good." Every meaningful command should have a release word such as "okay" to communicate that the exercise is over and the dog can be a dog again. After he completes an exercise, use a release word with lots of verbal and physical praise.

NO

The command "no" is used far too much and enforced far too infrequently by the average dog handler. Most dog owners or trainers use "no" for every misconduct. If the dog gets up from a sit-stay before being released, the trainer may yell, "No, Sit." The dog that eats food from the ground hears, "No, Drop it." "No" is used so often, the word is meaningless for the average household dog. Making it even less effective, "no," is rarely backed up with a meaningful correction. For the broken sit-stay, some people just place the dog back into position, and when the dog takes food from the ground an owner may just pull the leftovers out of his mouth. Neither action is a meaningful correction that will discourage the undesirable behavior. A proper correction must follow the command. Also, "no" can be a much more meaningful command if used only in one context and enforced.

"No" is an excellent command to use for aggressive acts, because for most people, the word comes to mind very naturally in tense situations. A trainer who sees aggression building will often automatically, out of alarm, yell "No!" in a firm and harsh tone. When aggressive behavior is building, there is no time to think of proper commands, particularly, when the word "no" is so natural. However, in order for the command to be effective and meaningful to the dog, you must only use the word for the specific purpose of stopping aggressive acts, and follow it with a correction to give value to the word. The intact male that stiff bodies up to another male should be quickly admonished with a harsh "No" and a strong pop on the collar. The dog learns "no" by hearing the command as he is misbehaving and at the same time receiving a collar correction. If you back up the command with a correction 100 percent of the time, the dog will eventually avoid punishment by ceasing the undesirable behavior immediately upon hearing the command. After the dog is trained and reacting to the command, you should intermittently back up the command with a correction to maintain the strength of the command.

SIT

The sit is a good exercise to control the movement of the dog for various reasons. The dog that dances around with excitement whenever you take out his lead to prepare for a walk wastes valuable recreation time. Unfortunately, dogs do not understand that the more time they spend getting dressed, the less time there is for walking.

In teaching the sit, place your right hand in the dog's collar to keep him from moving forward. Command "Sit" and gently pull him back into a sit by the collar as you run your left thumb and index finger down his back with moderate pressure on each side of his spine to the base of his tail. Apply pressure at the base of his tail until he sits. Then praise the dog for sitting.

After a week's worth of sessions, command the dog to sit. If he does not sit, tap him on the base of the tail, holding the collar in your right hand to keep him in position. Deliver a harder tap if he doesn't sit after the first tap. Do not push the dog into the sit, because he will only resist and continue standing. The contact must be hard enough to motivate him to avoid the tap. Give immediate praise when he sits.

GET DRESSED

"Get dressed" tells the dog to place his head through the collar rather than fidgeting and dancing around when you want to put the collar and lead on. To teach the behavior, place the collar on the dog's neck to control his movement. Command him to sit. If he moves from the sit, place him back into a sit by the collar. When he sits, command "get dressed," and place a second collar over his head. Praise him

To teach the dog to sit, place your right hand on the clasp or in the dog's collar and position the index finger and thumb of your left hand on each side of the spine starting at the shoulder blade. With moderate pressure, slide your left hand to the base of the tail.

immediately if he sits still while you place the collar. Don't attempt to put the collar on when he is moving around. You can hold a treat in the center of the collar as you command "get dressed" to induce the dog to stick his head through. When he does, praise and take him for a walk.

READY

The command "ready" tells the dog to make eye contact with you. If the dog is maintaining eye contact, he is generally paying attention and is better prepared to learn. You may choose to use other words like "look," "watch," etc., for the purpose of getting attention. Use the attention command every time you start a session or after a break in lessons, and before a new lesson is started. You can also use the "ready" command to get a dog's attention during a walk when another dog approaches. If the dog is paying attention to you instead of making eye contact with another dog, a fight may be avoided. There are two techniques to teach the dog to give attention on command.

The easiest technique is to use a treat. Command the dog to sit as you face him and hold his collar in one hand and a treat in the other. Move the treat from the dog's nose to your eyes as you command, "ready." He'll follow the movement of the treat to your eyes. Praise him for looking at your eyes. You can lengthen the amount of time you maintain eye contact if you move the treat from the dog's nose to your eyes a couple of times before praising him and giving him the treat. If the dog jumps up at the treat, place him back into a sit. Only give him the treat when he sits and maintains eye contact.

The other method of teaching the ready command consists of holding the dog's collar in one hand and his jaw in the other hand. Lift his head up and command, "Ready." When the dog makes eye contact, reinforce it with calm verbal praise and a scratch under his jaw.

COME

Never allow your dog to run free until he reliably returns to you. If you let him run free and have no way to enforce the command to come back, your dog will learn that you are powerless and the command "come" is meaningless. From the dog's point of view, an hour's jog through the neighborhood, past dogs and trash cans, might certainly be worth the consequence of your wrath. The one command dogs disobey the most is the recall or come when called. Puppies under five months are very dependent and are usually very reliable about going to their owner when called. After 4 1/2-5 months, when the dog becomes less dependent and the psychological umbilical cord is severed, the puppy would rather explore the environment than be obedient to the owner's call. You should start training your dog to come on command in early puppyhood, the day you acquire him, and certainly before he asserts his independence. The older dog that has already learned that returning to you on command is not necessary, will take longer to train to come reliably.

The motivators used to teach a dog to return on command must have a very high value. The motivators must be more rewarding than any other stimuli that may be present in the environment. The best motivators for training a dog to obey the call command are the two things dogs love most, chasing something and very tasty treats.

Puppy Recall

For the young puppy that has not learned to run off yet, start the recall training in the house. Stand right in front of the puppy with a delectable treat in front of his nose and call his name with the command "Come," as you back up a couple of steps. The puppy will follow the treat. When you stop backing up, get down to the ground or the puppy's eye level and praise as you give him the treat. After several repetitions when you are sure he is responding to at the least his name, begin to stand farther away before you call him, and run backwards as he approaches you. Do not do too many repetitions in one session because the puppy will get full and not put out as much effort for the treat. Continue to increase the distance, maybe even to another room where the puppy can't see you when you call him. Add distractions when the puppy is responding. For example, you may want to call the puppy when he is inattentive or engrossed in playing. If the puppy does not come, go back to calling from a closer position and try to find a tastier treat or other stronger motivator. At least one practice session daily will produce a very reliable recall.

The Older Dog

Attach a lead to the dog and move to the end of it. Regardless of whether the dog is attentive or inattentive, command "Come." If he moves toward you, run away about ten feet while holding on to the lead and give praise and a treat when he catches you. If the dog does not respond to the command, give a hard, fast snap on the lead as you run away from him without dropping the lead. Be sure to snap the lead instead of pulling it. If the lead gets tight, slow down to leave slack in it so as not to drag the dog. After approximately twenty steps, turn to face the dog and continue running backwards a couple of steps until he catches up. If the dog does not come close, give him another snap. When the dog is close, drop to the ground and praise him with petting and a treat. The first motivator introduced is the snap. The dog is motivated to obey the command to avoid the snap. The second motivator is the chase, and the third is the treat and praise.

When the dog is coming quickly and reliably on the training leash, take him to different places, such as the park, for practice. Do not let him off lead. After he is reliably returning on lead in the park, you can add a couple of feet of rope to the lead. After each successful session of the dog returning on command, add a few more feet of rope to the lead to teach him to return from long distances. Training should take place in environments where the dog will be distracted, or you may add distractions to old training grounds. A fuss and praise should always accompany very tasty treats when the dog returns on command.

Teaching the dog to return without a lead requires using a lighter lead made of something such as fishing line for at least three months before commanding the dog to return without a lead. The first few times you take the lead off, practice the exercise in a controlled area such as a totally fenced tennis court so that the dog cannot get away. Should the dog disobey, put the lead back on him for a couple of more weeks of practice before another off-lead trial. Even the well-trained dog will occasionally ignore the recall command for a good sniff. If the dog is well trained and normally returns 99 percent of the time, call his name again to ensure that he is paying attention. When the dog looks up, repeat the command "Come." Many trainers believe that the dog's hearing is so keen that it is impossible for him not to hear a command. However, dogs, like people, can become so absorbed in their work (for the dog it's sniffing), that they don't hear a call. If you cannot get the dog's attention, calmly and quietly walk up to him and give him a very strong snap on the collar with the command "Come." Then run or quickly back away so that the dog is coming on his own. Praise him when he is in front of you. Attach the lead to the dog's collar and review the recall exercise at least five times with praise for each time he returns to you. Take the dog back, on lead, to the interesting spot to become distracted or absorbed again. Call him and praise for obeying. The dog will obey because the lead is attached. You can then try him off lead again. Should he not obey at this point, retraining is in order, particularly with distractions and a little stronger motivator.

Misha was a very obedient Husky in all exercises except the recall. Before she learned the chase, she would run for miles if she got away in open spaces. Although the training seemed to curtail the running off behavior in open spaces, in enclosed places she would go about halfway to her owner when called and then turn and run around in wide circles until she exhausted herself. Misha was set up in an enclosed area on a concrete floor to do her recall. Her owner was instructed to equip herself with a very large set of keys. When Misha made her first turn, her owner threw the keys with good force so that they would hit the ground beside Misha as she passed. Just as the keys hit the ground, her owner commanded, "Come." The noise and flying object was startling and disrupted Misha's glee about running. Misha's tail went down as she crouched toward her owner. Her owner praised her for coming to her. The process needed to be repeated several times before Misha was convinced the noise would occur every time she disobeyed. Admittedly, it took several sessions for Misha to get her tail up again, and she did alert somewhat negatively to the sound of rattling keys for several weeks. However, the noise also served as a good reminder that running around in circles was unacceptable. The keys are a good aid because they can be comfortably kept in a pocket, whereas a can filled with pennies or pebbles is a little large for the pocket. Trainers use a device called a throw chain for the same purpose, but the keys are louder and noisier when they hit the ground. Some trainers also use the throw chain not just for noise but to hit the dog, which is not the purpose of keys. The keys should hit the ground, not the dog. If the dog is bent on running, which can be very dangerous to his welfare, and he is unaffected by the noise, you may want to consider using a device that will make impact without damage. This can be an appropriate use for a shock collar. A shock collar used intelligently under the guidance of an experienced professional is safer than chains or keys hitting the dog in the eye.

The "wait" command is what you can use to keep the dog in place and attentive when practicing the recall. Instead of waiting for the dog to become inattentive, command him to "wait" (see below). At the silent count of five, call his name and give the command, "Come," and then run away as above. The count for the dog to wait is silent and varied, making him sometimes wait longer, sometimes less, before you start calling and running.

WAIT

The wait command signals the dog to remain in position, temporarily, until another command is given. For example, when getting out of the car, you can command the dog to wait in order to prevent him from jumping out of the car until the lead is attached. You can also make the dog wait for safety reasons before you proceed down a flight of stairs. The wait is initially taught from the sit position. After the dog understands the wait command, you can tell him to wait while in the down or stand positions. The verbal command is accompanied with a flash of the hand in front of the dog's eyes. Command "Sit," and praise the dog for obeying. Flash an open hand in front of the dog's face and command, "Wait." If he moves, pop him back to the original position with the lead. Never reposition the dog with your hands. Repositioning him with the collar makes the correction more aversive and prevents him from interpreting the physical contact as praise for moving. You must place the dog back in the original spot from where he moved. Even if you were ready to call the dog and he only jumped the gun by a second or two before the command, put him back in the original position. Otherwise, the dog learns to move in spite of the command. If

The handler commanded the dog to wait before she proceeded down the steep staircase.

he inches closer to you and you don't correct him by placing him back, he is rewarded by being closer to you. The dog may move his head or tail without correction, but you should correct him for moving his feet or body.

You should vary the amount of time between the wait command and the subsequent recall command. If the amount of time between commands is always the same, the dog will anticipate when to move. Finally, reward the dog occasionally with a treat or praise for waiting before giving another command.

HERE

"Here" is a wish command. Use "Here" when you don't have control to enforce the command "come" because the dog either got away or is so far from you that you suspect he may not obey the recall command. The command "here" means the trainer "prays or wishes" the dog will come. The good trainer never uses a command that cannot be enforced. If the dog has not had enough training or gets away accidentally and you use a "come" command and then cannot catch him, he will learn that the command "come" is unenforceable. Instead, you should use the wish or throwaway command "here." You will be thrilled if the dog obeys, but if he doesn't, you may choose never to use the command "here" again. By using a different command, you have not made the recall command meaningless by giving the dog the opportunity to disobey it. If you use a command without being able to force the dog to comply with it, he will learn he does not have to obey. You can use the wish command "here" instead of the command "come." If the dog disobeys, only one command is lost. If the dog obeys, praise him profusely.

You can motivate the dog to return for the wish command by calling out his name in a very happy voice to get his attention. Once the dog looks over, command "here", and get down to the ground or run away from him. When the dog runs to you, praise him and give him a big treat.

LET'S GO

The command for walking on a loose lead without being in heel position or at your left leg is "let's go." A leisurely stroll through the park would not be very enjoyable for either you or the dog if formal heeling had to be enforced constantly. The command "let's go" tells the dog, "Take time to sniff the roses, but don't pull on the lead."

Attach a four-to-six foot lead to the dog's collar, and every time he walks off far enough to make the lead tight, command, "Back," accompanied by a hard, fast snap on the lead. The snap on the lead is parallel to the ground in the direction opposite to the one in which the dog is pulling. If the dog does not stop pulling, continue to snap the lead until he does stop pulling. The snap(s) must be aversive and annoying enough to motivate him to stop pulling. If you pull the lead instead of snapping it, the dog won't be annoyed enough to stop pulling and he will just pull harder. Immediately after the snap that ends the pulling, reward the dog with a slack lead and verbal praise. Repeat the parallel snap every time he pulls the lead tight, and praise him when the lead is slack.

HEELING

Heeling is important for keeping the dog close and in control to prevent any mishaps when crossing streets or being approached by other people and dogs. Formal heeling consists of the dog walking or sitting on your left side with a loose lead. The dog's right leg and shoulder should be parallel to your left leg. If he moves out of position, snap the lead parallel to the ground, in the direction opposite from the one in which he is going. If the dog is pulling ahead, snap the lead back. If he is pulling to the left, snap the lead to the right. When the dog is in heel position again, keep the lead slack and give him verbal praise and a treat. The timing of the snap determines your physical advantage. If the dog gets a whole body position away, you lose leverage because all of the dog's weight is working against the snap. You should snap the lead just as the dog starts to go out of position and before he gets a whole body position from you. Maintain a relaxed, straight arm. If you hold your arm rigid and bent at the elbow, it restricts the range of motion for the snap and usually places stress on your arm, shoulder, and back. If your arm is relaxed, the snap, a motion similar to snapping a whip or shaking out a towel, will only require wrist and arm movement.

SIT-STAY

The sit-stay keeps the dog in a stationary position and out of trouble. Teaching a dog the sit-stay could save a passing four-year-old's ice cream cone, or spare an elderly person from tripping over him.

During any stay command, the dog is not to move out of position until you return to him and give a release command such as "okay." Do not call the dog from the stay position; always return to him before you release him. Only call the dog from the wait command. This way you are consistent and the dog learns to stay until you return and will not anticipate being called. You can use the sit-stay in any situation where

Handler and
dog in heel
position.

the dog does not have to stay for more than five minutes. If he is required to stay longer than five minutes, which can be very tiring for him, use a down-stay.

To teach the sit-stay, first place the dog in a sit, with the collar positioned so that the ring of the collar and the clasp of the lead are between the dog's ears. Hold the clasp up to keep the leash taut. Flash your right hand, fingers spread, in front of the dog's eyes, and as you command, "Stay," step directly in front of him, and then quickly step back into heel position. Give the dog quiet verbal praise for remaining in heel position. Do not give physical praise because he may become excited and move before the entire progression is completed. Repeat the process with the hand flash and "stay" command, but this time, step to the dog's left shoulder before quickly stepping back into heel position. Again, give quiet verbal praise. Repeat the "stay" command process a third time, now stepping around to the dog's tail and then back to heel position. Once again, give the dog quiet verbal praise. Repeat the process for the last time in the sequence by stepping all the way around the dog to the original position. Back in the original position, give the dog a release command with verbal and physical praise.

If the dog moves during this progression, place him back into sit position by the collar, and repeat the last unsuccessful step until he remains in position. You should only proceed to the next step after the dog has successfully completed the previous step. The goal is to get all the way around the dog in four progressive steps without him moving.

After a week, give the lead some slack while practicing the progression. Keep a distance of one foot from the dog. If he moves, use the lead and collar to snap him back into position. Gradually increase the distance away from him to the end of the lead. When the dog successfully sit-stays through several entire progressions from the end of the lead, you may stand still at the end of the lead and gradually increase the length of time he performs a sit-stay. The goal is to have the dog sit-stay for five minutes.

When the dog moves, walk in calmly and correct him by using the collar and lead to snap him back into position. If the dog corrects his own behavior before you get to him, follow through with the planned collar correction anyway. If you allow the dog to self-correct, he will learn to avoid correction for moving by quickly returning to position when you move in his direction. The dog needs to learn that the only way to avoid a correction is by performing correctly, that is by staying in position. When he remains in position, you may walk in and give the dog a treat to reinforce the good behavior. If he moves for the treat, correct him for moving. Dogs are very capable of learning to stay in position when a treat is available. The dog will learn that staying in position earns a treat, and moving, even for the treat, earns a correction. If you only walk in to give corrections, the dog will learn to run to avoid the correction. If you reinforce good behavior, the dog will pay attention to you in an attempt to guess when the reinforcement is coming. Practice the sit-stay in many places and circumstances until the dog learns to stay under all distractions and situations.

Handler gives the stay command with flash of hand.

Handler steps in front of dog, and then returns to heel position and gives the release command. Only verbal praise is given until the end of the progression.

Handler gives another stay command and steps to the dog's left shoulder as shown, then returns to heel position.

Handler next commands stay and moves to the rear of the dog as shown here. Handler then returns to heel position.

91

Handler commands stay and steps completely around the dog. The handler then gives the dog a verbal release command and physically praises the dog for staying in position.

DOWN

The down is handy when grooming the dog and cutting his nails. You teach it in several steps before you ultimately require the dog to drop on verbal command only. The lesson is taught gradually because the down position can be threatening to the dog, and cause stress and even aggression in some dogs. These reactions may stem from the social hierarchy of the canine in which the underdog is pinned to the ground during a fight. This position is a very threatening position as the dog looks up to snarling white fangs. Therefore, when you physically pin the dog to the ground, the action is very threatening to him. The dog that dreams of having control or becomes fearful can lash out with a bite while you are in a most disadvantageous position. Teach the down gently in small steps to minimize provoking aggression or fear.

First Step

Attach the lead to the collar and place the dog in a sit at your left side. Kneel next to him with the lead placed under your knees to prevent the dog from leaving. Pick up one of his front legs at the elbow and let the leg relax a little before letting it down and picking up his other front leg at the elbow. After the second leg relaxes a bit pick up both of

The handler picks up the dog's front legs and uses her forearms to pin the dog close to her side.

The handler stretches the dog's legs forward into a down position.

the dog's legs from the elbows and use your forearms to pin him very close to your body to keep him from pulling away. Command the dog "Down," and stretch him out from a sit to a down position on the floor. When the dog is down, place your right thumb or hand in his collar, applying just enough pressure toward the ground to keep him in the down position. With your left hand, slowly and firmly stroke the dog's back encouraging him to stay down. After a few seconds, use a release word to let him know it's okay to get up. Allow him to get up and praise him verbally, physically, and with a treat. Repeat this exercise for one week before progressing to the next step.

If the dog protests being placed to the ground at any time by placing teeth on your body or by growling, discipline him with a good shake or cuff correction, and then repeat the exercise. (See Chapter 8, Discipline.)

Second Step

After a week of practicing the down by pulling the dog's legs out, place your right hand in his collar, under the chin, and your left hand on the dog's back, on the muscle directly below the shoulder blade. Command the dog, "Down," and with two fingers on each side of the muscle, no more than an inch apart, apply pressure to the muscle as your right hand guides the dog's head to the ground by the collar. When pressure is applied firmly around the muscle, there is an involuntary reaction from the dog to fold his legs. Praise him when he is down. Once he understands the command "down", after several lessons and many repetitions, he should willingly go down with a command and slight pressure to the collar.

Third Step

With your hand on the clasp of the lead, command the dog "Down," and apply pressure straight to the ground. Praise the dog immediately. He should now understand that the command "down" means put yourself in a prone position or be quickly placed to the floor by the collar. The only way the dog can avoid being quickly placed to the floor by the collar is to go down on command.

DOWN-STAY

Once the dog is down, you can use the flash hand signal and command the dog to stay. Repeat the four-step progression used for the sit-stay. The goal is to have the dog not move until you complete the four-

With the dog in a sitting position, apply downward pressure on the collar as your left thumb and index finger pushes on the muscle below the shoulder blade. Your fingers should be half an inch apart around the muscle.

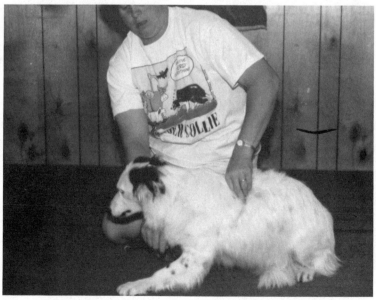

Do not let up pressure until the dog is on the ground.

Puppy Down

Another method for teaching a dog to lie down is often used on puppies. Hold the puppy by the collar to prevent him from scooting forward. Command, "Down," and hold a treat on the ground in front of him. As he bends and stretches to get to the treat, maintain enough pressure on the collar to discourage walking to the treat. The puppy does not get the treat until he is lying down. The puppy will tire of his head being on the floor to sniff and the rest of his body in an awkward upright position and finally lie down to reach the treat. Praise him verbally and give the treat.

The puppy down.

step progression. You should use the down-stay rather than the sit-stay when the dog has to remain in position for longer than five minutes. The dog is not to move from the down unless you return to his side and give a release command. After a week, repeat the progression, keeping a distance of one foot from the dog. If he rises, use the muscle and collar technique as a correction to place him down again. When the dog stays in the down position, go to him and reinforce the behavior with a treat. Practice the down-stay until you have taught the dog to stay for five minutes. Eventually, you can correct him for moving by just snapping the lead to the ground instead of using both the muscle and lead.

SETTLE

The settle command also means the down position. The command tells the dog to lie calmly and quietly, or "chill out," close to you, for longer than five minutes. There is no release command and you do not have to return to the dog to release him for this exercise. The dog may get up after a while for a drink of water or to change positions, as long as he does it calmly.

To begin with, command the dog to "settle" and place the dog down with the handle, lead, and muscle. At the start, have the dog remain in the settle position for five minutes; over a period of a week, increase the time he is in the settle position with each session until he remains for thirty minutes. Every time the dog gets up, place him back in the settle position again by applying pressure on the collar to the ground until he learns to settle for thirty minutes. After the dog is conditioned to settle for thirty minutes, he will learn to remain in a settle position unless stimulated by another event, for example, visitors at the door, or you moving to another room, or the need for a drink of water.

Since there is no release command for the settle, there is a basic difference between this and the more formal "stay". If the doorbell rings, the dog is not discouraged from alerting at the door, because he is allowed to leave the settle position without first being released. However, if the dog were commanded to stay and he ran to the door, he would be breaking the command that means "do not move until I release you." If the dog gets up from the stay to alert at the door without a release command and is not corrected, he learns that in some instances he may get up without a release command and in some instances not. The dog will test the pattern by breaking the stay and may learn that he doesn't have to obey the stay command. When he is taught the settle command, he learns to relax in the down position for an indefinite time. When the dog gets up calmly, or in response

The settle command tells the dog to lie calmly even with people present.

to the doorbell, he does not receive a correction for getting up from the settle. However, if the dog gets up and is rowdy for any other reason than alerting you to the door or another appropriate situation, you again place him in the settle position until he calms down. The settle exercise is also intended for longer periods than the down-stay. If you use the down-stay for longer than five-to-ten minutes, you may forget to release the dog from a long down-stay.

The settle command can also tell the dog to go to a specific spot, such as his bed. If you want the dog to learn to go to a specific spot, every time you command him to settle, take him to the area. If he gets up, use the collar to return him to the settle area. After several sessions of taking the dog to the specific area, command "Settle" and take him within a foot of the area, and let him go the rest of the way alone. You can throw a treat to motivate him to go the distance. He gets another treat and praise for going to the designated spot. After the dog is successfully going to the area alone from a foot away, try sending him from two feet, continuing to increase the distance you send him to settle with each session.

LEAVE IT

The command "leave it" tells the dog not to sniff or touch an object, or even another animal such as a cat. When the dog starts to pick up an object or sniff an animal, command, "Leave it," and give a snap away from the object with the lead or handle. The "leave it" command can be a life-preserving command considering the objects dogs may find and eat. A large piece of chocolate dropped at a party is life-threatening to a toy dog, and a command such as "leave it" may save his life. In addition to using the collar to enforce the command, you can also deliver a strong tap on the front of the dog's muzzle as he reaches to take an object or piece of food. Practice until the dog doesn't go for the object. Praise him verbally and/or give a treat from your hand for obeying the command. Do not confuse him by allowing him to take the object from the floor unless you give another command for picking things up from the floor. I use the command "vacuum," which communicates to my dog that the food may now be picked up.

DROP IT OR GIVE

To teach a dog to relinquish an object, offer him a rawhide or some other object he will be anxious to take in his mouth. Attach the lead or handle to prevent him from running off. After the dog takes the object and holds on to it for a few seconds, command him to "give" as you offer the dog a tasty treat. When the dog drops the object, give him the treat and praise. If he doesn't give up the object, firmly take the object out of his mouth and command, "Give" or "Drop it." Be prepared to deliver a very strong shake or cuff if the dog growls or snaps. Repeat the process until he willingly gives up the object.

OFF

The command "off" tells the dog to keep paws on the ground. Therefore, the command can be used when the dog jumps on people or on objects, such as furniture or kitchen countertops. When he jumps up, command, "Off," and snap the collar toward the ground with the lead or handle. Give the dog a sit command and praise him for being on the ground and sitting.

MOVE

The command "move" tells the dog to get out of your path. Most pet owners walk around or over the dog when he is in the pathway. Invariably the dog gets up just as you step over, and the scene is not pretty when you have a big dog and a short owner. Even a little dog can

The leave it command can save a vulnerable plate of food.

send you crashing to the floor by darting the wrong way. The president of a company, the individual who pays the salaries, does not move out of the pathway of an underling employee. The pet owner buys the dog food, the dog gets to move. Besides, making the dog move gives him more exercise.

"Move" is taught on lead. Lead in hand, command the dog to "move" and shuffle your feet toward him. As soon as the dog moves to avoid your feet, praise him. Repeat the procedure as many times as it takes for the dog to learn to move on command. When he appears to get the idea, reduce the shuffle steps. Practice the exercise until the steps can be eliminated altogether and the dog moves by command. If he doesn't move on command, pop his collar back and shuffle into him. When the dog moves, praise.

BY ME OR CLOSE

The "closer" or "by me" command tells the dog to get next to you in no specific position. The dog does not have to go into heel position.

This exercise is useful in any tight spot, like the waiting room of the veterinarian's office, particularly when another animal passes. Command the dog, "By me," and encourage him to move closer by patting your leg or offering a treat. Stroke and praise the dog, and give him a treat when he gets close. If the dog does not come closer because of a very tempting distraction, snap the lead several times if necessary, until he comes close. Maintain a loose lead and praise him for being close.

KNOCK IT OFF OR QUIT

A quick, harsh, firm "knock it off" can strongly convince a dog to stop all activity. Enforce the command with a snap on the collar, or a shake. An excited dog that is prancing around on the lead may benefit from a good "quit" command as you snap the lead. You can then command him to settle, down, or sit. Praise him for obeying.

JUMP

The "jump" command is another handy one to save the pet owner some work. You can use this command to get a dog in a tub, on a grooming table, or into a car. The easiest way to teach the command is to get a very delectable treat and throw the food into the car. Command the dog to "jump," and most dogs will jump in to get the treat. If the dog needs more encouragement, you can get him started on the way to jumping by placing a treat on the seat of the car or on a table and command "paws on" as you tap the surface. Praise him and give him the treat when he places his paws on the table. After he places his front paws on the surface, lift his rear and command, "jump." Give praise and another treat. You gradually do less rear lifting and the dog does more jumping. It may be best to start off with very low surfaces, six-to-eight inches at first.

QUIET

There are few things more annoying than a dog that barks and refuses to stop when you are trying to talk on the phone or answer the door. Teaching the dog to be quiet on command does not discourage barking at strangers. The command just gives you control to stop the barking when the noise no longer serves a purpose. The "quiet" command also eliminates any attention-getting barking.

Place a squirt bottle, on hard stream, filled with very cold water near the phone and door. Attach the dog's handle to his collar. The method is not very effective when you do not have lead control and have to run after the dog. When the dog has barked enough, three or four barks for people coming into the house, or when barking is inappropriate, such as when you are talking on the phone or greeting a person at the door, command, in a very firm harsh voice, "Quiet." If the dog does not stop barking, squirt him right between the eyes, several times if necessary until he stops barking. Short of aquatic animals, no animal, regardless of his love for water, enjoys cold water squirted at his face, in between his eyes, particularly when the squirt is paired with a harsh, "Quiet." Praise the dog for being quiet. Correct him every time he barks. If he is undisturbed by the squirt bottle, back it up with a glass or several glasses of water splashed in his face. If the dog continues to bark after several glasses of water, try a large pot of water. Eventually, he will respond to just the squirt bottle.

8

Discipline

A dog's confidence level and resulting behavior is greatly dependent upon the form of discipline you use to correct misbehavior. To raise a mentally healthy canine, corrections must not be brutal, and the dog must understand which behaviors cause punishment. When discipline is necessary, choose corrections carefully to make sure the punishment is appropriate and associated with the behavior.

Discipline the Dog Understands

Too often, dogs do not understand why they received punishment or which behavior produced the punishment because pet owners attribute unrealistic reasoning abilities far beyond the animal's mental capacity.

The owner may believe the dog knew he was doing wrong because he looked "guilty" when the owner yelled, "WHAT IS THIS ON THE FLOOR!?!?" and pointed to a mess. The belief that the dog knew better incites the owner to severely punish him despite the fact that the destruction occurred several hours before the owner got home. The dog connects the punishment with the owner coming home, not with the misbehavior from several hours ago. The next day, the owner is prepared to find a mess, and the first thing he or she does upon arrival home is search the house for evidence of dog damage. The posture of an owner searching for a pile of unmentionables is not at all friendly and loving. The owner's hunched over shoulders and wiggling nose, searching for a mess, make the person look mean and contorted. The verbal greeting may go something like, "So what did you ruin today?!?" The "guilty" look is the dog's response to the owner's weird behavior. The dog is remembering previous inexplicable punishments. From the dog's point of view, the scenario might go like this: at 10:00 A.M., cruising the territory for predators, he discovers (accidentally, of course) a strange smell emanating from the trash. To rid the house of such an abnormality, the dog decides to track down the object and recycle the offensive matter. To be thorough and make sure he doesn't miss anything, he spreads the rest of the trash around the kitchen. At 5:00 P.M., the owner walks in the door, and as he is going through the happy greeting ritual, the owner notices the trash. Through clever deduction the owner surmises that the culprit is the dog. Seven hours have passed, and the owner punishes the dog. In fact, if the owner's reaction or punishment is severe, the dog's reaction may be apprehension every time the owner arrives home. In the dog's mind, greeting the owner at the door elicits punishment. The dog forgot about the trash hours ago. Punishment long after the crime, rather than during or immediately after the act, has no purpose other than to confuse or make the dog fearful.

Many owners report that they do not even suspect a problem when they walk in the door, and yet the dog still looks guilty. Maybe there have been enough messes for the dog to realize that a mess on the floor is a good indication that a correction is forthcoming when the owner arrives. However, the dog cannot or will not connect that refraining from chewing at noon will prevent a punishment at 5:30.

There is no evidence to suggest that dogs deliberately misbehave to make their owners angry. Dogs misbehave because they were not taught proper behavior, or they are bored, frustrated, and anxious, to name a few reasons. Dogs chew, bark, etc., to satisfy their immediate needs and emotions, not to spite their owners. Dogs want to please their owners, not spite them.

Effective Corrections

Corrections need to be effective without being brutal. If a dog is punished too severely, he may become meek, unsure, fearful, and reluctant to venture past the familiar. On the other hand, a dog that never receives corrections for inappropriate behavior may have no qualms about stomping on anyone. Holding a grudge or staying angry at the dog for a long time also does not teach him proper behavior. Neither does depriving the dog of social contact by locking him in a room alone or turning your back to him. The locked up dog will start barking or destroying the room, and the owner who turns the other cheek usually gets nipped. Dogs do not comprehend grudges and isolation. At most, the isolation distracts them or they just become weary of their owner's unusual behavior and resent the confinement.

As mentioned previously, the intensity of the correction needs to fit the transgression. A puppy who steals a sock does not do so to watch the contortions of his owner's face. Retrieving is part of being a puppy, as is investigating new stinky items, carrying them around, flipping them in the air, pouncing them to death, and ripping their guts out. A proper correction for retrieving a taboo item would be to happily call the puppy and replace the catch with an acceptable chew toy or treat. Delivering a tough correction would discourage future retrieving. Conversely, the dog that bites an arm does not deserve a trade of body parts.

Alpha Rollover

In the recent past, most trainers corrected aggressive behaviors by taking the dog to the ground and pinning him until the behavior stopped or he displayed submissive body language. This maneuver was labeled the "alpha rollover" and was used to establish dominance over the dog. The method is very conducive to getting the alpha person bit and further intensifying the dog's anger. Restraint, particularly in a situation where the dog is either in a frenzy or seriously aggressive,

Tackling a two-hundred-pound dog to the ground for a correction may be unrealistic.

only serves to make him more exasperated. Tackling an aggressive dog to the ground (particularly a very large aggressive dog) and successfully pinning him may require a bit of a superhuman person. While the wolf may get good results when the puppy is three pounds, people are not wolves or the dog's mother, and will very likely have difficulty taking down an aggressive adult dog. The dog also understands that his owner is much slower and more vulnerable than the bitch that can bite back. A dog will not take his owner as seriously as another dog in terms of corrections meant to imitate dog's behaviors. Consequently, this correction places the owner in a very weak position and can be very dangerous. A trainer must carefully evaluate his or her physical ability in relation to the dog's size and capabilities before using a correction such as the alpha rollover for an aggressive act. A better punishment for aggression which reduces the chance of being bitten and gives the owner more control is the shake correction.

Shake

An effective correction for aggression is a firm "No" paired with strong eye contact as you lift the dog off the ground. Lift the dog off the ground by the loose skin on both sides of the jaw just far enough so his front paws are not touching the ground. Once the dog is off the ground, give him a firm shaking.

To begin the correction, take hold of the loose skin in each hand while holding your forearms close together under the dog's jaw as you lift him up high enough to take his front paws off the ground and shake him. Keep your forearms close so the dog cannot bite them, if so inclined. The shake should last long enough and be strong enough to re-arrange the dog's neurons (better known as an attitude adjustment) and disorient him for a second. After five-to-ten seconds, when the dog ceases the behavior and displays signs of submission, drop him back to the ground. The first sign of submission is usually the dog's eyes turning away. Other signs of submission are a limp body as he plays dead weight, whining, licking, urinating, defecating, or all of the above. Do not praise or console him immediately after the correction. Instead give him a command and praise him when he obeys.

The shake correction effectively communicates to the dog that you are bigger and stronger, because removing his feet from the ground places him in a very insecure position. While the shake is an excellent correction technique, it may not always be the right correction.

Aggressive dogs should not be approached straight on, so the shake may not be a good option if you are facing the dog. An aggressive animal is generally faster than the human and has the advantage in a face-to-face confrontation. If the dog is on a leash, a strong snap of the collar and a firm command such as sit or down may distract him

and defuse the aggression until you are in a better position to correct him. In my experience I have found that the shake is ineffective when used in connection with interdog-aggressive behavior. The dog does not appear to connect the correction with ceasing aggression toward another animal. The most effective correction I have found is a very harsh snap of the collar, and afterwards, a strong obedience command such as the sit or down.

For most aggression, especially when timing is crucial, a cuff under the jaw is effective. The cuff is a particularly efficient correction for the recalcitrant dog who mouths or nips and is undisturbed by being shaken or having his tonsils tickled. (See Chapter 9 for correcting teething and mouthing.)

Cuff Under the Jaw

The cuff under the jaw consists of swatting the dog under the jaw with a closed fist and commanding a firm "No" or "Knock it off." The cuff need not be hard, just strong enough to make the lower jaw meet the upper jaw. The hand always comes up under the jaw, never on top of the muzzle, where many olfactory nerves reside. This correction is a strong one and should be used when you are in a compromising position, the dog gets more aggressive or stimulated by the shake or other hands-on corrections, or has not responded to the other corrections.

Collar Corrections

Collar corrections or snaps on the lead are also good alternatives to the shake correction when the dog is on a lead. The collar correction eliminates having to put your hands on the dog, which can be interpreted by him as aggression or even petting and play. Some dogs become more aggressive and excited the more they are handled or touched, particularly, if the owner cannot maintain calm, firm handling. Strong collar corrections, which force the dog to pay attention to the handler, may distract and defuse the dog from reacting to fearful or aggressive stimuli. A quick snap on the collar with the command "No" can be effective for deterring sniffing and dog-to-dog socializing when such behavior is inappropriate. Of course, if one snap does not convince the dog to stop the behavior, give as many snaps as it takes to get his attention and cease the undesired activity. The collar correction is also handy when the dog attempts to pick up inappropriate objects to eat.

An effective snap of the collar followed by a "Heel" or some other command can be very effective in directing the dog's energy away from the undesirable stimulus and toward working for the handler.

Hanging

Lifting and holding the dog off the ground by the collar or clasp of the lead is defined as hanging the dog. This correction is very drastic and should only be used in extreme emergencies. An emergency arises if the dog is in a frenzy, and a person or another dog is in danger of being bitten, or if the dog is biting and will not let go. To hang the dog, take hold of the back of the collar or the point where the clasp of the lead and the collar meet. Take the dog off the ground just high enough so that his front feet are not touching the ground, and just until he gasps for air. Drop the dog to the ground when he is more interested in breathing than biting. This correction is not to be used lightly or frequently, but only as a last resort when the dog is not heeding other disciplinary measures and is exhibiting dangerous behavior.

Squirt Bottle

A squirt bottle, set on hard stream, filled with ice cold water is the most obtrusive, nonviolent, and effective correction for canine misbehavior.

109

The dog is receiving a shake correction for growling at his owner. This correction is effective because it places the dominant dog in an insecure position.

The bottle method can be used for many different behaviors, such as, but not limited to, jumping up, herding, barking, and chasing cats. Dogs do not like water, particularly, ice-cold water squirted directly at their face between their eyes. You shouldn't add any other substance to the water. Recently, several clients have mentioned that they were told by different trainers and veterinarians to add vinegar, lemon juice, or Bitter Apple to the water for an effective correction. This advice shows an obvious misunderstanding of the principles behind the water correction. Cold water by itself is shocking, aversive, distracting, and very effective when paired with a very strong command. Inflicting pain is not necessary to get a point across. Even though the Bitter Apple spray and other substances are intended for the mouth, not everyone is a good shot, and it could easily wind up in the dog's eyes.

The cuff under the jaw is a fast and strong correction
for the dog that snaps.

Pair squirting the dog in the face with a strong, harsh-sounding verbal correction. Your admonishment and the water will distract the dog from the behavior and is aversive enough to discourage him from repeating it. The dog that nips at heels will not find the act nearly as pleasurable if every time he nips, water is squirted in his face. Be careful not to laugh at the dog or his reaction; laughter will only turn the correction into a water game. Many owner's have claimed that their dog either likes being squirted or does not mind the correction. The first time I squirted my Portuguese Water Dog for barking he reacted in a manner that seemed to say, "Thank you, I was thirsty." After several unheeded squirts, I got out several glasses of water which seemed only to refresh his heated body from barking. Determined, I filled several large pots of water and placed them on his crate. He got the point and stopped barking after the first pot of water was thrown on him. I was then able to go back to the squirt bottle which to this day stops any misbehavior or barking with one squirt if my command is disobeyed. Persist with the water and success will come. You can leave a battery of bottles around the house for fast and easy access. A water bottle simply left in the dog's sight is often a good cue to remind him not to engage in inappropriate behavior. For instance, you can use water to correct barking in a crate. If you leave the bottle outside the crate in the dog's view, it will be a reminder not to bark. Water corrections can be used to discourage an array of misbehavior from a distance, depending, of course, on how far the water bottle can squirt water and the accuracy of the trainer.

For backyard misbehaviors, a power nozzle attached to a garden hose provides a very strong, annoying stream of water for good distance corrections. Toy battery-operated water guns can also send strong streams of water and are more fun for the child in all of us. For distance corrections, loud noises are also good corrections. The noise might be a cap gun or a board hitting a hard surface. The noise distracts the dog and is also aversive. The noise is made as the dog is misbehaving such as digging. When the dog looks up and stops digging, you verbally praise him and call him to you. When he reaches you, give him more praise. Many dogs are afraid of loud noises. The surprise noise can make the dog fearful and nervous, so you will have to determine whether the noise does more damage than good. On the other hand, some dogs habituate to noises and learn to ignore them. The effects of the cold water appear to endure over time.

Rolled Paper

Corrections with rolled up newspapers were used frequently in the 1950s and 60s. Rolled newspaper corrections were strongly discouraged because people abused the correction by hitting the dog on the nose or beating the dog for house training problems. The premise behind the correction was to physically distract the dog from the misbehavior by popping him with the paper without hurting him. In addition to the distraction, the noise of the paper was very aversive to the dog. However, a pop on the base of the tail with a newspaper is not ordinarily painful and far more humane than a choke collar correction. For instance, you can roll a small section of the newspaper into a tube and secure it with a rubber band to make a pretty impressive sound to distract the dog. A small section rolled up will make more noise than a bigger section. The tube does not have to contain so much paper that it becomes a weapon. When the dog misbehaves, you may either pop the rolled paper on a hard surface to make a loud distracting noise or pop the dog on the base of the tail. Pair a verbal correction with the pop so that eventually just the verbal correction will be enough to discourage the dog from misbehaving. The rolled newspaper correction might be a good alternative for the dog that jumps on the counter. Bait him by leaving tempting food on the counter, and when he jumps on the counter, pop him on the rear with the paper and command, "Off." Then, praise him for being on the ground. Like the water bottle, the paper can be left on the counter as a visual reminder of the correction should the dog jump up again.

Aftermath

Following a correction the dog will often look for ways to appease you in an attempt to repair the damaged relationship. It is important not to confuse the dog by consoling him immediately after the correction. But you should give him an opportunity to appease, and he can do so by obeying a command. Give the dog a command, in a normal tone, to do something simple such as sit. After he sits, and most remorseful dogs will immediately obey, you can praise him. You have given the dog a chance to appease, and you have clearly demonstrated reward for good behavior and correction for inappropriate behavior without confusing the two issues.

Alternatives to Punishment

A strategy used to reward proper behavior and ignore inappropriate behavior can be successful in some situations. As an example, behavior modification is a good strategy to use when a dog jumps up on people. Command the dog to "stay" or "wait" in a sit position every time the doorbell rings. The dog cannot physically sit and jump up simultaneously. Don't open the door until he's in a sitting position, and praise and pet him for keeping all four feet on the ground. Sometimes corrections can be avoided by simply replacing the maladjusted behavior with an appropriate behavior.

Creative Corrections

The very sly, creative dog owner can also avoid physical corrections by setting up natural consequence corrections in which the dog is corrected as a result of the environment per se. A good example would be if a dog jumped on the door to bolt out of the house and the door slammed shut on his tail. In the future, this natural correction would most likely make him fearful of running out the door, and encourage him to wait for someone to hold the door. One day while training my Standard Poodle in the park, a cat passed. I didn't notice the cat until my dog took off in serious pursuit, and the lead was out of my hand. The next thing I saw was the cat heading for a tree. I yelled my dog's name to get her attention and she suddenly stopped dead in her tracks. I was just a little shocked when she stopped because I didn't think we had gotten that far in training. I walked up to her and discovered that she had not stopped of her own volition; rather, when passing under the tree, a low branch had caught her ear, and she was snagged. Although the snag cost us stitches, the timing could not have been better. From that one experience, whenever she is running and hears her name, she stops and turns in my direction. Natural consequences, which might be the preferred method of correcting undesired behaviors, are very effective, but, unfortunately, difficult to plan or set up.

Good Prevention

Inappropriate canine behaviors and the damage they often cause can usually be prevented and discouraged from becoming permanent habits with proper management. In the case of a puppy who is teething, (a temporary developmental phase) you can prevent significant damage by confining him to a chew-proof environment until he is past the teething stage. Problems cannot be corrected if no one is present when the behaviors occur. If you don't correct a behavior, the dog will learn that it is acceptable. Therefore, anytime you can prevent, channel, or avoid a behavior, the relationship between you and your dog will be more positive. Positive training methods may sometimes take longer, but if they result in the development of a good friendship between you and your dog, the time and effort will be worthwhile.

Some problems can be prevented. Trash should be covered
or placed out of reach.

9

Aggression

Most dogs communicate aggression through body language. Signals of aggression are growling, snarling, strong direct eye contact, raised body hair, particularly in the shoulder region, and a tense, rigid body posture. The dog may appear to walk on his toes or be stiff legged. The position of the tail and ears depend upon the circumstances behind the aggressive behavior. A dog that displays aggressive behavior such as growling and snarling is not sending idle threats. The dog is sending a warning to back off. If the threat perceived by the dog either intensifies or does not disappear, he will snap or bite.

Snaps or bites that are preceded by growling and snarling are very conspicuous signs of canine aggression. Besides these, there are other levels of aggression that are more subtle but that may also lead to snapping and biting unless corrected. Aggression may start with innocent puppy play, and if the aggression is not corrected, it may gradually increase to serious biting whenever the dog either does not get his way or feels challenged. Regardless of the reason aggression develops, the behavior must be controlled and corrected from the very start, which often means from puppyhood. The aggressive puppy generally develops into an aggressive dog. And, as has been emphasized, the aggressive dog is dangerous and a serious liability emotionally and financially for the dog owner.

Puppy Nipping and Aggressive Versus Vicious Behavior

Terms such as nipping, mouthing, herding, biting, snapping, and nibbling are used to describe different types or levels of canine aggressive behavior.

NIBBLING

Some dogs appear to nibble at a person's skin in the same fashion that they might nibble at themselves to cure an itch. Nibbling is probably a vestige of group grooming, and should be discouraged. A dog that is permitted to nibble or mouth may accidentally injure a child or a visitor. Any act that involves the dog putting his teeth on the human body must be discouraged with either a shake, cuff, or snap on the lead accompanied with a sharp "No." No matter how gentle the dog may be, there is a risk of injury when teeth come in contact with the human body.

Very young puppies sometimes exhibit herding instinct.

HERDING

A chase game that some puppies love involves nipping human feet, which is sometimes a remnant of herding instinct. They love chasing and nipping the heels of any passing feet. Puppies particularly like to "herd" children, because the children usually run and scream, which makes the game very rewarding. Like nipping and mouthing, this game is not necessarily meant to display aggression. However, the dog's nipping usually progresses to bold chasing and biting at heels, which may result in serious injury, particularly if a child is tripped. Shake corrections are very appropriate for chasing games but may be difficult to implement, particularly if you can't catch the dog on the first try. A water bottle hooked to a belt buckle is more effective for the wise and hard-to-catch critter. The water bottle can correct the dog at a distance even if he has learned to run when a correction is impending. Squirt the water straight at the dog's face and accompany it by a harsh "No."

MOUTHING

Nipping, teething, and mouthing do not typically start out as aggressive behavior. Young puppies commonly gnaw or mouth fingers and hands to relieve the pain of teething. Unfortunately, puppy mouthing progresses to nipping if the mouthing is not corrected. Nipping is also a form of aggressive play between dogs. Although puppy nipping is not intended to do serious harm, it can develop into

The owner is correcting the puppy for nipping
by sticking his fingers down the puppy's throat.

biting. The puppy learns that the action of nipping gets people to back off, and it can be a fun game to boot. Specifically, the puppy nips, the person yelps (sound of submission), pulls away, and the puppy gets to chase the hand. Certainly, the person did not intend to teach him that nipping causes retreat; however, from the puppy's point of view, nipping gives him the upper hand, so to speak. If the puppy was successful in getting the person to retreat as a result of nipping, he may logically assume that biting should produce even greater results. As the dog gets older and wishes to occupy a more dominant position in the household, the nipping may quickly turn into biting.

The best correction for puppy nipping is to stick your fingers down the puppy's throat. As the puppy is nipping, instead of pulling your hand out of his mouth, push it in farther, far enough to tickle the tonsils. The puppy will gag and learn that chewing on fingers is very uncomfortable. As the puppy is gagging and opens his mouth wider, you can remove your hand without getting it scratched by the sharp teeth. Additionally, the puppy will be too busy gagging to chase the hand or snap at the moving hand.

SNAPPING

Snapping in its least aggressive form is a reflex. For instance, the sleeping dog that is startled when tripped over, may wake up and snap at the closest object out of reflex action. In this case, the dog is like a person who is startled and automatically strikes out. The bite is usually quick and without enough pressure to do more damage than make a red mark or a slight break in the skin. If a dog startles easy, you should warn him when a person enters the room or gets close. You can use the command "move" to get him out of the way. If the household is full of children running in and out, either crate the dog or confine him to a part of the room away from foot traffic to prevent people from tripping on him.

At its worst, snapping is an aggressive reaction from the dominant or fearful dog. Such snapping must be corrected with a cuff under the chin. The dog that snaps without being corrected, particularly the dominant dog, will become more confident about snapping for control. The fearful dog must be socialized and desensitized to frightening stimuli.

BITING

Typically, a bite is defined as when the dog uses enough jaw pressure to puncture the skin. A dog that intentionally punctures skin, tears flesh, breaks a bone, hangs on to the victim, or delivers multiple bites is considered vicious. For the safety of everyone, the aggressive dog must wear a muzzle whenever in public or in a hostile, provoking situation until the aggression is resolved. These dogs are very dangerous to anyone around them, including their owners, and should not be handled without expert professional advice and help.

Origin of Aggression

Aggressive temperaments in canines are usually the result of both genetics and the environment.

A dog's environment can trigger aggressive behavior, particularly if he has a propensity toward aggression. For instance, people often blame a dog's aggression on being abused or teased by children. Fortunately, a dog's environment can be modified to protect him from abuse and teasing. You can and should insulate the dog's space from negative interactions and incidents that might prompt aggression you cannot control. A chain link fence does not adequately protect the dog when the owner is at work or away because individuals or poorly supervised children may have access to him through the fence. Leaving the dog inside the house or constructing a double fence or a run far from the street fence are safer solutions. Protecting a dog from the environment is his owner's responsibility.

Aggression may also be the result of an injury. An injured dog may not understand the origin of the pain. As a result, he may snap at any object, including a helpful hand, that approaches the injured site. In cases of extreme pain, the dog may even lunge at anyone walking close. No matter how gentle a dog's temperament is under normal circumstances, take precautions such as using professional handling gloves, a muzzle, or at the least, wrap cloth around your hands before touching an injured dog.

Bitches with litters will often exhibit aggressive behavior around their puppies. Aggression associated with protecting the young is a natural behavior, and correcting the bitch may produce unnecessary negative interactions. The majority of bitches will allow trusted individuals to handle their puppies. Take time to gain the trust of the bitch before attempting to handle her puppies.

Many bites are the result of an unsuspecting passerby or visitor invading the dog's perceived territory. No one should walk into another person's (dog's) yard or house uninvited, and certainly the house or yard should not be left open for people to enter. High fences can prevent children from scaling them to retrieve lost balls, and security locks on gates are good deterrents for the average person. Even the mildest mannered dog may feel threatened by people walking in or invading his territory, especially when no one is home.

Then again, there may be no apparent provocation for the dog to bite. This type of attack is known as rage syndrome or idiopathic aggression, and it is very dangerous. When a dog bites for no apparent reason, the victim is least able to avoid the bite. There may be no cues to indicate an impending attack. This type of aggression has been associated with a few specific breeds, but there have been reports of unprovoked attacks in many breeds. Because of its unpredictability, dealing with idiopathic aggression is difficult. A veterinarian should thoroughly examine the dog to insure that there are no underlying physical reasons for the attacks. There are several disorders such as epilepsy or skin allergies that can cause the dog to be very irritable or touch sensitive, and a good medical exam may detect such an underlying problem.

In all instances of aggression, from nibbling to outright biting, the dog can feel either challenged or threatened. A dominant dog feels challenged, whereas a fearful dog feels threatened.

Dominance and Aggression

The canine is a social animal that strives to either be part of a group or head of a group. The dog that vies for the leadership position is called the dominant animal. Dominant dogs are more likely to challenge female household members than the male household members because they perceive human males as more dominant by virtue of their size, manner, and deep voice. A dominant dog will often protest the owner's commands. A command such as "down" may be perceived by the dog as threatening enough to justify a growl or even snarl.

A snarl or show of teeth is the dog's display of force. The teeth are the dog's primary offense and defense, and showing them sends the message to back off. In other words, the owner's position is being challenged. This display does not mean that the dog does not love the owner, only that the dog would prefer an infrastructure shift. In fact, many people who have been bitten by their dominant dog report that the dog is very loving most of the time, and particularly after an attack. If a challenge is allowed to go undisputed, future protests may escalate to bites, so it is important not to let any aggressive act go without a correction. For example, if the dog is on the couch and the owner goes to sit down or tells the dog to get off the couch, and the dog growls, the owner must force him off the couch and correct him for growling with a shake and a firm "no" command. If the dog is not corrected for growling, the couch becomes his possession, and the next time anyone attempts to sit or remove him from the couch, the dog may bite. The shake correction is usually very effective for dominant or possessive behavior. Other situations in which dominant dogs readily challenge the owner include: being removed from the bed, hands in food dishes, taking hold of the collar, brushing or grooming, nail trimming, and being placed in the down position. A dominant canine will also paw or mount people. Each challenge or display of dominance should be met with a shake correction. If several shake corrections do not appear to have any affect in altering the dog's behavior, beef up the intensity of the correction or switch to one of the other correction techniques. You can often avoid challenges by never allowing the dog into a situation that may cause a conflict. For instance, if you don't allow him on your bed, he will never challenge you over being removed from it. Unfortunately, mere avoidance of conflict does not resolve the dominance issue. Confrontations about dominance issues are inevitable in most human-canine relationships. A more effective strategy than ignoring or preventing the aggressive behavior may be to set the dog up for a confrontation when you are prepared to resolve the matter. A possible setup might be to give the dog a very tasty knuckle bone and after a few minutes take the bone from his mouth. If he tenses, growls, or shows any signs of protest, correct him immediately with a shake and a sharp "No." This exercise will let you know what to expect from the dog when push comes to shove. After a well-delivered correction or corrections, there should be no question that you are in charge. In addition, neutering the very dominant dog may contribute to a more controllable temperament.

Neutering the dog will not directly help the owner achieve the dominant position, but the procedure may help stabilize the dominant dog's temperament. In the male dog, the hormone testosterone will be reduced greatly by neutering, which may significantly reduce his aggressive tendencies. With testosterone levels low, the dog usually does not maintain a great urge to be dominant. The effects of neutering on temperament may also be dependent upon the dog's age. The older the dog when neutered, the less dramatic the effects of neutering may be on his behavior. In a dog with a well-established aggression problem, aggression becomes a learned behavior that must be un-learned through training. However, a reduction of dominant aggressive behavior has been noted in dogs neutered as late as 5 and 7 years old. These effects may be observed in the dog almost immediately to several months later. For maximum reduction in aggression, dogs should be neutered as early as 6 months of age. Currently, experimentation with neutering dogs as early as 8 weeks old has reported very good results. To date, the effects of very early neutering appear to be very promising.

Neutering bitches will eliminate the heat cycle and the subsequent hormonal changes associated with it. These hormonal changes do produce undesirable behavioral changes in the majority of bitches including irritability, false pregnancies, and other emotions that may lead to aggressive behavior. All in all, neutering the bitch stabilizes her temperament drastically.

Trained Aggression

The most popular, comprehensive, and respected aggression training program is Schutzhund training. The dog is trained for obedience and attack work. The animal is required to obey unconditionally in both areas. Schutzhund training has not only become a method for police dogs but a serious sport as well, in which members of Schutzhund Clubs compete for titles. Schutzhund training requires great effort, knowledge, and an expensive mentor. The enormous effort and work one has to put into Schutzhund training to earn a title often drives the average person who wants an attack dog for protection to a variety of less exacting sources. Most people buy a heavy-duty breed such as a Rottweiler and then seek any trainer, regardless of his or her qualifications, to train the dog to attack. For many of these private protection training schools, the only requirements of the dog and owner may be the amount of money the owner has and the dog's willingness to bite. Temperament testing for suitability and reliability may not be a requirement. Because the average person is not knowledgeable or strong enough to handle and control an attack-trained, heavy-duty guard dog, the dog can be a danger to the owner and to the community. One must seriously and objectively evaluate his or her own motives, the suitability of the dog, and the liability incurred in training a dog to protect or be aggressive. If your motive is to have a watchdog, you need only train obedience and teach the dog to bark and alert. Dogs naturally alert, and most obedience dogs will naturally protect if push comes to shove. If the sight of an obedient dog does not deter the aggressor, the aggressor has unpleasant ways of dealing with the dog regardless of the dog's training. Several years ago, a salesman came to my door. At that time, I owned a rescue Doberman that had been abused and shot by her previous owner. When I adopted Doxy a few months earlier, she was scared to death of her shadow. We had only been working in obedience for a month, and the work had helped her confidence level considerably, but not enough to go to the door when the salesman rang the doorbell. I quietly half carried and half dragged Doxy to the door. At the door, I loudly said, "Doxy, Sit-stay." I opened the door and commanded, "Doxy, Watch." I didn't really have to tell her to watch; she was so petrified she was not about to take her eyes off of this fellow. The sit-stay training paid off and she stood her ground. The salesman asked, "Is that dog trained?" When I replied with a simple "Yes," he said "Thank you, I have the wrong house," and left. Doxy in her scared state remained obedient, and that was all she needed to do to change this fellow's mind about selling magazines or whatever else he had in mind. The home can be just as secure with an obedience trained dog as with an attack trained dog. More so, in fact, without the dangerous liability of an animal trained to attack. There are countless stories of protection dogs backfiring on their owners, and there are more reliable ways to protect a home and its occupants.

Games

Some professionals recommend that dog owners refrain from playing certain games with their dogs to avoid surrendering dominance to the dog. These professionals are concerned that the dog will perceive the game as an opportunity to challenge the owner's position, and that a successful challenge could lower the owner's social status in the relationship, resulting in more frequent challenges. The game of tug-of-war is most frequently discouraged as a dominance issue game. Tug-of-war is a game that dogs play among themselves, and a game dogs seem to truly enjoy. There is no evidence to support the theory that dogs that are allowed to play tug-of-war with their owners are more aggressive or dominant than dogs that are not allowed to play the game. Games which involve winning do not cause a loss of domi-

Tug-o-war is a game that both dog and owner can enjoy together without jeopardizing the owner's social status.

nance. If dominance is lost, the handler never had control in the first place. The only time tug-of-war or any rough game should be avoided is when a dog owner cannot control the dog from nipping. If the dog nips hands while playing a rough game, a shake or cuff correction is appropriate and usually effective.

Wrestling is another game that people and dogs alike seem to really enjoy. But wrestling, like tug-of-war, can cause problems if the owner allows the dog to mouth or nip at body parts. The dog that is allowed to mouth as a form of play may mouth visitors or children. The visitors may not understand the dog's intention to play and may react by pulling away. If the person pulls away, the dog will close his mouth to hold on tighter and may injure the person. The best way to prevent injuries from nipping or biting is to eradicate mouthing under all circumstances. Once mouthing is eliminated, wrestling does have advantages in demonstrating dominance. Playing with the dog roughly and maintaining physical superiority communicates to the dog that the owner is stronger and more dominant. Demonstrating this type of control in play rather than when the dog is already angry or aggressively charged, such as in the alpha rollover correction mentioned earlier, can be much more effective for displaying dominance and less dangerous to the handler. As long as the owner maintains physical authority and controls mouthing, rough games are another way to positively interact with the dog. However, a child who may not have the strength to maintain the dominant position, should not roughhouse with the dog.

Children and Dogs

Contrary to popular belief, children and dogs do not go together like peanut butter and jelly. Leaving a young child alone with a dog in the house or backyard is like leaving a couple of 2-year-olds alone with loaded guns. Unless you want trouble, never leave a young child alone with a dog. Children must have guidance, discipline, education, and supervision throughout their childhood to learn how to interact appropriately with, and be nurturing toward a dog.

Children are curious creatures who may continually test a dog's patience and tolerance. A young child may get an enormous thrill out of chasing a dog or jumping on a dog that is lying quietly in the corner, and it takes a very rare animal to tolerate such roughness without snapping. The inhibition or tolerance levels for biting are different in every dog. Some dogs may bite with little provocation, and some dogs are more tolerant. Every dog that has teeth is capable of biting and the best way to prevent injurious conditions between children and dogs is to supervise the interactions. Children inclined to tease or be rough with the dog must be taught to treat and interact with him properly. Even the most tolerant dog may have bad days or sick days and lose patience with a child. He may try at first to escape; however, a persistent child who does not understand or does not heed the dog's body language/warnings may eventually receive a nasty bite.

Even the older child may experiment with or be curious about the dog's reaction to painful or unusual situations, and may subject the animal to frightening circumstances that elicit snapping. Children must be taught that animals can be frightened, hurt, and defensive; children must learn compassion and nurturing. Supervision, management, and modeling nurturing behavior will protect children from dog bites much more effectively than corrections after the fact.

The dominant dog often views the young child as a subordinate and a good subject to control. He may chase, herd, jump on, and in-

Leaving dogs and children together unsupervised is not safe.

jure children. The dog may even go as far as pushing them to the ground and mounting them. The majority of children do not know how nor do they have the coordination and muscle to correct and stop the dog. A supervising adult will be able to correct the dog immediately.

In addition to supervising children, you can prepare the dog for them by desensitizing the dog to rough handling. Devise games for pulling tail, ears, hair, skin, tough patting all over the dog's body, and shoving. If you act playful, the dog will accept the rough playing as a game. If the dog becomes fearful, you may want to start out with firm touching and gradually build up the roughness. Should he become aggressive, he needs to be corrected. Desensitizing the dog to rough handling in a positive, fun manner can save a child from being bitten by a surprised or unsure dog.

Fearfulness and Aggression

When an animal, or human, for that matter, becomes threatened or frightened, the brain produces specific chemicals that place the body is a state of heightened alertness or preparedness to react. This response is referred to as the "fight or flight" response. The animal will first attempt to get away, and if no escape route is found, will defend himself with a bite. The bite is usually a fast, hard snap with enough force to impair the perceived attacker long enough for the dog to find an escape route. While all dogs become fearful of something at one time or another in their lives, the fearful dog referred to here is the animal that is afraid of many things a great majority of the time. These dogs rarely investigate frightening stimuli on their own and are either slow to recover or never recover to a relaxed state. Correcting a fearful dog, particularly by the method used for a dominant dog, is a great mistake. A correction to the fearful dog only serves to affirm his fearfulness, at the least; more likely, it intensifies his fear. You must enforce obedient behavior and firmly deal with the dog in a manner that promotes confidence and reduces fear as is discussed in Chapter 10.

A fearful dog may learn to be aggressive. If the dog snaps because he cannot get away, the victim pulls away and the dog learns that snapping will make the person back off. The fearful-aggressive dog is also referred to as a "fear biter." Fear biters have a very bad reputation with trainers. They are believed to bite unpredictably with little warning, and great speed. The dog is considered unpredictable because the body language does not communicate intense fear. After the dog has bitten a couple of times and learned that he can defend himself, he rarely tries to escape, rather he maintains a fairly natural stance neither appearing friendly or overtly aggressive. Cameron, a two year old mixed breed, neutered male had shown fear of people since he was taken home by his owner at the age of 6 weeks. The owner was a young college student who lived with several roommates. While Cameron was growing up, friends of the roommates were always coming and going, and when Cameron displayed fear by backing away, the visitors sometimes chased him down to pet him. Cameron had no escape; if he went under the couch, he was pulled out and petted. When Cameron was 1 1/2 years old a visitor came in the door and Cameron backed up to the couch. The visitor continued to approach and Cameron snapped, but did not connect with the person's hand. The fellow reacted by stepping back from Cameron. The next time a friend came in and approached, instead of backing up Cameron snapped and connected leaving a minor puncture wound. The owner contacted me for a behavioral consultation, and when I met Cameron he displayed fear, but warmed up to me and approached me for a treat. After several weeks of training, Cameron appeared to be improving and seemed comfortable, even wagging his tail in a happy manner in the training class with other dogs and people present. He even allowed scratching under his chin after he took a treat. The owner missed a couple of classes and I called to find out if there was something wrong. Cameron's owner reported that he had snapped at another person who came into the house and approached him. When I inquired about the severity of the bite, the owner reported that it was not a "bad" bite, and did not require stitches. When Cameron came back to class, I offered him a treat and without warning, he viciously attacked my hand leaving three severe wounds. After the bite, his stare quite obviously communicated to me to back off or be eaten. Several weeks later, I was told by one of the owner's roommates that three weeks prior to the attack on me, Cameron had viciously attacked two visitors, without provocation, on two separate occasions. The roommate explained that one person was a frequent visitor who had previously gotten along with Cameron. This visitor was sitting down when he offered a piece of popcorn to Cameron, and Cameron reacted by viciously attacking his hand. Cameron had learned that biting was very effective in keeping people away, and he became more aggressive with each snap and bite. Once the fearful dog learns to be aggressive, the attacks will be more severe and frequent with little predictability. The prognosis for rehabilitating a dog like this through correction or any other means is very bleak because working with the animal is dangerous.

DOMINANT/FEARFUL AGGRESSION

Labeling people and animals with psychological disorders has become very popular in the last decade. Besides classifying their dogs as either dominant or fearful, people have recently perceived their dogs to suffer from ADD (Attention Deficit Disorder), LD (Learning Disability), schizophrenia, and psychotic behavior. What ever happened to the dog that was just simply out of control! Labeling is dangerous, particularly if the label is inaccurate. When an animal is labeled, the trainer may follow a specific program to rehabilitate the dog that may not correctly address all the problem behaviors. For instance, depending on the circumstances, a dog may be dominant in one situation and fearful in another. Smug was a rather large Labrador Retriever cross that displayed distinct dominant behavior with the wife and children when on the couch or approached too closely at the wrong time. The wife would only verbally correct Smug and his dominant behavior toward her began to generalize to more and more situations. But, if Smug was approached by the husband, he displayed fearful signs such as tucking his tail, laying his ears back, and licking for appeasement. If the husband caught the dog in a misbehavior, the ensuing correction was quite harsh, making the dog so fearful that he eventually attacked the husband when cornered during a correction. The harsh correction intensified the dog's fear of the husband, while the wife's weak corrections strengthened the dog's dominance. Smug had at least two distinct problems. Rather than label a dog and use only the therapy that applies to that label, each behavior or event should be dealt with individually to insure that the corrections for the behavior are deserved and appropriate.

CONFRONTATION WITH AN AGGRESSIVE DOG

A dog attack generally occurs very fast, and any direct confrontation with an aggressive dog should be avoided if at all possible. If the dog appears to be fearful, provide an escape route for the dog. If the dog is accidentally challenged and cannot be avoided, stand still without staring at him. He will interpret direct eye contact as a stronger challenge. Instead, just glance at him to keep track of his actions. Do not attempt to run, because a dog's responses are much faster than any human reaction. Try to keep a relaxed body, and avoid screaming. Screams or high-pitched voices will clue the dog to a person's state of panic and vulnerability. Although you may not be in the mood, soft and low humming or singing may help relax you. Never stamp your feet or make any fast movements. Fast movements will provoke an attack.

A deep-voiced yell at the dog sometimes bluffs the animal into backing off, but there had better be an alternative escape route such as jumping into a car or over a fence. Another method of escape may be wandering slowly and nonchalantly away from the animal. However, do not turn your back on the dog, because he may get bolder about chasing you away and attack from the rear. The hope is that a non-threatening presence will become boring to the dog, and he will become distracted and uninterested as you quietly wander away. If he should attack, curl up in a very tight ball, covering your face neck, stomach, and chest until help arrives. In calling for help, yell in a loud, low pitch; do not scream.

Joggers and people who like to take their dogs out for walks are always, rightfully, concerned about loose aggressive dogs. A fold up, pop out umbrella is a good weapon. If an aggressive dog approaches, popping out the umbrella will surprise him. He will need a couple of seconds to reorient himself, allowing, if all goes well, enough time for escape. You can also use the umbrella as a barrier from the approaching dog until you can find better protection. The umbrella may also double for a weapon, if necessary, against the dog's attack. Mace, although illegal in many states, is also easy to carry and very effective against aggressive dogs. Unfortunately, if you miss you are in trouble and the mace doesn't provide a protective barrier like the umbrella.

CORRECTION FOR THE AGGRESSIVE DOG

Attempts to correct someone else's aggressive dog usually ends in disaster, with a serious bite and nothing accomplished. A dog is more likely to bite an unfamiliar person than a family member so a trainer should limit corrections to his or her own dogs.

Occasionally, the more a dog is handled, the more aggressive he becomes and the appropriate correction may be the one with the least amount of physical handling such as the cuff or hanging. If the dog is serious about attacking, your safety is very important and a drastic correction such as hanging may be justified. For some owners, these corrections may sound very cruel to the dog. The owner who is confronted with an aggressive or vicious dog must keep in mind that the dog is intending to do harm and is very capable of disabling a person with his teeth. In these cases, extreme measures are warranted for personal protection and safety. If the owner cannot implement an effective correction or physically handle the dog, he or she should seek professional advice. After the dog is corrected for aggression, he should be made to obey a command. When the dog obeys, he should receive praise. Through this technique, aggressive behavior gets corrected, and obedient behavior is praised and strengthened.

Never attempt to physically confront or correct a dog if you are hurt or afraid. Research has suggested that pheromones, a scent emitted from the body, cues animals about our emotions, particularly fear and pain. The dog will pick up on your disability and/or fear and take advantage of your weakened condition. If you must correct the dog and cannot confront him physically because of fear or even mere size, make the dog work at heeling or some other moving exercise. The dog cannot think of two things at once so the obedience will distract and appropriately channel the aggressive behavior. You must still praise the dog when he obeys the command, regardless of your emotions as a result of the aggression.

OBEDIENCE TRAINING

Obedience training establishes appropriate communication between the dog and owner. Teaching exercises such as the down and down-stay will earn the owner dominance over the dog. Because the dog will test the owner's ability to control and dominate him, obedience training may also reveal the extent of the dog's dominant tendencies. This is valuable information, because some dogs may never challenge their owners until they are required to do something such as perform an obedience exercise. Obedience training prepares the owner to meet and win the dog's challenge. A successfully met challenge under controlled circumstances may give the owner the edge in later critical situations.

Obedience training can also appropriately channel an aggressive dog's behavior by giving him guidance and, best of all, a leader to follow. In general, constant guidance, leadership, and consistent and reliable communication breeds trust and enhances control.

Aggression Toward Other Dogs

As previously noted, dogs taken from the litter or mother and placed in homes when they are too young generally do not know how to properly communicate with other dogs and are uncomfortable around them. Should it be impossible to leave the puppy with the litter longer, until he is at least 9-10 weeks old, there are socialization classes that will expose the puppy to other puppies and grown dogs in a positive and systematic manner. But even with proper socialization, dog fights are common. Bitches will fight with bitches and dogs will fight with dogs. Bitches and dogs will also get into occasional altercations, but not as frequently as animals of the same sex. It is common for older dogs to beat up puppies. Usually the older dogs do not hurt the puppies, but in cases of extreme jealousy or threat to the older dog's status, the adult may do some serious damage.

JEALOUSY AMONG DOGS

Multiple-dog homes often produce jealousy or rivalry among the dogs. Males may fight over a bitch that is coming in or is in heat, although such fighting may cease immediately after the bitch goes out of heat. Most dogs work out the infrastructure among themselves with little intervention from the owner. Very often fights between two dogs in the same household produce more noise than injury. You may hear World War III coming from the dogs only to discover after the fight that there is not a tooth mark on either dog. (Be extremely careful checking for bites, because puncture wounds from bites are very difficult to de-

The Malamute and Border Collie are roommates
who often get into harmless spats.

tect until they become infected and swollen.) When neither dog is hurting the other, your intervention may make matters worse by causing more jealousy and rivalry. If there are no injuries, allow the dogs to work out minor changes in the relationship.

Minor arguments among dogs, even among those who appear to be the best of friends, will occasionally sprout, particularly when the social structure changes. The canine social structure in a multiple-dog home will change several times during the life of the dogs as they become older, ill, or a member is deleted and/or added to the group. Again, if carnage is not a problem, allowing the dogs to work out their own social structure is best. But if the dogs are fighting and hurting each other, you must intervene. When more than two dogs are in a household, there is a risk of a pack fight. If two dogs fight, the other dog(s) will likely attack the underdog or the dog that yelps. Historically, dogs have ganged up to kill one dog. For the safety of the pack, crate the dogs next to each other when no one is around to break up fights,

The larger Samoyed stops chewing and directs a strong stare at the puppy to communicate that the rawhide bone is not community property. Should the puppy ignore the cues, a snap is sure to follow.

supervise, or lead the pack, but avoid isolating them from each other.

When there is a conflict/fight between two dogs, ideally you should correct both dogs. Give each a series of strong collar corrections by the handle attached to their collars. Then place them both on a down-stay in the same room about four feet apart. If they do not know a down-stay, they can be tied in position, four feet apart until they are taught a reliable down-stay. You can also muzzle untrained dogs when they are together. Correct the dogs with a hard snap on the collar and a harsh "No" at any sign of renewed aggression. The dogs should not even be allowed to make eye contact with each other without receiving a correction for the attempted challenge. The dogs will continue to be pumped up, ready to fight, for several minutes to several hours, and a simple stare or growl from either dog is enough to set them off again. After a ten-minute down-stay, you can release them with a calm, unex-

135

cited "Okay." Keep the atmosphere calm to prevent them from becoming excited again.

If the dogs are separated, they will not learn to get along. Instead, they will learn that fighting rewards them with separation. In making them do a down-stay, you establish control and teach the dogs to tolerate each other in the same room. Every time they are separated, even for short periods of time, they have to be reintroduced or reunited. The reuniting often results in a new fight to reestablish social status and territory. The dog that is in the house first, by the dog's perception, owns the territory, and the dog coming on the turf is at a disadvantage. The dominant dog will not miss an opportunity to let the underdog know that walking on owned turf is dangerous to his health. In fact, most fights begin when two dogs are reunited after a separation period. A fight may start when the underdog simply comes back in the house after going out to the yard to relieve himself. To prevent arguments, send both dogs out together, and they should return together. If they do get separated, make sure the underdog returns to the turf first. The underdog will not pick a fight, and the dominant dog will generally respect the other dog's position of being on the turf first and not start a quarrel. Sometimes, no matter what you do, the dogs will not tolerate each other and you must intervene or separate them. Intervention may consist of having the aggressive dog wear a muzzle whenever the two dogs are together or reunited. Separation may consist of a high, strong see-through gate between rooms or for outside, separate pens or dividing the yard in half with a fence.

Always introduce two strange dogs on neutral territory so that neither dog perceives a home-turf advantage over the other. Should either dog display aggressive behavior, give repeated sharp collar corrections, coupled with the "no" command, until the dog ceases the aggressive body and/or verbal language. Maintain a loose lead when the dog is not being aggressive.

Fights may also start over possessions, or over the owner's attention. If possessions such as bones become objects of argument, each dog should have a bone or toy, or for that matter you may choose to remove the possessions altogether. Even if each dog has toys, arguments may still occur. In that case, you may choose to only give the dogs their toys in their crates.

Jealousy can also erupt when the owner pets one dog and not the other. One dog starts pushing the other out of the way. Should this happen, place both dogs in a sit or down-stay and pet them both. You may also just end the petting session and place both dogs in a settle or stay position. You may pet them both or each dog separately when they are in the stay position. If they growl, push, stare, or show any signs of an impending argument, correct them verbally along with strong collar corrections until they cease the aggressive behavior. A shake correction is not always a good option when two dogs are present. The shake correction places the dog being corrected at a disadvantage, and the other dog may attack the vulnerable dog during the correction.

MINIMIZING AGGRESSION BETWEEN DOGS

When two dogs have been known to fight with and injure each other, it is very important to monitor their body language and correct any signs of aggression before the situation becomes a full-blown fight.

Correct any signs of aggression such as staring, raised hackles, leaning over or mounting the shoulder region or any other area immediately with collar corrections before the dog intensifies the aggression. Do not allow the dogs to become too excited in the house or yard when visitors arrive. Once the dogs get excited and start running around and barking, they will get into a frenzy and a fight will surely begin. Games such as fetch may also incite a fight if both dogs are running after the ball at the same time. Play with one dog at a time if they have a tendency to get into arguments, or pick another game that doesn't cause them to get overly excited. Play sessions can also result in fights if one dog gets pinned or injured. If the dogs have had serious fights in which one was injured or became frightened, don't allow the play sessions to get too rough. You may want to stop the playing and make them do ten-minute down-stays to calm them.

Avoiding situations that produce fights may not stop fighting altogether. If you want to teach the dogs to play together, or teach one dog to do a down-stay while the other is playing, ask someone to help train or be available for assistance in correcting inappropriate behavior.

While it may not be possible to get two aggressive dogs to love each other, teaching them to tolerate each other may be quite feasible. Although teaching dogs to tolerate each other does not mean they will never have another fight, there should be fewer of them.

BREAKING UP FIGHTS

Getting between two fighting dogs is a very good way to get bitten, but few people can refrain from physically breaking up a fight when their dog is involved. Before jumping in and chancing a bite, try very cold water in the dogs' faces. If cold water does not work, very hot water may do the trick. Although hot water may burn the dog, a burn is easier to treat than a severed jugular. If water is unavailable, and you feel that your only choice is physical intervention, take time to wrap any handy extra clothing, such as a jacket, around your arm to cushion misplaced bites. Take your time to find the right moment to grab the dogs by their tails or the back of their collars. Please remember when two dogs injure themselves in a fight it usually ends with stitches. However, if your hand gets bitten while breaking up the fight, you could lose the use of your hand. Even if your dog would never bite you under normal circumstances, when dogs are fighting and in a frenzy they are out of control and do not realize or plan where they bite. If the dogs are small enough, you can separate them by lifting them off the ground and holding a dog in each hand by the base of the tail or the back of the collar. They will have a very difficult time biting if they are hanging from their tails or collars. The dogs will loosen their grips to gasp for air. If the fight is between dogs too big to lift off the ground, try to insert

Every breed is capable of aggression. Training is an important tool
for curbing and controlling aggression against people or other dogs.
Photo by Missy Green.

something like a stick between them that they can attack rather than each other or you. The minute the dogs separate try to get one behind a barrier such as a door. The barrier is important, because when one dog is pulled off, the other one will continue to attack. After you break up the dogs, you should leash them and make them do a stay. Be sure to correct any signals of aggression they display during the stay.

DISPLACED AGGRESSION

In discouraging a dog fight, be careful not to get the brunt of the dog's aggressive backlash. When a dog readies for a fight, his system is totally charged and cannot be turned off instantly. The dog that is distracted from a fight by a correction may transfer the aggression aimed at the other dog to the person who interfered with the confrontation.

Dogs also transfer their emotions to other dogs. If the owner corrects one family dog, the corrected dog may attack the other family dog without any apparent provocation. Should a dog exhibit anger displacement, take him out to a quiet, distraction free area or another room, and let the dog calm down.

Aggression Toward Other Animals

Aggression toward other animals almost always occurs if a dog is allowed to chase animals. Most dogs love to chase and catch small animals, and if the dog happens to catch the creature, the creature usually struggles and the dog becomes increasingly aggressive to maintain the hold on his catch. The dog that is successful and emerges from the encounter unscathed finds the whole experience very rewarding. On the other hand, dogs rarely bother cats that do not run. The majority of dogs that have had an experience with a fully clawed cat become very respectful of the claws. Similarly, dogs that have been chased by horses will refrain from chasing horses. If chasing other animals were to become unrewarding or downright frightening, the dog would probably refrain from aggression toward them too. Consequently, the dog needs to be set up in a situation in which the victim becomes the aggressor and the entire scene becomes very scary or threatening for the dog.

Since most dogs are distracted by and dislike loud noises as much as water in the face, prepare to provide as much noise as possible by filling several pop cans one-fourth full of rocks or pennies and taping the tops closed. The more threatening, confusing, and chaotic the chasing environment becomes, the less rewarding the chase becomes for the dog. Next, for the cat chaser, find an aggressive cat that will not run and will stand all claws up to the dog. When the dog attempts to chase the cat, be very demonstrative with corrections such as shouting and spraying him with very cold water between the eyes, several very strong collar corrections, or throwing a noisy can near him. Do not hit him with the can; the noise is enough to scare him. If the dog consistently chases the cat into a certain room, another person may hide behind the door in the room, readied with pop cans or water. When the dog comes to the door, have your helper throw a pop can toward him or squirt water in his face from a squirt bottle or even a bucket. Water does not usually stain and is easy to clean up.

If the dog is chasing horses, get a rider and horse who are not afraid of dogs to chase him down. The rider may become aggressive, shouting at the dog and throwing noisy cans near him, not at him. When the dog turns and runs from the horse and rider, call him to come, and praise him for returning. For this correction it is, of course, essential to use a horse that won't spook at all the commotion.

If the dog is chasing small animals such as chickens and rabbits, you can use a dead chicken or rabbit to set him up for a correction. Attach the dead animal to a string and stick. Ask a helper to move and work the stick so that the animal at the end of the line appears alive and aggressive toward the dog. When the dog starts chasing the animal, the helper can make the dead animal (through stick movements) very aggressive, jumping all over the ground and attempting to attack the dog. (Keep in mind this might backfire and turn into a fun experience for the dog if he has had a long and successful career at catching and killing aggressive animals.) Once the dog retreats, call him and praise him for returning.

Unfortunately, there are dogs that continue to chase animals no matter what the consequence. These dogs must always be on leash or be confined to an area such as a fully enclosed pen. Some trainers resort to the use of shock collars to discourage chasing behavior. Such device should not be used without the guidance of a qualified professional, because a shock collar used improperly can produce serious behavior problems in even the strongest-tempered dog. Should you need to explore training options such as shock devices, be sure to check the trainer's credentials and qualifications before adopting his or her advice. When dealing with the emotional health and well-being of a dog intended to be a fifteen year companion, you will want to be assured that the advice is sound and not harmful to either the dog or your relationship with him.

When Nothing Works

There are times when obedience training may fall short in resolving or completely controlling a dog's aggressive behavior. If the dog is overly aggressive, it is critical to seriously weigh the dog's value against your safety and the safety of other humans and dogs. A priceless child or a part of a child's body that an aggressive dog damaged cannot be replaced. No dog is worth the pain, suffering, and anguish caused by bites. More than likely, the aggressive dog is not happy either as a result of always feeling threatened, isolated, or corrected. The owner who believes the dog can simply never be given the opportunity to bite is unrealistic and overly optimistic. Someday the owner will make a mistake, or events beyond the owner's control will arise. The fence will blow down, or the door will be opened unexpectedly or without authorization and supervision, and the dog will have the opportunity to bite. Even the dog that is aggressive toward children but does not live with children will someday come in contact with a passing child. There is nothing a dog owner can do to make up for the injury the aggressive dog inflicts. Aggressive dogs that do not respond to training and behavior modification easily and quickly may not be worth the risk. These animals are dangerous to the trainer, owner, and community, and are difficult if not ultimately impossible to manage and control.

When a dog becomes aggressive and cannot be controlled through training, other options must be considered and evaluated carefully.

Unfortunately, short of euthanasia, there are no foolproof remedies. A muzzle is not a good option for the very dangerous dog because he may be able to remove the muzzle, or you may simply forget to put it on in a particular incidence. Drug therapy using hormones to reduce aggression can sometimes be effective, but this option must be thoroughly discussed with a knowledgeable veterinarian who is experienced with using these drugs and their possible side effects. The owner must also be religious in maintaining the drugs. In addition to the drugs, therapy for the dog must include strict training and behavior modification to make him reliably controllable. Another option is to pull the very aggressive dog's teeth. The aggressive dog cannot do much damage without teeth. This is an expensive procedure, and, of course, the dog must be provided with soft foods for the rest of his life.

The last option is euthanasia. The dog is given an injection that results in a painless death. Before euthanizing an aggressive dog, seek the advice of a professional behaviorist and a reputable veterinarian. Once made, however, the decision to euthanize a dog that is very aggressive or has been diagnosed with idiopathic aggression should not be a source of guilt, although the decision will be very difficult and painful for the owner in most cases. The emotional and financial liability of continually and knowingly risking injury by keeping the very aggressive dog far outweighs the pain of putting to death a dog that can disable a person for life. Ethically, professionals can only give the dog owner options. The owner has to make the final decision. When euthanasia is one of the serious options, I always recommend several people for the owner to talk with, and suggest that they continue to seek different professional opinions until they feel comfortable with their decision. However, one thing I try to stress and make sure that the owner clearly understands is that they do not have the option to give away a dog that has bitten to another person or family. The owner must also understand that if this same dog is surrendered to an adoption agency, he or she must inform the agency that the dog has bitten. An aggressive or fearful dog is less tolerant of people he does not know, and he will be more likely to bite unfamiliar people. If the new people don't know the dog's rules, or the dog does not know their rules, and someone attempts to correct the dog, he may retaliate with a bite. Even if the new owners understand that the dog is aggressive and vow to control him, there is no reason to assume they will be any more successful at it than the original owner. Providing the dog with more space is no solution, either. Even on a 1,000-acre farm the dog will come in contact with people. The legal and ethical liability and responsibility for the animal's demonstrated aggressive behavior remains with the original owner. If the dog bites, even when living in another home, the original owner may still be named in the lawsuit and have to incur the expense of hiring a lawyer. In some states, the original owner stands to be as much a part of the lawsuit, usually on the losing end, as the new owners. Importantly, the pet owner who has an aggressive dog must investigate the reason for the behavior and ensure that the situation is not repeated with another dog. If the reason is genetic, the owner must learn how to better pick the breeder and puppy. If the reason is lack of control, the owner must seek advice and material on how to prevent the situation from reoccurring with another dog.

=== 10 ===

Shyness and Fearfulness

Like the aggressive dog, the fearful dog may be the product of genetics, his environment, or both. The sire and dam pass genetic coding to the puppies that may affect their behavior, and the puppies also learn behavior from the dam. Puppies become fearful as a result of being startled or mistreated, particularly during developmental periods when they are especially sensitive. The owner's interactions with the dog during a startle or fearful reaction can also greatly influence the dog's fear threshold. Regardless of the apparent source, there are different levels of fear. Terms such as reserved, shy, and fearful have been used interchangeably to classify a dog's level of fear. These terms are used freely, and sometimes for self-serving purposes. Sometimes the breeder will explain to a prospective puppy buyer that the sire of the litter is not fearful, "He just won't let anyone touch him because he is reserved," or "The puppy is in the corner alone because she is just a little shy." These terms are subjective and therefore can be misleading.

While there are no canine models set in concrete to compare to these terms, a general description of them may help you recognize a dog's temperament, and so his potential.

The Reserved Dog

Webster's defines "reserved" as not exhibiting emotion or welcoming intimate contact with others. The reserved dog does not display fear or appear threatened. Instead, he is unconcerned or uninterested about the people or environment. If a person approaches, the dog does not back up, hide, or growl. He may hold his ground without approaching, or may walk up and sniff the person a moment before moving on to other things. The dog neither avoids human contact nor needs it. He may calmly walk away from petting, but he never quickly ducks or backs away. A loud, unexpected noise may startle the reserved dog (and person for that matter); however, unlike the shy or fearful dog, the reserved dog recovers to a normal or fairly relaxed state quickly and has little or no difficulty investigating the source of the noise immediately. While such a dog is not outgoing, neither is he shy or fearful.

The Shy Dog

"Shy," according to Webster's, is defined as showing timidity and having difficulty establishing personal relationships with others. A young dog that moves away from a person or object because of uncertainty and caution may be termed shy. In contrast, a truly fearful dog does not just try to move away; he tries to escape for fear of his life. The shy dog that is startled will recover fairly quickly, a few moments to several minutes later, and investigate whatever it was that unsettled him. He will generally take longer to recover or investigate than the reserved dog. Shy periods often manifest in young dogs between the ages of 8 months and 2 years from lack of experience or socialization. Even well-socialized dogs may appear to go through sensitive stages and have episodes of uncertainty or mild fearfulness around the ages of 8 months and 15 months. These sensitive stages are often more apparent in the male dog. The eighth month may be associated with hormonal changes and the rear molars erupting. The sensitive period at approximately 15-18 months may also be associated with hormonal changes, this time while moving from puberty to adulthood. My first Gordon Setter was 7 months old when I acquired him and was a very outgoing, rambunctious fellow. At 16 months, I observed his first fearful reaction as he looked up and saw the living room ceiling fan turning. The ceiling fan was not a new addition or a seldom-used appliance. He had just never noticed that big bird on the ceiling before and came unglued. For three entire days, whenever he entered the living room, he would look up, crouch, bark, and pass the monster as fast as he could. Even the most admirably bold dog can have startled reactions or "goosey streaks." Every organism is fearful of something. If the dog has never had a startle reaction, he has just not been exposed to everything. One startle reaction does not mean that the dog will become fearful of everything. However, proper handling is important when a startle reaction occurs so that the fear does not generalize to other situations. While just one reaction to an object or person does not warrant labeling a dog shy, the dog that regularly exhibits uncertain and cautious behavior can be justifiably called shy. The typical shy dog will stretch out to sniff an approaching stranger and immediately pull back or dart away if the person continues to approach. The tail is usually tucked, the head is tipped, the ears are held somewhat close to the head, and the eyes are very watchful. The shy dog rarely bites unless pushed to it by a person aggressively attempting to corner and/or restrain the dog. If the dog is given time to orient and habituate to the environment or event on his own, he will usually relax and interact very cautiously. These shy dogs can just as easily pass through shy stages and develop with lovely temperaments as they can become fearful if not handled properly.

The Fearful Dog

The fearful dog hides under or behind something, the tail and ears are plastered to the body, and the whites of the eyes are visible as the dog looks at the person or object obliquely. The dog may tremble, or growl softly. If the threat continues to approach, and the dog cannot get away, he will bite. The bite is fast, and only intended to provide an escape route, unlike that of the dominant dog that may hang on to get in a couple of bites. Often the fearful dog that lashes out with his teeth does not connect with the first snap, but the second snap is sure to connect. Timber, an 18-month-old pretty, black sleek mix about the size of a medium German Shepherd was very fearful and had snapped at the owner's father when she finally sought help. Although Timber did not connect, the owner took the warning seriously and brought him in for an evaluation. Timber was so scared of everything and everybody that he had to be dragged into the office, and he spent the majority of the hour under his owner's chair. His owner loved him dearly and committed to work with him every day with positive socialization techniques and training. One year later, after tremendous time and effort on the owner's part, Timber is being prepared to show in obedience trials. He wags his tail when he is working and even approaches most people on his own. Timber now is best friends with the owner's dad. The owner's enormous success with Timber was by no means the norm. Fearful dogs may learn to cope with frightening situations, but they do not generally become bold.

Fear of People

Dogs that are fearful of people must not be cornered or approached improperly. The person who persistently approaches a fearful dog intensifies the dog's fear, and in effect confirms his idea that the person is to be feared. The approaching person who does not heed the dog's fearful body language by backing off will very likely provoke a defensive bite. Bites from fearful dogs can be avoided with systematic socialization and proper handling.

Frequently dog owners react improperly to their dogs' fearful episodes. They either hold the dog with a tight lead or collar, which communicates to the dog that the owner is worried; they push the dog closer to the person, which intensifies his fear; or they comfort him, which reinforces the fearful behavior and makes it rewarding. The dog owner may further reinforce the fearful behavior by talking in a soothing voice and stroking the dog or by allowing the dog to hide behind his or her legs which also reduces fear and rewards hiding. The more comforting the owner is the more rewarding the fearful behavior is for the dog, and the more likely it is to be repeated.

In an attempt to prevent fearful behavior, many owners of fearful dogs avoid exposing the dog to frightening situations. To become brave, the dog must be positively exposed or socialized to people or other frightening stimuli. The dog must learn through repeated positive interactions that people are safe and pleasant to be around. At the least, the dog must learn to tolerate people and not bite or run away, which he cannot do if he is isolated. Dogs that live in households without children are commonly frightened or nervous around children because they are rarely exposed to the young humans and their mannerisms. The dog must be consistently and systematically socialized to children, new people, and novel events in a positive way to feel comfortable with them.

In order to socialize the fearful dog to people, ask a person of whom the dog is moderately fearful to stand still and hold out a treat to the dog. The food must have a very high value, steak, cheese, or anything the dog loves enough to tempt him in spite of the fear. If the dog is not a serious chow hound, withhold his food so that he is hungry. Command the dog to "sit-stay." The person must not approach the dog, and the dog should not be forced or pushed toward the person. The idea is to get the dog to approach the person of his own volition and at his own pace. If he is forced or pushed, or if the person approaches, he will feel more threatened. If the dog starts to approach for the treat, give him a release command such as "okay" and verbally praise him. The sit-stay command is used to prevent the dog from backing or ducking away. If the dog is allowed to back away, his anxiety will be reduced by the distance from the frightening stimulus and he will be reinforced to back away. If the dog moves backwards, correct him and place him back in a sit-stay. If the dog does not take the treat, have the person drop the treat on the floor. The dog will usually take the treat from the floor rather than the person's hand. Dogs will not take food from a person until they are willing to trust him or her. Repeat the process a second time. The dog will usually take the second treat from the person's hand, particularly if you cup your hand under the person's hand. Repeat the exercise until the dog is readily approaching people.

Sometimes the fearful dog becomes so comfortable with people that he starts jumping on them to get the treat. Correct the jumping only with the command to sit. Give the dog the treat when he is in the sit position. If you correct him for jumping instead of giving him another command ("sit"), he may associate the correction with the person and again become fearful. When the dog is taking the treat confidently, the person should attempt to scratch him under the chin while you hand feed him a treat to chew on while being touched. Chewing on the treat distracts him from the person and begins a pleasant association with the person and treat. After the dog allows the person to pet,

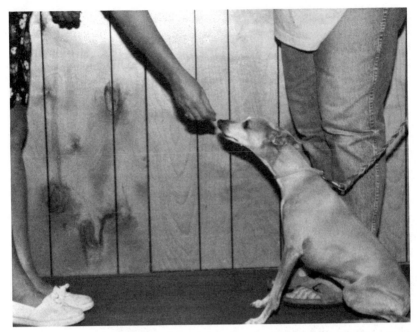

The dog was commanded to sit-stay. The leash is loose while the dog reaches out to sniff the treat.

praise him and give him more treats as reinforcers of the social behavior. Touching should be extended to all parts of the dog's body very gradually, perhaps over a period of a couple of months. Once the dog is accepting of petting for a treat, he must then tolerate the petting before he gets the treat.

If the dog refuses to approach or take a treat, the person should continue to offer the treat anyway, and under no circumstances should he be allowed to hide or back up. Command him to "sit-stay." If he backs up or growls, give him a collar correction. The collar correction will distract the dog from the frightening stimulus and require that he pay attention to you. If the dog is not on a stay command and is corrected for moving when a person approaches, he will associate being corrected with approaching people, and his fear will be reinforced. If he is commanded to "stay" and gets up, the correction is associated with disobeying the command rather than the approaching person. When the dog stays and is quiet, praise him verbally.

Repeat the dog's exposure to people in this same manner as often as possible. As he becomes more relaxed after repeated exposures, the

The Malamute exhibited fear toward the bike and the owner is using the touching chain to encourage the dog to investigate.

person approaching him may gradually get closer and closer while you continue to offer treats to him. Do not feed the dog before the sessions so that he is motivated to take the treat. If he doesn't take treats, you may want to use his dinner as a motivator. The dog must hold position with an approaching person in order to have his dinner. As the dog becomes more comfortable, the person may get closer, and eventually may even attempt to pet him. The process, to be effective, must be carried out very slowly. If advances are too fast, the dog may become fearful and lose ground. If it takes a year of repeated exposures, several times a week, so be it.

A method that can be used to help the dog investigate people or objects is the "touching chain." Command him to sit next to you and do not permit him to back up or move away. Use either the wait or stay command. If the dog moves from the stay or wait command in any direction other than toward the frightening person or object, correct him for moving from the stay or wait position before the release command. But as soon as he begins to stretch out to move toward the person or object, give him a release command such as "okay." You then may cup the person's hand in yours or touch the object with one hand and keep the other hand on the dog. The dog will usually become curious and venture closer. As he begins to move closer, praise him. Verbal and physical praise, along with a treat, is very rewarding for the dog in this situation. This approach works particularly well when socializing dogs to people. The dog trusts you, and your endorsement of the person or object through touching, will give him the courage to investigate. Also, if you cup your hand under the person's hand, it is quite unlikely that the dog will bite either hand. After he has investigated and finds the threat from the object or person unfounded the dog will relax and go about other business. Try to replicate the situation to insure that the dog does not have the same response to the same person or object at another time. Continue to repeat such exercises until he does not respond fearfully.

Fear of Events

Unfortunately, many things that frighten dogs are not within our control, such as cars that backfire, fireworks, or thunderstorms. When the dog becomes frightened, you can distract him by playing and/or talking happily. He will usually turn his attention to you and be enthralled with the game. The distraction discourages him from concentrating on the object of fear. Dogs cannot fully concentrate on two things at once, and by preventing the dog from focusing on the frightening stimulus, there is a greater chance the upsetting experience will not imprint on or remain with him. If he focuses on the frightening situation and fear intensifies to a traumatic level, he will always be afraid of the particular event and may generalize the fear to any similar situation. In extreme cases a dog can become nervous and fearful all the time.

A severe thunderstorm at the wrong time and place created quite a problem for a particular dog show exhibitor. The show was held in a tin barn-like building. The wind became fierce and rattled all the metal walls and big heavy bay doors. The exhibitor's 3-year-old dog became frantic. The exhibitor immediately took the dog out of the building and put him in the safety of his crate. The following week the exhibitor attended another show in a tin building and the dog refused to go into the building. The exhibitor's mistake was removing the dog from the first building during the height of fear. The dog was rewarded with the refuge of his crate for becoming frantic, bolting, and pulling out of the building. Dogs that are afraid of certain buildings or enclosures is fairly common. You can use treats as a distraction by throwing them in the air and making the dog catch them mid-air. If the treat falls to the ground, get it before the dog to make the game hard for him. Playing catch with treats is not to be construed as rewarding the dog for being nervous. The concentration in eye and mouth coordination that is necessary to catch the treat takes the dog's mind off the scary stimulus. The exhibitor should have remained in the building and attempted to distract the dog. Occasionally, the older dog, in particular, refuses to be distracted no matter how jovial and interesting the owner's actions. If the dog is extremely frightened or stressed, his system shuts down to such an extent that even the chow hound will turn up his nose at a gourmet treat. If you cannot distract him from the frightening stimulus, remain calm and talk to him in a normal voice. Command the dog to sit-stay close to you. Enforce the stay even if you have to physically restrain him by the collar. The dog should be handled firmly, without anger, and not allowed to get up while in a hysterical state. If the dog is allowed to bolt, he will learn to bolt out of places to reduce anxiety or fear. If the dog is restrained until calm, he will learn to concentrate on obeying your command to avoid correction, rather than focusing on the fear. If you are angry or tense, it will only serve to further stimulate or energize him. Verbally praise the dog only after he relaxes, and for obeying the command, even if he had to be held in place. There should be no petting until the release command. Do not remove him from the frightening area until he begins to calm down. He will learn that frantic behavior does not open an exit. If the trauma is so great that he cannot calm down, particularly in the dog 2 years of age or older, again give him a command and enforce it. After he correctly performs the command, you may want to remove him after a few minutes. In the case of isolated incidents, do not bring him back to the same or similar surroundings for a least three weeks to give him ample time to forget the unpleasant incident. If you dwell on the problem, the event will become very prominent in the dog's memory. After three weeks, you may again gradually introduce the scary stimuli, and in the case of our dog show exhibitor, without the benefit of wind and thunderstorms. Take the dog into the particular scary building for short periods of time until there is some evidence that he is coping with the environment. Gradually increase the time the dog is forced to remain in the building over several repetitions. High-value treats or junk food that the dog does not often get will very likely motivate him to walk into the building. If he is uncooperative and refuses to walk in the building on his own, give a "heel" command and enforce it with pops, if necessary. The object is to have the dog sit in the building until there are signs of him calming down. If he remains in the building without incident, the association of fear will eventually be extinguished. In some cases, no matter the effort, the dog will never be rid of fear associated with some particular incidents; nonetheless, he can be taught to cope with the fears rather than become hysterical and out of control.

Fear of Noises

Although many events that dogs fear are beyond our control, loud noises are something they can be exposed to in a nonthreatening manner. A noise can be created in another room, across a field, or at some distance while the dog is distracted with food or play. If the dog shows no reaction, the distance between the dog and the noise is shortened in very small increments, a couple of feet at a time. If there's a startled reaction, talk normally, distract the dog, and wait until he's relaxed and engrossed in a pleasurable activity before repeating the sound. Depending on how severe the dog's reaction is, repeat the noise either farther away or at the same distance. The noise should not be made louder or closer if a startle reaction is apparent from the dog. Only make the noise louder and closer after the dog does not react to the previous distance. Desensitization does not have to be accomplished all in one day. As a matter of fact, if the training session is too long, the dog's stress level may rise. Clumsy handling of metal food dishes while preparing the dog's food or slamming cabinet doors while he's eating also helps desensitize a dog to noise. There are also cassette tapes on the market with noises such as thunderstorms recorded for the purpose of desensitizing dogs. Although this method of desensitization has been somewhat successful with people, it is very questionable with dogs. The tapes just do not sound like the real thing.

Commonly, hunting dogs become gun shy because the trainer does not take the time to desensitize the dog to noises. Instead of shooting the gun in the distance to desensitize the dog during initial training, inexperienced trainers just take the dog out to the field where guns are going off as if it were a trap shoot. Some hunters will even shoot right over the dog's head just to determine if the dog is gun shy. Shooting over a dog's head without properly training him is sure to result in gun shyness. Even one startling shot can make the dog shy.

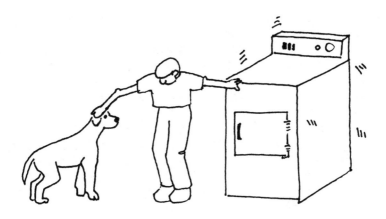

Gun training should be systematically presented, and only after the dog is so motivated to hunt birds that the only thing worth living for, next to steak treats, is hunting, despite the noise of the guns.

Fear of Surfaces

Unusual surfaces such as grates or slippery floors can also scare a dog. Approach these surfaces slowly and permit him the time and space to investigate the flooring. After the dog has had ample time to inspect the surface, command, "Let's go." If he does not go across, tempt him with treats. If the dog still will not walk on the surface, take him across by the collar. Lead him back and forth repeatedly over the surface until he walks on the unusual ground without jumping across or going around.

Detecting Fearful Behavior in Puppies

There are several tests available for puppies designed to predict their temperament. The most reliable is to monitor the puppy's heart rate after exposing him to frightening stimuli such as a loud noise, being restrained, or scary-looking moving objects. This test can be con-

153

ducted when the puppy is as young as 7-10 weeks old. The difference between a startled fearful dog and a startled bold dog is the time it takes the dog to recover from the fearful/anxious state to a normal or investigative state. Even the brave dog will experience an increase in heart rate and jump fifteen feet in the air, bark, and raise his hackles at an unexpected rattle of a bag. But the bold dog's heart rate will return to normal within approximately thirty seconds once the stimulus is removed. The fearful dog will freeze, tremble, or try to escape, and it will take several minutes for his heart rate to return to resting rate after the stimulus has been removed. How quickly the puppy's heart rate returns to normal is a good indicator of how bold or how fearful he will tend to be as an adult. Other more obvious signs of nervousness are panting, pacing, and sweating through the pads; one need not necessarily measure the heart rate to determine if a dog recovers quickly from frightening stimuli when these signs are present. Dogs that have slow recovery rates need special socialization if they are going to adjust to their environment. Fearfulness may never be totally eliminated, but socialization is the best tool we have to help the dog tolerate and adjust to his environment. Since there are always new circumstances for a dog to encounter, socialization is an ongoing process. As time goes by, the more things the dog experiences positively, the fewer he will fear.

11

The Crate and Problem Behavior

Behavior problems are easier to prevent than they are to eradicate. For a dog to learn that a behavior is not acceptable, he must be consistently corrected in the act of misbehaving. For example, if you are not home to correct the dog for misbehaving, he learns to misbehave when no one is home. When the behavior cannot be corrected, it should be prevented. The best way to do that is to use a crate. The crate is a safe and secure place for the dog to be left when no one can be home to oversee his behavior.

A Natural Environment for the Dog

By nature, dogs prefer denlike structures. They will generally not lie in the middle of an open area. Instead, most domestic dogs will seek covered areas to lie down, such as under a table or bed. When covered areas are unavailable, they will lay against a wall or the side of a couch. The crate provides the covered, isolated security that dogs naturally seek, and it can also be used as an enclosed dog bed. Not all dogs accept the crate as their den or bed on their very first exposure to it. However, with proper reinforcement and training, the dog will either come to love the crate, or, at the very least, tolerate it.

Security and Protection

The crate can supply important security and piece of mind for the dog owner. It is a safer environment than confining the dog in a small room or chaining him up in the yard. The crate is also safer in areas where windstorms may blow down fences or where people may intrude on private property. A room is too large to seem like a den to a dog, so many dogs left in houses feel insecure and become anxious. These dogs can become destructive, scratching or chewing through walls and doors to escape. Chaining the dog in the yard makes him a sitting duck for roaming aggressive dogs that may enter the yard. Confining or chaining a dog in the backyard can also cause him to be aggressive with other people, and develop behavior problems such as excessive barking, digging, chewing, and circling. If no one is home to correct the dog, the problem behaviors can disturb the neighbors, who may complain to local animal control agencies. When a dog is in a crate, he cannot damage the home, get into mischief, or disturb the neighbors. The crate allows you to relax, knowing that you will return to a house that is in the same condition it was left. Thus, you and the dog will have a stronger relationship, untroubled by the stress, expense, and frustration of chronic behavior problems. The crate, used properly and not as a prison or punishment device, can prevent and correct many behavior problems, and keep them from becoming serious, hard-to-fix habits.

Problem Prevention

CHEWING

Dogs are curious, social animals that may become frustrated, bored, anxious, and lonely when their human companions leave for a

This dog enjoys and finds security in her crate.

Photo by Margie Thayer

busy, long day. To relieve these emotions, they often chew. Even when chew toys are available, dogs often prefer to chew on furniture, clothing, or anything else that may smell like the occupants of the home. Once a dog begins chewing to relieve anxiety and frustration, the behavior becomes habit if it is not corrected. In the case of puppies, chewing is often a relief from teething pain and a natural developmental phase. If the puppy is not directed to chew only on appropriate items, all household items, including dangerous objects such as electrical wires, may become permanent targets for his teeth. The crate eliminates the opportunity for the dog to chew unacceptable items while you are distracted or absent.

HOUSE SOILING

Crating encourages proper toilet habits in the puppy as well as in the older dog. The dog may not see any reason to control his bladder functions when allowed to roam the house freely. Dogs generally detest having to eat or lie near their own urine or feces, but if a dog has an abundance of space he has little reason to make an effort to control his bladder. Once a dog starts to mess in the house without correction, the habit is difficult to break. The crate prevents him from messing in the house. It provides a good incentive for him to control urine and feces, because the offensive mess is inescapable. However, do not leave the dog in the crate so long that he had no choice but to relieve himself in it. Frequent messes in the crate can desensitize a dog and nullify his desire to be in a clean environment.

BARKING

Dogs will run and bark in the yard when there are visual or auditory stimuli such as the approach of the mailperson or trash truck. These visitors may break the monotony of the dog's life, and he may find barking so rewarding that long bouts of barking may become a habit to relieve boredom. If no one is there to correct this, the dog will form the habit of inappropriate barking at every sound and everything that moves. The dog that barks for any and all reasons can be crated and insulated from many of the things that elicit barking. Any barking the dog does in the crate will be much less audible to the neighbors than if he were left in the yard.

DIGGING

If the dog is in the crate, he cannot dig in the backyard when you are gone. Digging, like other problem behaviors, will become habit if not corrected. More importantly, wonder dogs that can escape through a mole hole, dig to China, or jump the fence cannot be safely left in the backyard. In the crate, the dog can neither destroy the yard nor escape from it.

Other Advantages

The crate has more advantages for the pet owner than just preventing behavior problems from becoming habits.

TRAVELING

The crate is a safe way to transport a dog in a vehicle, particularly an energetic dog that likes to jump around the car or jump into the driver's lap. The crate can be tied down in the bed of a pickup truck and should be covered to protect the dog's eyes, ears, and nose from road debris. Dogs must never be tied or allowed to ride loose in the bed of a pickup. Traffic accidents or severe road damage have jarred pickups enough to throw dogs out of the vehicle. If that happens, the dog either gets hit by a car or if he is tied, hung. In many states if the dog is the cause of a road accident, the dog owner is responsible for damages to the parties involved. If you are vacationing with your dog, a crate can prevent possible damage to cars, hotels, or a host's home.

ILLNESS

If a dog should have to stay at a veterinary hospital, he will be kept in a cage similar to a crate. The veterinarian may even prescribe crate confinement for injuries and illness. Dogs that are already crate trained

159

will be less stressed by the experience and recover more quickly than their untrained counterparts.

FRIGHTENING OR DANGEROUS EVENTS

A crate is invaluable during the summer firecracker and thunderstorm season. The crated dog will be insulated from those potentially terrifying events. The sounds of firecrackers and thunderstorms will be muffled if the dog is crated in the house, and he will be comforted by the perceived safety of his den. Thousands of dogs are lost and killed by cars each year during the thunderstorm and firecracker season because they become so fearful they escape and try to run from the noise. Some dogs are so fearful of these noises that they will break out of the house through windows and scale unbelievable obstacles, including six-foot fences. In addition to protecting the dog from noises, the crate can be a shelter from extreme weather, such as cold, heat, hail, and blizzards, which can be dangerous to a dog left in the backyard.

In the multiple-dog home, the crate insures that there are no serious altercations going on between the dogs when no one is home to supervise them. Crating is also advisable or necessary for rival dogs to prevent them from fighting.

VISITORS

Another important advantage of crate training the dog is the comfort of visitors. Visitors who are fearful of dogs can feel safe and comfortable if the dog is crated, and the crate can be kept in the same room with them so that the dog does not feel resentment about being isolated. When the visitors are young children who must be supervised around a dog or who are just too energetic and rough for the dog, the crate offers a place where the dog can lie unmolested without feeling locked up.

When and How to Use the Crate

The dog is placed in the crate whenever he cannot be supervised. Therefore, the dog is in the crate when everyone is sleeping, no one is home, or everyone is too busy to watch him. The crate can also give humans a break from that rambunctious animal.

Many people are concerned that a dog who must be crated all day will suffer from lack of exercise. Unless the dog finds some mischief to get into, such as chewing on the couch, barking, and/or digging, he

The crate is used to prevent mischievous behavior
when no one is at home.

sleeps or rests most of the day. Dogs, with the exception of very young puppies, do not generally exercise themselves or exert any unnecessary effort on their own. Crating the dog during working and sleeping hours is not cruel or inhumane as long as you spend time with him and allow him to be out of the crate for a good majority of the time when someone is home. The active periods for most dogs are early morning and evening. You can allow the dog to be inside the house under supervision before you leave for work and after you arrive home rather than just leaving him in the yard. A little time during the morning and evening to obedience train, play, or walk with the dog is good quality time out of the crate.

Puppies should start off sleeping in the crate for an average of eight hours a night. A dog should sleep through the night, and there is no reason why he should not sleep in a properly sized crate.

During the day, place the dog in the crate when you leave for work or when everyone is genuinely too busy to keep one eye on a mischievous problem dog or puppy. When everyone is sleeping or away from home, the dog should not be doing anything except sleeping or contentedly chewing on a safe chew toy, which he can do in the crate. Anything else the dog may find interesting to do when the family is sleeping or not home is probably mischievous or dangerous. Ideally, during the day, after approximately four hours, the dog or puppy should be let out to relieve his bladder. Hiring someone to let the puppy out of the crate after a few hours during the day is a good option for the busy household. Under normal circumstances, the adult dog should be fine for eight hours in the crate. While many people wince at the thought of eight hours in a crate with no bathroom break, they surely expect the housebroken dog who roams the house freely to constrain his bladder for eight hours during the night or when they are at work. Of course, anytime there is an opportunity to come home, or have someone come in and let the dog out in the yard for a while, you should take advantage of it.

Crate Training

There are several ways to train a dog to willingly accept the crate. The first thing to remember is never to use the crate to punish the dog. Always place the dog in the crate with praise, a treat, and a normal-toned command. If the crate is used as a punishment, the dog will find it aversive and will avoid it. If you must crate a dog after a scolding, the negative association between the crate and scolding can be broken if you command the dog to do a simple exercise such as sit, then praise him for sitting before placing him in the crate.

Some crate training methods can take longer than others. If there is no desperate reason to have the dog safely confined, you can use a slower approach, such as placing him in the crate with a treat or toy for short periods of time, starting with one minute and gradually increasing the time in the crate. You can throw a treat or toy into the crate as you command the dog to "crate," "bed," or whatever command you wish to use. If the dog does not go into the crate on his own, physically stuff him into it, if necessary. No fuss or consoling speech such as "Oh, baby, I will be right back, don't you worry" is appropriate when putting the dog in the crate. Deliver one firm, command in a normal tone of voice and close the door. Give the dog another treat through the door before walking away. After one minute, or several minutes if the dog is quiet, let him out of the crate. A fuss when crating or letting the dog out of the crate makes it an emotional event that may cause unnecessary expectations and anxiety for the dog. If the dog is whining or barking, hit the top of the crate and command him to be quiet. Hit the top of the crate as often as necessary. If the dog is very persistent about barking and whining in the crate, try shaking the crate, earthquake style. Once the dog is quiet, praise him verbally and let him out of the crate. Increase crate time a couple of minutes at a time, and do not let the dog out of the crate when he is whining or barking. If you let the dog out of the crate when he is "verbal," he will be reinforced for barking and whining and will continue to be "verbal" until the door opens. If necessary, repeat the process several times a day, increasing the time the dog spends in the crate. Always give him a treat and/or toy in the crate.

Unfortunately, most dog owners buy a crate as a last resort, after their couch has been chewed up. In this case, for the safety of the home and to insure that the dog continues to have a place in it, a quick method for crate training is imperative. Place the crate next to your bed with the door left open so that the dog can freely explore the new den. Place the dog into the crate at bedtime, and leave him in it overnight. You need to place the crate next to your bed just long enough to complete the crate training process, approximately three days, then if you want, you can put it in any part of the house that you wish. Also, it's handy to place the crate next to your bed so that you can correct the dog for whining or barking in the middle of the night without having to get out of bed. If the crate is far from the bed, most people will just put a pillow over their heads rather than get out of bed to correct the dog's barking. Using this method, crate time is not built up gradually.

If the dog complains in the crate, plan to train him during a week when no one has to get up early in case the protests continue for a few nights.

If slapping on the crate is not effective and the dog continues to fuss, fill a spray bottle with cold water and place it on top of the crate. When he fusses, spray the water into the crate aimed at his face and pair it with a very harsh-toned "Quiet." Even if the dog likes water, a firm squirt in the face and a harsh command will take the fun out of it. If the squirt bottle doesn't work, a glass or even a bucket of cold water may do the trick. Few drowned dogs continue to bark.

During the day, you may place the dog in the crate while you run errands or spend time in another room. When he's quiet, let him out of

Crates are made in various sizes.

the crate. The crate can and should be placed in busy parts of the house during the day to ensure that the dog is around people and the goings and comings of the household. Although the crate is not the most expensive looking piece of furniture, you may be able to put a decorative cover over the top of it and let it double as a side table.

For a little more pizzazz, I teach my dogs to sit outside in front of the crate, and I close the door without locking it. I throw a treat in the crate and tell the dog to "go to bed." The dog paws the door until it opens and then goes in to get the treat. Once the dog gets the idea, I can send him to the crate from across the room and he will open the door on his own.

You must be consistent and persistent in putting the dog in the crate and correcting the verbal protests. The dog will adjust to the crate eventually. While puppies usually adjust to it very quickly, the older dog may resist for a couple more days. Persistence and patience will pay off and the dog will adjust. The cost of furniture and the safety factors for the dog can far outweigh any temporary protests. Even the most resistant dog will be happier complaining in his kennel than sitting in an animal shelter cage awaiting a very unfortunate fate.

Crate Sizes and Types

Crates come in various heights and widths for different size dogs (see size chart on page 166). A crate that is just large enough for the dog to lie down, turn around, and stand in with minimal clearance between the shoulders and top of the crate is a good fit. The crate need only be tall enough to allow the dog to stand with his head at shoulder level, not all the way up. In fact, if the crate is too large, it may lose its effectiveness as a training aid for some behavior problems.

Commercial crates are made either of smooth, molded fiber glass or of all wire. Fiberglass crates are completely enclosed with the exception of two small wire mesh windows for ventilation on each side and a wire mesh door. The fiberglass crate consists of two smooth pieces, a top and bottom held together by steel screws and plastic nuts. If the crate is an older or used one, make sure the screws and nuts are not zinc. Puppies and even older dogs may eat the zinc screws and nuts. Zinc is toxic and has been reported to cause death in dogs if consumed. Replacement plastic nuts and steel screws are available through the manufacturer of the crate. There are also crates available that clip closed and do not have screws. Such crates are specifically designed so the dog cannot chew or get caught on any sharp edges. They are also easy to take apart for cleaning. The top half fits snugly into the bottom half for easy transportation and storage. To give the dog additional comfort, you can cut a piece of pegboard to fit the bottom of the crate. Heavy-coated dogs may prefer the bare, cool molded floor or a wire mesh crate which provides more ventilation.

The wire mesh crate folds up compactly for easy transportation. A steel pan inside the crate provides a solid base and can be easily removed for cleaning. You can cover the top and/or any side(s) of the crate with a sheet or blanket to give the dog additional secu-

The wire crates provide good ventilation and fold up compactly.

SIZE CHART

Kennel Size		Dog Size
100	16"W x 21"D x 15"H	Toy breeds (Toy Poodle)
200	20"W x 27"D x 19"H	13 inch Beagle, Lhasa Apso
300	22"W x 32"D x 23"H	Shetland Sheepdog, Corgi
400	24"W x 36"D x 26"H	Labrador Retriever, Setter
500	27"W x 40"D x 30"H	Rottweiler, Greyhound
700	32"W x 48"D x 35"H	Great Dane, Borzoi

rity and privacy. You can also put a washable blanket or pad on the floor of the crate if the dog won't chew it. Small water and food dishes specifically made for the crate are available.

Crating does not have to be a lifetime sentence or a permanent solution. When the puppy grows out of the chewing stage and becomes reliable about not soiling the house, or if circumstances change for the older dog and problem behaviors are resolved, he may then have the freedom of the house or yard. The dog's trustworthiness can be tested by leaving him out of the crate for short periods of time. For instance, you can leave him out of the crate when getting the mail or taking a shower. If the dog was responsible, gradually increase his unsupervised time outside of the crate. If there are no mishaps, leave the dog alone in the house for longer periods of time and eventually the entire day. Occasionally, the dog will regress and an old habit may reemerge. Reintroduce the crate and try freedom again several weeks later.

Some dogs are never trustworthy enough to be left in the house alone, and the crate may in fact be a lifetime facility. The crate option is still a lesser evil than the negative emotions for you and the dog that can stem from chronic behavior problems.

12

Repairing Problem Behaviors

Modifying or extinguishing problem behavior in dogs requires consistency, persistency, patience, and a lot of effort. In many cases a long time habit is not cured overnight, just as an "inherent" behavior such as chasing small animals may take several sessions to eradicate. Understanding the source and the dynamics of a particular behavior can help the owner deal successfully with it while maintaining a positive relationship with the dog.

Barking

Excessive barking is a major problem for many pet owners and their neighbors. There are few people, particularly neighbors, who are not disturbed by excessive barking.

WHY DOGS BARK

Contrary to the myth that many dogs bark excessively for no reason, there are several reasons why a dog barks.

Certain breeds of dogs were bred for their tendency to bark. To do his job, a watch dog must bark to alert his owner to the presence of an intruder. Unfortunately, dogs bred to bark may acquire the habit of barking when they are not working.

While some barking is the result of breed-specific tendencies, it may also develop as a consequence of the dog's environment. Dogs that are left alone in the backyard for long hours each day may become sensitive to sounds. Boredom, frustration, and anxiety are often to blame for a dog that barks at any visual or auditory stimulus. Chained, tied, or staked dogs will bark for the same reasons. Lonely dogs often find barking in chorus with other neighborhood dogs an enjoyable pastime.

Dogs left in yards where passing children have access to them through a chain link fence may get teased, taunted, or even petted. The frustration of being teased or the desire to be petted may stimulate a dog to bark as people pass.

Dogs will also bark when someone intrudes on his perceived territory. The dog's perceived territory may include a much larger space than just your property; it may include your neighbor's property, or even the entire block. Such a large territory in a busy neighborhood can make barking a full-time job for a dog.

THE WATCHDOG

While most people acquire dogs primarily for companionship, the natural tendency of the dog to bark and alert the household to intruders or other dangers is an added benefit much appreciated by most dog owners. However, the dog that barks constantly at all sounds and movements is not a good watchdog. In fact, the dog that barks inappropriately at everything becomes an annoying nuisance and is tuned out, like the boy who cried wolf. The dog that barks appropriately, only in the presence of unusual occurrences, is taken seriously by the household, neighbors, and intruders.

APPROPRIATE BARKING

1. The dog alerts the household to a visitor, then quiets down immediately when the owner is in control and gives the dog the "quiet" command.
2. The dog barks when someone is in danger, injured, or property is being invaded.

3. The dog barks at strange and novel sounds.

INAPPROPRIATE BARKING
1. The dog barks continuously after the owner has commanded "Quiet."
2. The dog barks when the trash person, mail person, or other routine visitors approach the property.
3. The dog barks at the neighbors when they are in their own backyard.
4. The dog barks because the rest of the neighborhood is barking.
5. The dog barks at people passing the property who are using public access such as the sidewalk.

Training the Dog Not to Bark

Most people who own dogs are aware that barking is annoying to neighbors and they sincerely try to prevent the dog from barking continuously. Common methods people use to stop barking are either yelling at the dog and/or calling him into the house. These methods can unintentionally teach the dog several lessons:
1. The dog learns that barking causes the door to open.
2. Barking gets attention from the owner. Even though the attention paid may be negative or unpleasant, negative attention is better than no attention at all.
3. Barking is not acceptable when the owner is home. Unfortunately, the dog does not learn to be quiet when the owner is away from home.

In order to prevent the unintentional training, confine the dog in an area where he will not be tempted to bark or be heard by the neighbors, such as in the house or crate, until he is trained.

The first step for correcting a barking problem is to train the dog to stop barking on command. A garden hose and/or water squirt bottle are the most effective, nonviolent, methods for correcting the problem. The garden hose and water bottle provide a long distance correction.

Physically correcting the dog by holding his muzzle or scruffing him for barking irritates him; often the dog nips in an attempt to avoid the correction. Harsh physical corrections can teach a dog to mistrust the approaching handler, and the dog learns to run off to avoid the correction. The struggle to catch the dog lowers the handler's authority position, whereas the water can reach him from a fairly good distance with little physical effort.

TOOLS FOR TRAINING THE DOG NOT TO BARK

1. A lawn hose that does not freeze. These hoses are available at most hardware stores.
2. A power spray nozzle to fit on the end of the hose.
3. Several water squirt bottles.

TRAINING THE DOG TO STOP BARKING ON COMMAND

In the House. Ideally, just telling the dog "Quiet" when he is barking and praising him when he stops would be the most desirable method of training a dog not to bark. Unfortunately, few dogs make life that easy. Therefore, place a squirt bottle filled with cold, plain water strategically in each room of the house, particularly at the front door. Ask a friend or neighbor to come to the door and knock and/or ring the doorbell. Allow the dog to bark three or four times, or as many barks as it takes you to get to the door. Once you are at the door, command the dog "Quiet" with a very firm, harsh voice. Your tone of voice is very important to let the dog know the correction is to be taken seriously. If he doesn't stop barking, squirt him in the face, right between the eyes. When the shock of the water hits the dog, he'll stop barking, and you can praise him. Avoid the temptation to laugh at the dog's reaction to the water, which, admittedly, can sometimes be quite amusing. Laughing can make him interpret the correction as a game. If he believes you are playing a game, he will not take the correction seriously, particularly if he loves water. When the dog barks again, repeat the squirt and the praise. After about the third squirt, most dogs will get the idea: bark and get squirted, be quiet and get praised. After the dog appears to have gotten the point, ask the neighbor to leave and come back in about fifteen minutes so that the process can be repeated. If the dog stops barking on command, don't squirt him. Repeat the procedure until he stops barking on command. You should leave the squirt bottle near the door for several weeks to remind the dog to stop barking on command when people approach the door. The squirt bottle can be used in any room anytime the dog doesn't stop barking on command. The squirt bottle won't discourage the dog from barking when appropriate circumstances arise, because you are teaching him to stop barking on command, rather than not to bark at all. The dog will continue to bark at visitors or intruders, and cease barking on command.

In the Yard. Attach a garden hose with a power spray nozzle to an outside faucet. Or you can attach a hose to the kitchen sink through a window that leads out to the backyard to correct the dog more quickly. If the dog is barking at a visitor approaching the house, allow him a couple of alert barks before commanding "Quiet." If he doesn't stop barking, aim the power nozzle at his face and shoot. When he stops barking from the shock of the water, praise him. The dog will probably start barking right after the praise, so be prepared to spray him again, and praise him a second time when he quiets. If the dog doesn't stop barking on verbal command, but stops only after the hose is in sight, follow through with the correction anyway. Even if he runs, follow him with the hose and spray him. Keep addressing the dog verbally from the time the command is given until you reach him with the water. The stream of words connects the command to the correction. If there is silence between the command and the water correction, he won't associate the command with the correction, or with the idea to stop barking. If you follow through with the correction even though the dog stopped barking after the hose was in sight, he learns that the only way to avoid the water is to stop barking on command instead of when you bring the hose out. If you don't follow through, you'll have to bring the hose out every time you command the dog to stop barking, and he'll never learn to be quiet simply on command.

To correct inappropriate barking behavior and teach the dog to be quiet on command, persistency and consistency are very important, so the water tools must be conveniently placed and in working order. If you don't correct the dog consistently, he'll only learn that sometimes barking is allowed, and sometimes it's not. He'll continue to bark to determine when barking is permitted. Barking will, in effect, be reinforced.

Water corrections won't teach the dog to fear or hate water in general. He'll simply learn to avoid the water correction by not barking. The dog that loves to play in water will still love it, but he'll also learn to respect the spray bottle, hose, and "quiet" command.

If you keep the dog in the house or crate to control barking when no one is home, you can also turn on the radio or television to further insulate the dog from outside noises. The noise of the appliances will mask outside noises and drown out the dog's barking, should he bark in the crate. The radio and television may also provide a sort of companionship for him.

When You Are Away. Training a dog not to bark during the day when no one's home is a little tricky and time consuming, but worth the trouble if you plan to leave him in the yard. Dogs are very aware of routine behaviors, and can differentiate a weekend from a weekday by his owner's behavior. The most obvious cue to the dog may be how late you sleep on the weekend versus the weekday. In order to train him not to bark when no one is home, you must set him up to believe a Saturday or Sunday is a weekday.

Set up a hose outside the fence in an easily accessible place. On a designated weekend, go through the exact going-to-work routine, including getting up at the same time, leaving the house, getting in the car, if that is the normal mode, and driving down the block. Then quietly sneak back to the house and hide where the dog cannot see or hear anyone approaching. When the dog starts barking, command "Quiet," reach over the fence with the hose, power nozzle attached, and spray him between the eyes. Once the dog is quiet, praise him and leave again, only to double back, quietly, and repeat the process several times until he remains quiet for longer periods of time. You may have to repeat the routine for a couple of weekends before the dog remains quiet for several hours at a time. Keep him confined in the house or crate during normal working days so that he doesn't get away with barking when no one is home; otherwise, the weekend efforts will be a waste. After he appears to be responding to the weekend lessons, hire a responsible person or ask a neighbor to hold vigil with the hose and report on his progress. Most neighbors would not only be thrilled to drown the dog for barking, but would probably pay for the opportunity. Once the neighbors report that the dog is quiet for your routine hours away, leave him out in the yard unsupervised for short periods a couple times a week. If the dog remains quiet, gradually work up to leaving him in the yard for longer periods of time. A tape recorder can also be used to monitor barking. You may have to repeat the correction process periodically. You can also install privacy fencing which will reduce visual stimuli and give the dog less reason to bark.

NO BARKING TOOLS

The Mikki muzzle is available on the retail market and when fitted properly, allows the dog to drink water while preventing him from opening his mouth wide enough to emit a loud bark. Depending upon how the muzzle is fitted, he'll be able to eat a small treat, but probably would not be able to regurgitate if necessary. The dog will still be able to whine. It may be a viable alternative for preventing him from barking either in the yard or crate, however, any device, collar included, that you leave on him when no one is around to supervise is potentially dangerous. The muzzle should not be a punishment. You should give the dog a treat every time you put it on him.

Shock collars are also available for sale in certain supply and hunting catalogs. Inexpensive shock collars, priced at about $100 can be extremely unreliable. Often these collars deliver shocks inappropriately or do not deliver shocks when needed. Inappropriate shocks, such as when the dog coughs or burps, will make the dog neurotic. Furthermore, shocks are often not delivered effectively unless the collar is fitted very tightly. The heavy-coated dog usually has to be shaved on the neck so that the skin is exposed where the collar touches for an effective correction. Bark activated shock collars have been known to deliver shocks to the dog when garage door openers or other electrical equipment happens to be set on the same frequency as the shock collars. The dog also learns that he must not bark when the collar is on, but when the collar is off, barking is okay. In order to maintain quiet behavior, the dog must wear a dummy collar, a collar that feels like the shock collar but does not shock.

A last resort cure for barking is the surgical procedure of debarking. Surgery is performed on the dog's larynx to control the volume of his bark. This procedure does not prevent the dog from barking; instead, it modifies the bark into a raspy, low, throaty sound that may only be heard close to the dog. Surgery is never without risk or postoperative pain and should only be considered as a last resort. If you have exhausted all humane procedures to stop the barking, and the only alternatives are to stop the dog from barking or be forced to get rid of him, debarking may be justified. Consult a veterinarian for a complete discussion of the advantages and disadvantages of all procedures available.

Mikki muzzles come in all sizes.

TEACHING YOUR DOG TO BARK

Teaching a dog to bark is simpler than teaching a dog not to bark. When the dog barks at the door, for instance, you can pair the word "speak" with the bark, and praise the dog. After the praise, if the dog is still barking, command him to be quiet. If he stops barking, praise him. If he continues to bark after the command, use a water bottle to enforce the command.

If the dog does not bark readily, a very tasty treat in front of his face may motivate him to bark. Pair the command "speak" in a jolly, playful tone with the bark. A reinforcement or treat held in front of a dog's face generally excites him, and he will become more and more active and verbal. As soon as he barks or makes any sound, give him the treat and praise him. Many repetitions will usually result in the dog barking on command. If he is taught to bark on command, he must also be trained to stop on command. These commands teach the dog to bark appropriately, which makes him a good watchdog and an animal who is not a nuisance to the community.

Chewing

Chewing is usually a developmental phase that puppies pass through to relieve the itch and pain of cutting new teeth. The majority of dogs stop chewing everything in sight once their new teeth are fully erupted, at about 9 months old. The few dogs that do not cease chewing by age 1, either have acquired the habit of chewing from boredom, anxiety, and frustration, or have acquired an unusual gourmet appetite. Regardless of the reason a dog chews, the behavior of chewing can be very expensive and very dangerous to the dog's physical well-being.

Correcting chewing, or any other behavior problem, requires that someone be present to catch the dog in the act. Showing the dog a shoe that was chewed several hours earlier and yelling at him may make you feel better, but there is little chance that he will connect the correction with the idea that chewing shoes is wrong. An unsupervised puppy left to roam the house may develop a taste for dangerous chew toys such as electrical cords, cleaning supplies, and other toxic items. The landscaped yard filled with possibly toxic plants, or rocks and wood that can obstruct the dog's intestines is a similarly dangerous environment for the unsupervised puppy. Dogs that chew and swallow rocks or other sharp objects often require costly and risky emergency surgery. To avoid mishaps when you cannot keep a watchful eye on the dog, confine him in an area where only appropriate chew items such as dog toys, rawhides, or knuckle bones are available. You must exercise caution in which chew toys are left in the crate, because dogs have been reported to choke on some toys and rawhides. If you confine your dog to a crate during unsupervised periods, you don't have to worry about him chewing up prized possessions and furniture, or doing himself harm. Occasionally, "Jaws," the super-chewer, is able to work over an airline-type crate. A wire mesh, heavy-gauge metal crate is a good alternative for the gifted chewer.

You may choose to dog proof the house by removing any prize possessions until the dog has passed through the chewing stage. Products such as Bitter Apple or Tabasco sauce may be sprayed on furniture and possessions to keep the dog from chewing, but check for staining before using them. Ninety-nine percent of the dogs find the taste of these products repulsive, but a few dogs think they are a gourmet delight. One product that may not be attractive to any dog is ammonia. Be careful not to spray the ammonia when the dog is close by; it could damage his olfactory system and eyes. Read the instructions carefully to determine what is safe to spray on valuable possessions.

The chewer should be well supplied with acceptable chew items such as old socks, safe dog toys, rawhides, chew hooves, and knuckle bones. Only knuckle bones are safe; other bones will splinter and get caught in the dog's throat or intestines. If you are worried that your dog will not discriminate between an old chewable sock and a new sock, you may want to take time to play fetch with the dog and an old sock so the item will become his favorite toy. The old sock will carry the scent of the dog, whereas the new sock has your scent. The dog quickly learns the difference between the socks when you praise him for playing with and chewing the old sock and reprimand him for chewing on socks with your scent.

CORRECTING THE DOG FOR CHEWING

When you catch your dog with a prized possession in his mouth, do not run after him or approach as if to kill, otherwise, he will run. Dogs are not stupid. Be a little tricky in preventing him from chewing and/or running off with the item. A treat and an acceptable item such as a sock or rawhide for him to chew is a good exchange for inappropriate items. Show the dog the toy and treat, and in your happiest voice, no matter how much constraint it takes to remain calm, call him. You must not run after the dog no matter how tempting it is or how much you want the item back. If you chase him, he has taught you a

Substitute a rawhide chew or appropriate toy
for the inappropriate item like this thong that the puppy wanted to chew.
Photo by Elaine Wishnow.

new game, "catch me if you can." In the process of the chase, the dog
will also sink his teeth into the item just to hold on tighter. You have a
much better chance of getting the prize back undamaged by calmly
calling the dog. When he comes, praise him for coming and offer him
an exchange, the treat and toy for the item he stole. Gently take hold
of the dog's collar - do not grab at him, and give a release command
such as "drop it," "give," or "thank you" as you take the item out of his
mouth. Even if you have to pry his mouth open, praise him following
the exchange of items. If he brings you an item and you don't have a
treat or toy handy to exchange, gently take the gift and praise. Keep
the verbal praise going as you walk over to the treat jar or to get the exchange toy.

If the dog does not come when called for a treat, drop to the ground and act very silly. Curiosity will get the best of him, and he will come over to see what is going on. This trick only works a limited number of times, so it would be prudent to enroll the dog in an obedience course to teach him to return on command.

The drawback for exchanging stolen items for treats and praise is that the dog will learn to bring you everything for a treat. If he gets overzealous about retrieving, omit the treat most of the time and just verbally praise him. However, the best prevention for fanatic retrieving of household items is for you to put things away. A dog that retrieves everything for you is much more enjoyable to live with than one that sneaks an item off to a secluded part of the house and secretly chews the prize to pieces.

Digging

Although digging in the yard may do aesthetic damage, the real danger is the dog digging out of the yard.

WHY DOGS DIG

Canine excavation may be a breed-specific trait. Some breeds of dogs were genetically engineered and perfected for their ability and willingness to dig. The terrier, for instance, is usually very willing to dig to China to get to the vermin in a hole. Digging is a natural behavior for dogs that like to store up goodies, such as bones, for a rainy day.

Dogs will dig in the hot weather for a cool place to lie down, particularly if there is no shade available. Dogs will dig to get out of a fence to roam the neighborhood. Bitches will dig in pregnancy or false pregnancy as an act of nesting.

Finally, as in all behavior problems, dogs dig out of frustration, boredom, and anxiety.

PREVENTING DIGGING

Digging is easier to prevent than to cure, since most digging occurs when the dog is in the yard alone for long periods of time.

To prevent digging:

A Samoyed tunneling to China.

1. Provide plenty of shade.
2. Trim the dog's nails short. If his nails are short, he will find digging with the pads of his paws very uncomfortable. If digging is uncomfortable, he won't dig.
3. Leave play toys outside to keep the dog busy. If he buries things, avoid giving him toys, bones, or other items that are tempting to bury.
4. Fence off tempting plants and shrubs that are fun for the dog to dig up.
5. Neuter the dog; it will reduce his desire to escape the yard.

If the dog cannot be supervised and corrected for digging when he is doing it confine him in either a crate, the house, or an outside pen designed to eliminate digging. Should you choose a pen provide shade or shelter against hot or bad weather. A pen need only be four feet by eight feet. Of course, a larger pen is quite acceptable. The pen should not be square or round, because these shapes encourage circling behavior. To prevent the dog from digging out of the pen, you can lay wire mesh or heavy chicken wire on the ground under the pen. The wire should be just slightly larger than the bottom of the pen so that you can bring the excess up the outside of the pen and attach it to the sides, providing a floor that the dog can not dig through. The dog will either dig at the wire mesh laid on the ground without the reward of escape or eventually give up digging, if digging gets him nowhere.

Leave the dog in the pen whenever he cannot be supervised closely. After several months, which should be ample time for him to lose the habit of digging, give him the freedom of the yard for short periods of time. If the dog does not dig, gradually increase the time you allow him to be in the yard. For example, on day one, allow the dog ten minutes in the yard. If there are no signs of digging, give him ten minutes of freedom in the yard each day for a week. If the dog resumes digging, confine him to the pen. If there are no signs of digging, increase the time to fifteen minutes for the following week. Continue to gradually increase the time in the yard as long as there are no signs of digging.

If the dog should sneak a hole here or there, fill the hole with rocks or other hard material. The filler must be large enough so the dog cannot swallow it. You can place dirt over the filler. However, loose dirt alone will only tempt the dog to further excavate the site, whereas rock will file down his nails and make digging uncomfortable.

Some dogs are just confirmed diggers. Despite correction, these dogs often regress to digging when left alone in the yard for long hours. The only solution may be to confine the dog to a pen with a wire mesh floor when no one is home to supervise him. If you do not mind the dog digging as long as he does not escape or destroy property, you can put a sand pile in the pen and let him dig to his heart's content. Hide toys or smelly knuckle bones in the pile to get him started.

CORRECTING DIGGING

Attach a power nozzle to a garden hose. Attach the garden hose to an outside faucet, or if accessible, an indoor faucet such as a kitchen sink positioned behind a window that leads to the yard. Keep the water on for fast shooting. When the dog digs, aim the nozzle right between his eyes with the command, "Leave it." The command must sound loud, harsh, and guttural to be effective. When the dog looks up and stops digging, praise him verbally. Repeat the process as many times as necessary until the dog gives up digging when you are home.

While the water procedure will teach the dog not to dig when someone is home, it won't teach him to not dig when no one is home. Therefore, keep the dog confined in the pen, house, or crate when no one is home to correct or supervise him. If the dog is allowed to dig even once without correction, all the prior corrections will be meaningless, and he'll learn to limit digging to times when no one is home.

The procedure used to train the dog not to bark when you are away can be used to teach him not to dig. Consider that the cost of landscaping and property damage may far exceed the cost of building a pen or run to prevent digging.

House Soiling

One of the reasons dogs are a preferred domestic companion animal is their natural tendency to keep a clean den. Generally, dogs prefer to eliminate a good distance from where they sleep and eat. They are easily trained to eliminate in areas other than their living quarters, unless they are:

1. too young to control themselves,
2. raised in an unclean environment,
3. exhibiting marking behavior,
4. experiencing physical difficulties,
5. improperly trained.

PUPPIES TOO YOUNG TO TRAIN

Puppies sold or given away before they are 7 weeks old are often extremely difficult to house train. These puppies do not have enough control of their bodily functions to choose when and where they eliminate. Reputable, knowledgeable breeders do not place their puppies in new homes under 7 weeks old. Even at 7 weeks old, the totally engrossed puppy at play may suddenly squat to urinate or defecate without any apparent forewarning. The 8-week-old puppy starts to show occasional control by halting the flow of urine or feces if caught in the act and swooped up for a trip outside. Around 10 weeks old, most puppies are aware that they have to go out about one second before it happens, and they usually sleep through the night dry. The 10 week old puppy may even start to whine, bark, or go to the door in an attempt to get out and eliminate away from the living quarters.

With positive training methods, the 10-week and older puppy will get more adept at controlling his bladder and sphincter muscles. In an attempt to keep a clean environment, the puppy will also become more reliable in cueing to go outside.

HOUSE SOILING AND UNCLEAN ENVIRONMENTS

Puppies raised in an unclean environment or a kennel can be very difficult to house train, and in fact, may never become reliably house trained. Puppies raised by breeders or caretakers who do not keep the dog's area clean of droppings and urine, or puppies raised in confined kennels where the droppings fall only a short distance from the cage, adapt to being close to their feces or urine. These dogs become accustomed to uncleanness, and to them, a clean den may not be worth the extra effort to communicate the need to get outside.

MARKING

Marking can be considered analogous to the dog leaving a signature. The dog urinates on a certain wall or object to convey the message "I have been here," not because of an uncontrollable need to relieve the bladder. Marking behavior is most commonly committed by male dogs. Bitches exhibit marking behavior less frequently. Neutering has had a high success rate in curbing marking behavior; however, because marking is a species-specific natural trait of the male dog, the behavior is very resistant to extinction or counter-training.

PHYSICAL DIFFICULTIES

There are a variety of physical ailments, infections, and illnesses that are difficult to detect but that can cause the dog to lose control and void in the house inappropriately. If the puppy is not catching on to house training or the older trained dog suddenly has a series of accidents, consult a veterinarian to rule out illness or physical problems.

Pregnant bitches or bitches in estrous may have accidents in the house because they need to urinate or defecate more frequently.

THE IMPROPERLY TRAINED DOG

The pet owner who does not find a pile or puddle for a few days may make the serious mistake of assuming the dog is house trained. The puppy may wrongly get the freedom of the house before being reliably house trained. When the puppy has an accident and is scolded for emptying in the presence of the owner, the puppy learns to go off into an obscure corner to urinate or defecate in the future. These spots may go undetected for days, and the owner may be under the mistaken impression that the dog is trained because there doesn't appear to be any messes. This is frequently the case with toy breeds. These tiny dogs leave such a small amount of waste that they may eliminate in the house unnoticed for months before there is enough volume or odor for the owner to see or detect. If you don't correct the dog for evacuating in the house, he doesn't learn that such conduct is unacceptable. Check the house and furniture carefully for any signs of unwanted presents before allowing him the freedom of the house without a watchful eye.

HOUSE TRAINING

Whether training the new puppy or retraining the older dog, the principle is the same: every time the dog eliminates in the house without being caught in the act and corrected, he learns that eliminating in the house is okay. You correct him after the fact, he only

---

HOUSE TRAINING TOOLS

1. A crate only large enough for the dog to turn around, lie down, and stand in a position where his head is even with his shoulders. If the crate is too large, it may not be an effective house training aid.
2. Effective cleaning, deodorizing, disinfectant solutions, and a repellent. There are several products on the market. Basic carpet or floor cleaner followed by a solution of vinegar and water will deodorize quite effectively. Dog repellents are also readily available at pet stores.
3. A strict feeding schedule, and a consistent schedule for either walking the dog or letting him out to eliminate.

---

learns that when urine or feces are on the floor, you are to be avoided. Dogs may certainly recognize the mess as their own, but do not learn that they can avoid a correction several hours later by not leaving a mess earlier. The dog does not learn where to eliminate or that eliminating in the house is wrong. In fact, he doesn't learn to stop eliminating in the house at all. He simply learns to find obscure places to leave the waste and to avoid you whenever you get close to the spot. Therefore, two critical aspects to house training are:

1. The dog must not be left unattended or unsupervised, even for a minute, until he is surely house trained.

2. The dog should be confined to a crate or the yard when you can't supervise him, which includes nighttime.

House Training the New Puppy

Puppies are not born knowing not to eliminate in the house, and a harsh scolding only teaches a puppy to be afraid of his owner. The best approach to house training the young puppy is to supervise him and not let him have the opportunity to have an accident in the house, particularly an undetected mistake. You must teach a young puppy gently and positively where to eliminate. A strict feeding and exercise schedule, a crate, clear direction, and patient vigilance is the positive approach to house training a puppy.

FEEDING SCHEDULE

The feeding schedule is a very effective aid in regulating how much is processed by the back end of the dog. The dog that has access to food constantly and eats a bite here and there all day will always have material to evacuate. To facilitate house training, feed the dog on a regular schedule and pick up any food he doesn't finish in fifteen minutes.

EXERCISE SCHEDULE

After feeding, take the dog outside to eliminate immediately. If he doesn't empty after five minutes, place him back in the crate and try again in fifteen minutes, and every fifteen minutes thereafter until he eliminates. Keep track of the time between feeding and eliminating. If the puppy empties after twenty minutes, take him out twenty minutes after every feeding. When a dog is fed on a regular schedule, you can develop a regular time to take him out to eliminate. More frequent feedings will require more exercise times. As the puppy matures and becomes more capable of controlling bodily functions, you can decrease the frequency of walks to perhaps three times a day for the young adult.

Puppies need to go out to eliminate several times a day, not just after eating. Young puppies need to be taken out after a play session or when they awake from a nap, and several times in between for good measure.

Go outside with the puppy on a leash to make sure that he empties instead of plays. Often a puppy will become distracted and not empty himself outside only to finish the business in the house the moment he is let in.

When the puppy begins to eliminate outside, take the opportunity to pair a command to the process. If the dog learns a command to eliminate, many walks in the snow and rain may be shorter. Use creativity for coming up with an appropriate command. The command "hurry" seems to work well without eliciting snickering from bystanders. When the puppy finally eliminates, give quiet verbal praise such as, "Good dog." Avoid excited praise because he'll become distracted and immediately cease eliminating. Similarly, a treat at this time may distract him from doing business. The puppy that learns to expect or anticipate a treat as praise for emptying can get in such a hurry to do the business for the treat that he may only partially empty and wind up finishing the job in the house.

If the puppy decides to play instead of getting down to the business at hand, confine him in the crate and wait another fifteen-to-thirty minutes and try again. Do not let him loose in the house until he empties outside.

For the first few weeks in his new home, keep the young puppy or new dog in a small area near the door he'll use to go outside. He might not be able to control himself through a big house on the way to the door. And if the dog has to be scooped up for a quick run outside, the distance is shorter.

ACCIDENTS

The majority of dogs have occasional accidents due to illness or not being able to get outside in time. Be sure to clean up the accidents properly to discourage marking behavior or repeat incidents in the same spot. If the odor of the urine and feces is not neutralized, there is a risk that the dog, and other animals in the house, will be encouraged to use the spot again. There are several products on the market that have been reported to effectively deodorize and clean canine urine and feces. Standard carpet or floor cleaner is not enough to discourage the dog from returning to the same spot. A 50/50 mixture of vinegar and water, applied after cleaning the spot with a basic carpet or floor cleaner, has been reported to be a good pet deodorizer. Sprinkling baking soda on the damp, washed spot will also help deodorize it. Club soda may help remove stain in the carpet. Spray a dog repellent to deter the dog from returning to the spot to relieve himself in the future.

On the brighter side, an accident can be a teaching and learning experience. Catching the dog in the act of eliminating provides an opportunity to teach him the proper place to relieve his bowels or bladder. The dog that is never caught in the act or has never had an accident may not learn that the house is the wrong place to eliminate.

CATCHING THE DOG IN THE ACT

When you catch the puppy in the act of voiding in the house, do not run up to him. He will startle and run in the opposite direction, trailing the mess throughout the house during the chase. Instead, briskly walk up to him and voice disapproval without anger. Saying "Stop" may be useful to distract the puppy and convince him to hold whatever is left. Pick him up or take him by the collar and show him outside. Most dogs will put on the brakes and hold the waste while they are carried out. If the puppy was caught before everything was left in the house, he will have a little leftover to spend in the yard for the purpose of praise. The "stop" tells him that the house is not a proper place to leave droppings, and the praise signals the yard as a good place to empty. If the puppy does not appear to have anything left and you bring him back into the house, keep an eye on him, because sometimes the trauma of being caught in the act temporarily suppresses the urge to finish the job. If you can't watch him, place him in the crate to be sure he does not slip off somewhere to finish the job. After a half an hour or so take him outside again to eliminate.

Dogs usually return to the same spot they left the recycled remains of their last meal. If the dog defecated in the house, pick up the feces and place them outside so that he can sniff the material later and be motivated to leave some more outside. You can put a urine soaked paper towel or a rag that you used to clean up the dog's mess out in the yard for a short time to encourage him to return to the spot. You can also place a special puppy pad, sold in most pet stores, outside to motivate him to use the yard. These sheets are specifically designed to attract the puppy to urinate and defecate on them. Make the pad smaller and smaller each time you place it outside, until the pad is eliminated altogether.

If the puppy or adult dog is very resistant to house training in spite of a strict regimen, and continues to have accidents in the crate or house, consult a veterinarian to rule out physical abnormalities.

PUPPY CUES

Ideally, life would be very simple if the dog would just cue someone every time he had the urge to eliminate. Some dogs naturally cue by whining at the door, while many dogs do not give any overt signals. Sometimes owners aren't aware of the cues their dogs use. Training a dog to cue to be let out can be a very simple task. Always let the dog out the same door. Every time he passes the door, whether he has just been out or not, say something like "outside" and open the door to help the dog make the association that being at the door opens the door. The dog will learn to go to the door to signal the desire to go out. To get him to bark at the door, talk excitedly. Reward any sound he makes by opening the door. Each time thereafter, talk excitedly and require louder sounds or finally a bark before you open the door. Save this type of training until the dog is old enough to hold his bladder for more than a few seconds. If he signals to go out and doesn't eliminate, that's okay. More important than a few unnecessary trips to the door is that the dog learns how to open the door when he needs to go out.

CRATE SCHEDULE

The crate schedule for house training will vary with the age of the dog. As the dog gets older and becomes more reliable in controlling bodily functions in the house, he will spend less time in the crate. During the night, letting a puppy sleep in a crate for eight hours is perfectly reasonable. However, an alternative to the crate is tying the puppy on a short lead to your bed or other stationary object. A U bolt may be attached to your bed or wall. A short chain with a swivel clasp on each end, so that the dog doesn't twist the chain and choke, can be designed to attach to the U bolt on one end, and the puppy's collar on the other end. The chain lead should be long enough for the dog to lie in different positions, but not long enough to let him move a body distance away. Dogs will not mess the floor where they sleep.

During the day, an eight hour stint in the crate may be mandatory for the puppy whose owner must work to buy puppy food. Until the puppy is trained, long hours in the crate are necessary. Most puppies sleep sixteen hours a day anyway. If the puppy is not sleeping, you can bet he is getting into trouble, so the crate will serve a dual purpose.

The crated dog must have evening time and weekends for a lot of running in the yard, playing, training, socializing, or just relaxed touching time. If you can, try to take off on a lunch break or have someone go and let the pup out during the daily working hours.

Keeping one eye on a puppy for several hours is not an easy task. A good way to keep track of him and prevent him from slipping off in a

Photo by Deloris Reinke.

corner for a quick mishap is to tie him to your waist with a six-foot lead. The puppy will not have any unnoticed accidents, and as an added advantage, he will learn to keep close to you without getting underfoot. Although tying a puppy to your belt buckle sounds a little inconvenient, amazingly it is not. The puppy will adapt very quickly and follow you around without getting stepped on. You can talk to and pet him occasionally, and you can warn him before moving if you haven't changed position for a few minutes. If you do happen to step on him, don't make a fuss over the incident. Command the puppy to "move" and continue with your work. If there is no fuss to reward the puppy for getting underfoot, he will be motivated to get out of your way. Tying a dog to your waist for twenty-to-thirty minutes a couple of times a day is usually more than enough activity for the young pup.

House Training the Older Dog

An adult dog brought into a new home is likely to have mishaps. The mishaps may be the result of confusion and ignorance about the house rules. Or perhaps the odor of a dog that was in the house previously triggered an instinctive reaction.

MARKING

To prevent marking behavior, have the house carpets cleaned and pet deodorized before you bring a new dog home. Neutering the male dog may also help eliminate or reduce marking. If possible, have the dog neutered before you bring him home. The effect of neutering on marking behavior is often dependent on the dog's age and the strength of an established marking habit. Although neutering may not completely cure marking behavior, it can only help, and it contributes in several other important ways to producing a much nicer house companion.

A common complaint from owners who live with marking males is that they can never seem to catch the dog in the act. Marking is usually done in rooms or areas of rooms that the dog doesn't frequent or spend a lot of time in, such as a formal dining room or a guest bedroom. The dog won't usually urinate where he has to sleep or eat. However, dogs will normally mark in the same spot. Dogs will often begin to mark when they reach puberty or if a new dog or bitch in heat comes into the house. The area must be properly cleaned with a product specifically formulated to neutralize pet waste. A general carpet cleaner is not enough. After the area is cleaned, spray the spots with a dog repellent. There are several products on the market such as Keep Off, Boundary, and a variety of others. Give the whole house a general light spray of the repellent, spraying a little heavier on the marked areas. Repeat spraying the used area later in the day, and twice a day for a week. The second week, spray the areas once a day, and the third week every other day. Continue to decrease the frequency of spraying the repellent each week until you are down to once a week or can eliminate spraying because the dog has stopped marking. Periodically, give the house and marked areas a general light spray. You can put a newspaper or paper bag on the spot so that when the dog starts to mark, you will hear the urine contacting the paper and be able to deliver a timely correction. If the dog is only marking in one area a Scat Mat can be very effective. The Scat Mat is a mat that sends a little shock to the dog when he steps on it. The shock is of the same intensity as you may feel when you screw a light bulb into a live socket and get a shock. The Scat Mat can be moved from one area to another after it has deterred the dog from marking on a particular spot. Another technique which helps to eliminate marking in favorite spots is to place the dog's bowl on the spot after you have cleaned it and feed him there. If feeding is very inconvenient in these areas, place the dog on a down-stay several times a day over the marked area. The best deterrent is to never let the dog out of your sight even if you have to tie him to your waist or chair to keep him in the same room with you.

Beyond discouraging marking behavior, training of the older dog is the same as training the young puppy. You need to watch the adult house soiler at all times or must confine him to the yard or crate when unsupervised. Although a newly acquired adult dog will be on his best behavior like anyone visiting a strange home, you should watch him carefully for about three weeks. Three weeks is a reasonable adjustment period, and if the dog has not had an accident, you can probably relax. Of course, not all dogs will read this information, so some may take more or less time to adjust to a new home.

After three to six weeks, once the dog appears to have adjusted to the new environment, you can allow him the freedom of the house for short periods at a time. Regularly check everywhere, especially in corners for mishaps. If there are none, leave the dog free for a little longer period. If the dog does mess, confine him in the crate when you can't supervise him. If you catch him in the act, briskly walk, do not run, up to him and command, "Stop" disapprovingly. Escort the dog outside and praise him when he finishes the job up outside. If he does nothing in the yard, crate him. The dog may become so nervous when caught in the act that his muscles will tense up and delay the process until he either relaxes or returns indoors. Thirty minutes later, take him out again to give him another chance to finish and be praised. If the dog has not had any accidents for a week, you may try giving him some freedom of the house. Crating may be necessary on and off until the dog is reliably house trained.

SUBMISSIVE URINATING

Bitches are more likely than males to urinate submissively. The dog that urinates when greeting people is not to be considered unhousebroken; disciplining her for submissive urinating will only intensify and escalate the problem. Harsh tones and looming over the dog will precipitate urination. Stooping down to her level and petting her under the chin does not produce submissive urinating for some dogs. Unfortunately, for others the level eye contact may still produce wetting. For these dogs the tactic of encouraging them to jump up to be petted is often more successful in avoiding wetting. It would also be wise not to encourage submissive behavior by scratching the dog's belly should she roll over. Eliminate greetings, particularly emotional, happy arrivals. Instead, acknowledge the presence of the dog with only a monotone voice in the process of calmly walking her outside to the yard. Don't pet her in the house or before she empties in the yard. After the dog empties, bring her in and go about your business until the excitement of your arrival has worn off. When the dog is calm, greet her. If the excitement is allowed to diffuse, you can still have a quality greeting without the dog urinating. If there is a big fuss or an emotional greeting after the dog comes back in the house, she may still have enough liquid left to wet. Likewise, your departures should be unemotional. A normal voiced, "see you later" rather than a long petting session and baby talk good-byes will prevent traumatic departures which lead to very excited greetings and urinating. Chances are your dog will eventually mature and grow out of the behavior, particularly if you are careful not to get her too excited. Obedience training also helps curtail submissive urination by building the dog's confidence.

One more word about waste. Every dog owner should be committed to picking up after his or her dog in public places. An easy way to pick up feces is to carry plastic bags. You can place your hand in the plastic bag as if it were a glove, and pick the droppings up without touching them. Then pull the bag over the feces, tie it shut, and dispose of it in a waste container. There are bags and products on the market specifically designed for this purpose which are light and convenient to carry in your pocket while on a walk. Disposable plastic gloves are another good option. Gloves and a bag to put the matter in, are easy to carry anywhere. If dog owners don't become more conscientious about doing this, dogs will continue to be banned from more and more public places. The only thing worse than a dog who is not house trained is an owner who is not trained to clean up after his or her own dog

Jumping

Friendly dogs will greet each other by licking or sniffing each other's face. Dogs try to communicate with people in the same fashion by jumping up to get close to a person's face. Although the dog is only attempting to greet people with a show of affection and excitement, jumping up can be annoying and cause damage. Dogs that jump up may startle visitors, knock people over, and damage clothing.

You can easily teach a dog either not to jump up at all or jump up only on command. The same training methods apply both to puppies and adults.

KNEE CORRECTION

When the dog jumps up, quickly raise a knee up, to waist height, if possible. The purpose is not to kick him but to block him from connecting with your body. Command, "Off" in a firm tone. Don't use the "down" command because "down" means to lie in a prone position. If you use the command "down" out of habit when the dog jumps, and you can't break the habit, use a different word to mean the obedience command "down." When the dog bumps into your knee, it will be uncomfortable for him. Dogs avoid uncomfortable activities. When he is on the ground, and only when he is on the ground, praise and gently pet him. Most people make the mistake of giving the knee correction without the praise when the dog is on the ground. In fact, they are usually yelling at the dog when he is on the ground instead of praising the good behavior. The knee correction paired with the praise when the dog is on the ground communicates that jumping is inappropriate and being on the ground is rewarding. Quite a few repetitions of the correction will probably be necessary before he understands that jumping up is unacceptable. Intelligent beings that they are, many dogs will figure out how to avoid the knee and jump up at the person's back or side. Be prepared

This surprised person is raising her knee to correct the dog for jumping.

for the modification and quickly turn and bring up your knee when the dog jumps at your side. When the dog jumps up at your back, just pick up a foot as if attempting to hop, and he will bump into your foot.

Use the command "off" or "sit" when you enter the door to remind the dog to stay on the ground.

THE WATER CORRECTION

An alternative correction is the squirt bottle filled with cold water. Leave the bottle by the door, and when the dog attempts to jump up, squirt him right between the eyes and firmly command, "Off." Praise and pet him for having all four feet on the ground. The water bottle is a good technique when company arrives, since most visitors are either reluctant or unable to raise their knees to block the dog. Set the dog up by inviting someone over to work on not jumping. Have the person ring the doorbell and command the dog to "sit" or use the correction. The dog only gets petted when he is sitting. Repeat the doorbell ringing and corrections as many times as necessary until the dog doesn't jump up on visitors. Several setup sessions may be necessary to eradicate the jumping behavior.

THE HANDLE CORRECTION

Attach a six-inch piece of clothesline to the dog's collar. When the dog attempts to jump up, command, "Off" and pop the cord quickly toward the ground. Always praise him when he is on the ground. The cord should not be left on a choke collar when the dog is unsupervised because it could get caught on objects, tighten up, and strangle him.

If the dog knows the sit-stay, sit and wait, or the down-stay commands, use them when people arrive. If the dog jumps up, correct him with a collar correction or pop for breaking the stay. The stationary commands will defuse the excitement of the people arriving in the house. Dogs jump when the are excited, and the excitement usually lasts about fifteen seconds. If you make your dog sit and wait or stay for fifteen or more seconds when visitors arrive, he will usually calm down and greet the people without jumping up after being released from the command.

JUMP UP ON COMMAND

Most dogs need little encouragement to jump up, so when the dog jumps up, tap your chest and say "Up." Praise and pet him for jumping up on command. When you want him to get off, use the "off" command. If the dog does not respond to the command in a second or two, bring up a knee. Praise the dog when he is on the ground. With consistency and persistency, the dog will learn that "up" means to jump up and "off" means to be on the ground.

JUMPING ON FURNITURE

The "off" command is also useful when the dog is on furniture. Use the handle attached to his collar and command "off." Give him a strong pop toward the ground and praise him for getting off the furniture. If he gets back up right after the correction, repeat the process as many times as it takes for the dog to get off on command. If he doesn't stay off after a couple of times, put him in a "down" or "settle" on the floor.

FENCE JUMPING

Strangely, when a dog is taught to jump over obstacles on command, fence jumping generally ceases. The explanation may be either that the dog does not jump because he was not commanded to jump, or more likely, the dog that is getting quality time through obedience training bonds closer to the owner and has less need to escape. There are several environmental remedies: a new higher fence; a fence built on the inside of the yard just a few feet away from the old fence making a double fence and a very difficult obstacle to jump; an addition to the existing fence using strands of wire on top; a strand or two of electric wire at the top of your fence (if lawful in your area); an enclosed pen that has a chain link roof; or a trench on the inside of the yard next to the fence so that the dog stands lower and has a higher distance to jump. If you can set the dog up to jump the fence, a cold water hose correction just as he is coming over it can be an effective deterrent. The invisible fence which delivers a shock when the dog steps over the boundary has been quite successful for many people, but it can be very dangerous if the dog is not trained properly and does not understand how the collar works. If the invisible fence is your choice, read the training instructions very carefully or hire a professional to help you train the dog. One other pitfall to the invisible fence system is that the fence does not keep other dogs out and should one get into your yard, your dog is as trapped as if he were tied to a chain.

Bolting

A good way to prevent the dog from learning that bolting out the door is a bunch of fun is to teach him from puppyhood, or when you first get him, to sit-stay at the door until you attach the leash and give the "heel" or "let's go" command. A sit-stay command when visitors come to the door not only gives the dog something else to think about besides jumping up on people or dashing out the door, it also teaches him to sit controlled at the door beside you. A trained dog at your side is good safety insurance when opening the door to strangers. Even if the dog is not a guard dog, he will look so well trained quietly and obediently sitting beside you on command that people will assume he is trained to alert, attack, and guard.

Photo by Cindy Noland

IF THE DOG HAS ALREADY LEARNED TO BOLT

The dog that bolts out the door must be set up in a situation that makes bolting very unrewarding. Purchase the kind of lightweight steel cable used on big game fish, and a steel bolt snap. Attach the snap securely to the wire. Then tie the end of the wire to a strong, heavy stationary object such as the rail of a staircase, and clip the bolt snap to the dog's collar. As you attach the line, distract the dog to steal his attention away from it. Make the line only long enough to go from the stationary object to the door frame. A helper should be positioned on the other side of the door to deliver a good correction, such as a bucket of water or a can filled with pebbles, when the dog attempts to go through the open door. Open the door, and when the dog bolts, as he comes to end of the line at full running force, have the helper throw the can near him, or a bucket of water at him. Call him to come just as the can hits the ground or he gets doused. When the dog returns, give him praise and a treat. If he doesn't return, pop the wire and reel him into the house. Dogs will not usually fall for this trick twice in a day. After the first correction, the minute the wire is attached, the dog figures out not to bolt. In fact, after a few days you may have to stop attaching a line and just go with the helper outside the door and correct the dog with water. Without the line, the helper will have to get scarier and more aggressive as the dog comes to the door.

You can prevent the dog from being rewarded with running out the door by crating, holding, or tying him, and using the stationary commands whenever the door is opened. When the dog does not attempt to bolt, a good reward would be to command him to stay and attach the lead for a short walk. For extra insurance, don't let him go out the door first when you go on walks. Command him to "wait" as you walk out the door to the end of the lead. If the dog tries to follow, pop the collar back as a correction. When he finally waits, command, "Heel," or "Let's go," and praise him. If the dog should bolt out the door during the training phase, he will learn that sometimes running out the door works and sometimes it doesn't. He will continue to try to bolt out the door at every opportunity, on the chance he might be successful.

Car Chasing

Car chasing is very rewarding for the dog. Dogs love to chase anything that runs, and the faster it runs, the better. To extinguish the behavior, you must negate the reward of the chase. Car chasing is most often done by dogs that have the run of the property and are not exposed to many cars. Expose the dog to traffic by making a point to walk on busy streets occasionally. Command him to remain in a sit-stay as cars pass, and snap the collar back if he attempts to move.

You can set the dog up for a car chasing correction by having a friend armed with several cans filled with rocks, for noise effect, drive up to or past the area where the dog starts chasing. Instruct the helper to put on the brakes as fast and noisily as possible when the dog is at a full chase. When the car comes to a screeching halt, have the helper jump out of the car and create enormous noise and chaos by throwing the cans near the dog. If the dog is not likely to bite, have the helper aggressively chase him home, throwing cans behind him. Repeat the setup with different cars, and if possible, different people, until the dog refrains from chasing cars.

You can also use the corrections for car chasing when a dog acquires the nasty, dangerous habit of chasing bikers, joggers, and horseback riders.

Coprophagy (Feces Eating)

Coprophagy, or feces eating, is surely considered by dog owners to be the most disgusting habit. However, stool eating will not harm or make the dog ill unless parasites are present in the feces. Coprophagy is more common in bitches. Speculation about the behavior in bitches suggests that they are more prone to this habit because of their maternal instinct to clean up their puppies' waste during the first few weeks of their lives. Boredom is also a possible cause for eating waste, as is the presence of undigested nutrients. Coprophagy may also be a serious sign of pancreatic enzyme deficiency, so a physical exam at the veterinary office may be appropriate to rule out any underlying problems.

Whether the dog eats poop because of boredom or taste preference, to prevent it, you must keep the yard clean by picking up the stool immediately. If taste preference is the cause, you can feed a food that is highly digestible and reduces the amount of waste the dog excretes. There are several good foods on the market that claim high digestibility and low waste. Some researchers feel that pancreatic enzymes in the food discourage the dog from eating stool. Your veterinarian may have more information about the use of pancreatic enzymes and where you can get the product. Consult a veterinarian whenever coprophagy is persistent and the dog is losing weight or the stool has an abnormal appearance.

As an attempt to condition the dog not to eat the waste, you should get to the feces first and sprinkle them with hot sauce or cayenne pepper. The pepper sauce should make the feces taste objectionable: however, some dogs love the taste of hot sauce. If the dog is a hot sauce gourmet, the only way to keep him from eating feces is to walk him on leash and use the command "leave it." The animal will revert to eating feces when left outside alone.

OTHER ANIMALS' FECES

To prevent the dog from eating other animals' feces on walks, you should teach him the command "leave it." Discipline him with a snap on the collar for diving for the feces, and pair the correction with the command "leave it." A good way to set the dog up for a prepared correction is to stroll him through a horse corral. To help the dog generalize and learn not to eat feces anywhere, take him to many areas where feces are known to lie, and correct him.

Preventing a dog from eating out of a cat's litter pan is difficult, because most dogs commit the act when no one, including the cat, is around to correct the behavior. A spray that might repel the dog from the litter box might also make the pan unattractive to the cat. The best option is to place the pan up high or in an area where the dog can't get to it. A barrier for the room where the litter pan stays is a good snack preventive. A gate with bars that the dog cannot fit through might be a good choice, because cats are generally smaller and can usually slip through, under, or over gates that dogs cannot penetrate. If you catch the dog in the act, command, "Leave it," and use the handle to give him a collar correction or tap him with the rolled newspaper if he continues to eat.

Excessive Licking

The dog that chronically licks himself, can be sprayed with Bitter Apple or other comparable products. Most dogs find the spray very distasteful and refrain from licking themselves. Spray the dog's coat fairly often to discourage and extinguish the habit. Provide him with toys soaked in broth or other items to redirect the licking. If your dog licks excessively, consult a veterinarian for an accurate diagnosis and treatment. Your veterinarian may prescribe a suitable drug to deter licking before the dog causes damage to his skin tissue.

When the dog licks people, use a squirt bottle and spray the dog in the face as you command, "Leave it." The dog who is licking can be placed in a settle away from the individual. Certainly, if you find licking undesirable, stop petting when the dog licks to avoid unintentionally reinforcing it. Squeezing the dog's lips against the canines as a correction for licking is a good last resort remedy.

Separation Anxiety

Sometimes a dog has such a strong attachment to his owner that he becomes extremely dependent on his owner's companionship. There is suspicion that acquiring a puppy younger than 7 weeks old contributes to a dog developing separation anxiety. The 6-week-old puppy is very immature and has not fully developed independence and exploratory behavior. At 6 weeks old, the puppy is a component of a collective system, the litter, and has not yet developed an individual personality. The puppy is just beginning to venture out independently and learn about social relationships with littermates and the dam. If he is forcibly separated from the litter before developmentally appropriate, he may transfer his dependency to the owner. The dog owner develops a tie with the dog similar to the parent-child relationship. If the owner doesn't actively work to help him develop independence through socialization and obedience training, he can remain very dependent. Separation anxiety may also develop if the owner never leaves the dog alone as a young pup. Often people arrange to get puppies during summer vacations or when a member of the family is home all day to take care of the puppy. There is usually someone home with the puppy every minute of the day, or the owners take the puppy everywhere they go. If there is a schedule change and the family member goes back to work, the puppy that is not used to being alone for several hours a day becomes very anxious. These dogs will whine, bark, dig, escape from the yard, chew, and even cause damage to themselves by chewing on their bodies when left alone or without their owners. There is a significant relationship between separation anxiety and behavior problems in dogs. While corrections for the behaviors an anxious dog exhibits can be effective in curbing his undesirable conduct, he also needs to be conditioned or desensitized to tolerate periods of solitude.

CONFINEMENT

The dog that vents his anxiety through destruction or barking must be confined to a safe area for his own protection and that of your property. But the confinement needs to be chosen carefully.

Confining a dog by a chain in the yard creates worse anxiety, because he may feel vulnerable and helpless. Room confinement also increases anxiety, because the area is too large for him to feel comfortable. In addition, there is always something available, like walls and doors, to chew on to vent the anxiety. An outdoor pen is another poor option, because he can be stimulated inappropriately to bark to vent emotion. The best option for confinement is the crate, which provides a small, den-like area. The dog is not over stimulated by outside noises and sights, and there is nothing dangerous he can do. The enclosure of the crate furnishes him with safety and security. For further security and comfort, you can leave a familiar-smelling blanket or pad in the crate. You can also turn the radio on to a soft music station to soothe the dog. Heavy metal, rock, or jazz may be a poor option for the dog that needs to relax. If you are an avid television viewer and he is used to the noise of the television you can use that on alternate days for familiarity. If there is another caged animal such as a bird, you might place the crate near the other animal for companionship. A second dog, a cat, or another animal the dog can interact with can provide companionship.

Unfortunately, a second animal can sometimes double the problems. If the first dog has behavior problems that have not been resolved, you should work those problems out first before acquiring more problems. Many people choose to get two puppies from the same litter or of the same age for companionship in hopes of preventing separation anxiety problems. The dogs will go through the same developmental phases at the same time, which can be difficult for the owner. Two house soiling, chewing puppies will require double the time. The up side is that both dogs will be through the puppy mischievous stage at the same time. There is always concern that the littermates will bond with each other and not the owner. But you can avoid excessive littermate bonding by providing individual time for each dog on a daily basis. Obedience training both dogs is an excellent opportunity to give each puppy individual, undivided, quality time. You should also crate puppies separately to prevent exclusive bonding, but near each other for companionship. Think carefully before you decide to acquire an animal for the anxious dog's companionship.

You can also keep anxiety down by placing chew toys in the dog's crate. A knuckle bone with the marrow intact in the middle may keep him busy for a long time relentlessly trying to lick out the marrow. Sterilized bones can be bought at many pet stores, and you can soak these bones in broth and fill them with goodies such as peanut butter or processed cheese spread. The better the chew toy, the busier the dog will be, and the anxious behavior will be appropriately channeled. Long hours of chewing will keep the dog's mind off the missing owner and tire him, making him sleep for longer periods of time. Do not give the crate chew toys to the dog on any other occasion so that the novelty of the toys doesn't wear off.

Place the dog in the crate with the toys fifteen minutes or so before you leave the house so he does not associate the crate with the negative emotions evoked by your leaving. Vary the time you place him in the crate before you leave, and don't make a fuss. Commiserating words such as, "Honey, I will be back soon, you poor thing" will only serve to heighten the dog's emotions, and he will miss your comforting presence even more. Give the dog a high-value treat and leave with nothing more than a "Bye." The purpose of the treat is to make your leaving a rewarding experience. Every time you walk out of the house, the dog gets a windfall. When you return, there should be no fanfare. If the reunions are emotional and overly rewarding, the dog will spend the day anticipating your arrival. When you get home, let him out of the crate and immediately take him out to relieve himself. A loving greeting is appropriate about ten minutes after the dog comes back in from the yard or walk. If the greeting is immediately after the dog comes in from the yard, he may not empty in his rush to get inside for the greeting. If there is an interval between your arrival and the greeting, the association between being left in the crate and your coming home will be broken.

Dogs that are exceptionally anxious and do harm to themselves can benefit from a mild tranquilizer during the initial stages of being confined. The tranquilizer and gradual positive training can ease the anxiety for the dog until he is conditioned to accept solitude. However, drugs can have serious side effects and must not be used without the recommendation and supervision of a veterinarian.

WHINING, BARKING AND SCRATCHING AT THE DOOR

If your dog is scratching, barking or whining to get in the house, do not reinforce his behavior by opening the door and letting him inside. Instead, open the door and dowse him with a bucket of water. Only let the dog in when he is quiet and not scratching at the door. A metal guard can be installed to prevent damage from claw marks until the behavior is eradicated. For doors inside the house, use a squirt bottle to correct scratching. Teach the dog to sit and stay a few feet from the door before he is allowed entrance through the door. Sitting a distance from the door before it is opened prohibits scratching.

EXERCISE

Physical exercise helps reduce anxiety. Scheduling exercise such as a game of fetch or a jog in the park in the morning can release the dog's pent-up energy and help him relax. Limit the amount of exercise to a level that will be easy and comfortable for you to maintain on a permanent basis. If the dog becomes used to the exercise and the schedule gets erratic, he will miss the activity and may end up more stressed than he was originally.

A very interesting phenomena which trainers often observe is that after a training session the dog is exhausted. You can run a dog for five hours and he will be ready to run five more hours, but use his brain for thirty minutes in obedience training and he's exhausted.

DOGGY DAY CARE

Recently doggy day care has become very popular with many dog owners. Staff members exercise your dog regularly, socialize him with other dogs and people, and sometimes even train him. The dog is never alone, and therefore, won't experience separation anxiety. Theoretically, the atmosphere fosters a well-adjusted animal.

But the trend is new and there may be some drawbacks that are not yet evident. The dog that is never alone, may not, later, adjust well to solitude if it later becomes necessary for him to do so. Day care can be very costly if the service must continue throughout his lifetime. And depending upon the facility, he may spend a good portion of his day in a pen or a crate, anyway. Some facilities put puppies together for puppy play time. If two puppies are equal in size and temperament, and well-supervised by a knowledgeable professional, the play time can be a very beneficial experience. If the play time is a free-for-all, a couple of pounces from a dominant puppy on a submissive one can have permanent negative effects. Conversely, the dominant dog may become more confident and exercise his new-found power in more situations. Puppy training by competent professionals is always beneficial; however, you must insure that the training methods are compatible with your own methods. Too often, puppy training is left to apprentice or novice trainers, who may not have enough experience to read the dog and adjust the training with alternative techniques when problems arise. The experience the puppy gets from being handled by many trainers is invaluable for socialization, as long as the training is consistent. If he is handled by only one trainer, the dog will naturally bond with that person. Day care can also help with house training if the staff takes the puppy out regularly and frequently. A good way to reap the benefits and avoid the possible pitfalls of day care may be enrolling him two or three days a week instead of every day.

OBEDIENCE TRAINING

Obedience training during early puppyhood can develop a communication tool which fosters security and trust. Obedience training can teach the dog to stay quietly and calmly in one place until the owner returns. For example, a down-stay practiced frequently can make the stay command to communicate to the dog that he must remain in place during brushing, cutting nails, cleaning ears, etc. If he doesn't accept being groomed, you don't have control of him. If he doesn't like grooming, you can change his attitude by daily sessions that include treats.

A 100-pound Akita hated his nails trimmed. Although he didn't bite his owner, she couldn't hang on to him to get the job done. At first it took three people to keep him on the table. The dog was desensitized to the nail trimmers with treats. Once he stopped having a fit when he saw the trimmers, he got treats whenever the trimmers touched him. During the trimming, while the groomer was extremely careful not to cut the nail quick, which would cause pain and a negative experience, she distracted him with treats. Eventually, he allowed his nails to be trimmed and received treats only after the job was done. After six sessions of nail trimming, the Akita did not love his nails trimmed, but he tolerated the ordeal and one person was able to do the job rather than three people holding him. Grooming must start the day the puppy gets to the new owner, before he gains the weight and strength to successfully protest. Even professional groomers will turn away a poorly behaved dog. The grooming fee is not worth a bite and loss of the ability to work.

13

Feeding and
Food Related Problems

Development of a healthy mind depends upon the development of a healthy body and bone structure. The quality of the food the dog gets is very important to his health. A poor quality food may affect the dog's energy level and behavior. The majority of dog foods are similar in content as far as the essential vitamins and minerals. Where foods differ is in the consistency, quality, and taste. The quality of dog food is measured by the source of its nutrients. Some of the same vitamins, minerals, and nutrients can be supplied by sources such as coal and shoe leather. The essential nutrients may be supplied to the dog by inferior sources in some commercial dog foods, making digestibility and the efficient use of the nutrients physically expensive for the dog. A dog food company with a good track record or reputation, and a serious focus on nutritional research and quality, keep animal nutritionists on staff and can provide reliable guidance and information addressing specific nutritional needs for dogs.

Behavior problems related to food can have a serious effect on a dog's general health, the safety of the people in the household, and the owner's worry level. Recent research suggests that dogs that bolt down their food, have a higher incidence of bloat. The dog that protects his food bowl may be a liability to visitors, particularly young children. The finicky eater may cost the owner much frustration, time, and worry. But most canine behavior problems that stem from food are within the owner's power to change.

How Much and When to Feed

Obesity is a problem with a great many dogs which can cause health problems and affect the dog's behavior and energy level. Free feed is not conducive to monitoring the dog's intake, particularly in a multi-dog household. Keeping track of the amount of food your dog eats may help you detect a health problem. The amount of food based on the dog's breed and height that food manufacturer's suggest on the bag might not apply to every individual dog's metabolism, so it is a good idea to monitor your dog's weight and adjust the food accordingly. Although most dog owners are capable of detecting weight gain or loss and can easily adjust the amount of food they feed, the veterinarian is a more reliable source for information about your dog's weight problems and food intake than the back of a food bag.

Generally, you should feed the puppy under six months at least three times a day. When the puppy loses interest in some of the feedings, this is usually his way of letting you know it's time to cut down. At six months old most pups are not attacking all the feedings and you can ration the food into two feedings.

Eating Problems

BOLTING FOOD

Some dogs attack their food as if it were their last meal. Food bolting will often develop when dogs are fed together and become concerned that the other dog will take their food.

To eliminate this cause of food bolting, feed the dogs in separate rooms, preferably rooms with doors between them, or in separate crates. If you don't have separate rooms or crates available for each dog, feed them alone at different times. You may want to feed the dogs from a pie pan or any similar large, flat pan to prevent them from picking up large amounts to bolt down. If bloat is a serious concern, feed smaller and more frequent portions.

Frequent feedings may slow down the bolter, because the food becomes less novel three or four times a day. A disadvantage to feeding several meals a day is that you will have to walk the dog more frequently. Timed automatic feeders are good options for feeding the bolter more frequently.

Finally, do not make the dog wait for the food or let him watch you prepare it. The excitement and anticipation of getting it will only encourage bolting.

THE FINICKY EATER

There may be several reasons why some dogs are finicky about their food. Finicky eaters may not like the taste or odor of the food, may not be hungry, or they may regulate their food intake based on the amount of exercise they receive. Regardless of the reason a dog becomes a finicky eater, do not contribute to the problem by cooking special tidbits or recipes, or adding delectable gourmet treats to the food. Once you give him dressed up food, often with additions that are not particularly healthy for him, he will not only come to expect the same wonderful diet every day but will learn to hold out for even better food. Recent research indicates that dogs are more interested in the odor of the food than in its taste. With this information in mind, if you feel you have to add something to the food to entice the finicky eater to the bowl, try lacing the food with garlic, a spice dogs seem to love. New studies have suggested that garlic is a natural healthy addition to food, whereas other choices may be more expensive and contain ingredients which are not necessary or may disrupt the vitamin balance of the food.

Some people reduce themselves to hand feeding, or staying in the room with a finicky eater to tempt him to eat. There are many stories about the bizarre deeds owners do to get their dogs to eat. If an owner stands on his or her head and the dog happens to eat that day, every night thereafter the owner may resort to head standing to get him to eat. The dog learns that part of the eating environment is his owner doing a head stand, so he waits for the performance before he eats.

Don't give a finicky eater free access to food all day. If it's available at all times, there is no novelty to being fed. A dog will be more interested in his food dish if it only appears once a day. If he's not interested, pick up the dish after fifteen minutes and put it away until the next day. The dog will eat when he is hungry. Don't make a fuss with

Dreaming of steak instead of kibble.

consoling phrases and tones—"Poor Poopsie, don't you feel good today?"—when he doesn't eat. How comforting and rewarding the fuss becomes, and all the dog has to do to get the attention is not eat.

Sometimes owners worry unnecessarily about a dog's food intake. Dogs often regulate the amount they eat according to the exercise they receive. The dog that does not get much exercise may not need to eat as much as you expect. Monitor his weight and consult a veterinarian to determine whether worry is truly necessary.

Some owners claim that their dogs become bored with the same food day after day, while others report that their dogs love the same food from birth to death. Switching the mildly finicky eater's food from time to time may result in renewed interest in eating. However, switch to comparable food rather than something totally irresistible like steak. If the dog starts receiving a gourmet diet, he will probably not go back to the original basic diet. A palatable switch may be between two different foods of the same brand. For instance, try giving the dog half a bowl of the chicken recipe with half a bowl of the lamb recipe from the same dog food company. If the foods are from the same manufacture

Dining with another dog can sometimes motivate
the finicky eater.

they may be similar enough so that the switch does not have to be
gradual. However, when you switch brands, start by adding a small
amount of the new food to the old food. Increase the amount of the
new food daily over a period of one week as you decrease the old food.
Switching foods too quickly, may give the dog a bad case of diarrhea.

Although dogs often prefer canned food, and semi-moist food,
most veterinarians will recommend dry food for sound teeth and the
health of the dog. If the dog will not eat dry food at all, try adding only
one tablespoon of canned food to the dry food. Persevere in getting
him to eat the dry food by placing it in front of him and picking up what
he doesn't eat in fifteen minutes. Put off feeding him again until the
next day, and don't give him any treats, tidbits, or scraps in between
meals or when he doesn't eat the regular meal. A healthy dog will not

let himself starve to death. If he doesn't eat after three to five days, consult a veterinarian.

When finicky eaters are made to wait or sit-stay for the food they are sometimes fooled into thinking that the food is a reward. (For owner's who want to avoid being mauled by their chow hounds, the sit and wait for food may be a survival technique).

Competition from another dog nearby may also motivate the finicky eater to clean his dish.

Feeding scraps to the finicky eater may be counterproductive. Scraps are probably more palatable, and the dog who doesn't eat very much to begin with, may turn up his nose at dog food when scraps are available. If you must feed scraps to the finicky eater, place them in his dish only after he has finished the normal meal.

Don't feed scraps from the table when the dog is begging. Place them in his dish or command him to "settle" before giving him a scrap. If he gets the scrap while he's in the settle position, he's rewarded for quietly laying by the table. If he gets up, physically place him back in the settle.

Feeding tidbits or scraps is a controversial health issue, and you should discuss it with your veterinarian. Some veterinarians feel that scraps may distort the nutritional balance of commercial diets, and therefore, are detrimental to the long term health of the dog. Other veterinarians believe that small amounts of scraps are not harmful. Most believe that an excess of scraps, or a diet consisting of just scraps can be very unhealthy. If scraps do not disrupt the dog's eating habits or diet, they can be very desirable treats or an occasional welcomed change from the same old dog food.

Food-Related Behavior Problems

BEGGING

Begging usually becomes a habit if you feed the dog from the table when he begs. He won't leave the table if he's reinforced for staying with tidbits. Command the dog to "settle" at the table and enforce it. He'll tire of staring up and will soon fall asleep if you don't reward him for begging. If you give the dog a scrap from the table, give it only when he's in a settle position. Some dogs are just born optimistic, and even though they have never received food from the table, they plant themselves at the table, hoping something will fall their way. Dropped food is a good beggar reinforcement, especially if you have a child who likes to make a game of dropping food on purpose. You may choose to train the dog to settle or down-stay in another room or at a distance from the table.

The dog must never bite the hand that feeds. To make sure that he doesn't, teach him the command "easy." Offer him a treat by holding the treat in your thumb and index finger keeping your palm toward your body and your knuckles facing the dog. If the dog grabs for the treat, pop him in the front of the mouth on the lips with your knuckles. Command, "Easy" along with the pop. After one knuckle pop, he will generally take the food from your hand gently.

MESSY EATERS

There are two types of messy eaters: dogs that knock over their bowls, and dogs that carry food away from their bowls. To cure the dish dumper, feed the dog in a large, heavy ceramic bowl. There are also bowls designed with flanges on the base to make knocking over the bowl impossible.

Begging is reinforced every time you feed the dog from the table.

For the carry out gourmet, you can use a large dish so that the food is already spread out rather than layered. Do not encourage the behavior of spreading the food by hiding goodies on the bottom of the dish. In addition, stand several feet from the bowl and when the dog starts to leave with a mouthful, block his path and send him back to the bowl with the stamp of your feet. If necessary, take him back to the bowl by the handle on his collar. You may also choose to feed him in his crate to prevent the mess.

FOOD GUARDING

In a multiple-dog home, food guarding is very common. Feeding time should be supervised so that each dog remains at his own dish. Allowing the dogs to roam from one dish to another may cause arguments. If you can't supervise them and are concerned about fights or that one dog might be getting more than his own share, feed the dogs in their crates.

Guarding food from the owner or provider is unacceptable. Every dog owner should check occasionally, starting at puppyhood and continuing through adulthood, to determine if the dog is getting possessive about food. Place your hand in the dish while the dog is eating and observe his reaction. It should not be anything more serious than mild interest. Each member of the family, and even visitors, should be able to place their hands in the dog's dish or pick up his dish without a problem. The dog should be taught that having someone place a hand in the food dish or pick up the dish is very rewarding. Pick up the bowl while the dog watches and place a tasty morsel in the bowl. If the puppy or dog growls or reacts negatively, deliver a shake correction and repeat the process until he doesn't react negatively. If he snaps, give him a cuff correction. Periodic checks are important to monitor and cure aggressive behavior over food. If the dog doesn't react, put a treat in his bowl.

Occasional hand feeding is a good tactic to let the dog know who controls the food. This is not to say that meal after meal should be hand fed, but once in a while starting dinner out with a couple of obedience commands and making the dog work for his food is not a bad way to maintain a position of control.

TRAINING WITH THE FOOD DISH

If the dog objects to a hand in his dish, it's time for some dish training. With a delectable morsel in hand such as liver, cheese, hot dog, etc., command the dog to sit and hand him the treat in front of his food dish. Offer the treats closer and closer to the dish until your hand is in it

The Husky is intensely watching as the owner removes the bowl. Another person is ready to correct any signs of possessiveness, if needed.

and he's taking the treat gently. You can also feed the dog by placing the food into the bowl one small piece at a time. The dog must learn that hands in the bowl are rewarding. If he growls or becomes aggressive, correct him with a shake correction or cuff under the chin. Repeat the process and correction every time he growls or appears aggressive. You should give him several training sessions a day. The more frequent the sessions, the faster he will become accustomed to having his food handled. Do not feed the dog anywhere but at the food bowl until he readily accepts this. You should put your hand into his bowl frequently, sometimes with a tasty treat, sometimes without, to reinforce the training and to check whether the dog is becoming possessive again.

After the dog comes to accept your hand in the bowl, have other members of the household repeat the process. Every member of the family should feed the dog. Don't leave the dish on the floor when visitors are present unless the dog has been desensitized to people handling it.

If he becomes very aggressive or attempts to bite around the food dish during the training process, use handling gloves as a safety precaution.

211

BONE POSSESSION

Bones and other chew toys can turn Jekyll into Hyde. Training the dog to give over or drop objects such as bones and toys can prevent him from becoming aggressive over what he perceives as his possessions. You may want to take the attitude that everything you give the dog is on loan. Out of the goodness of your heart you either share or loan the dog food, bones or toys. When you want the items back, the dog must give them up without a bite.

To train the dog to give up a really delectable bone, condition him to give up other, less desirable objects first. To begin with, attach his leash or handle so that he can't get away. Start with a new toy, or a toy that only generates mild interest. Offer it to him, and after he takes it, immediately command him to "give". Offer him a very tasty treat such as cheese, liver, hot dog, or steak in exchange for the toy. Most dogs will give up the toy and take the treat. If he doesn't, take the toy out of his mouth. If he growls, a good shake correction is in order. The theory is that the dog learns that a growl elicits a shake correction, and release of the object results in a treat. Practice the training frequently, gradually working up to objects of higher value for the dog, ending with the bone. As with food bowl possession, I do frequent checks throughout my dogs lives to ensure that they are not becoming possessive as they age.

If you give the dog bones, they should only be knuckle bones. Knuckle bones do not splinter, and the large bone is too big for the dog to swallow. Other meat bones or their splinters can cause damage. Give your dog rawhides only under supervision because dogs have been known to swallow and choke on them. I once gave my Portuguese Water Dog a round rawhide which he was able to put in his mouth whole while he chewed. As the rawhide softened from chewing, he tried to swallow it whole, and it got caught in his throat. He began choking and I wrapped my arms around his stomach area and jerked hard enough to make him cough out the rawhide. Since that incident I have tested many shapes of rawhides and found that my dogs only choke on the square or round chews. My dogs seem to do much better with the rectangle shaped rawhides. Regardless, I never leave my dogs unsupervised with a rawhide. Nylabones may be a good choice when no one is around to supervise the dog. These plastic bones do not break and can not be swallowed. Unfortunately, many dogs do not find the Nylabones especially tasty, although recently, the manufacturer has developed a flavored Nylabone that seems to be more appealing. You might also try to improve the flavor of a Nylabone by soaking it in meat broth.

14

Social Behavior

Dogs are bred not only for variation in appearance, but also for differences in temperament. An Airedale neither looks or acts anything like a Golden Retriever. The Airedale is a naturally bold and competent watchdog, whereas the Golden Retriever may offer an intruder a cup of coffee or the television set for a pat on the head. The individual idiosyncrasies in temperament for each breed are numerous as are the differences within the individuals of the same breed. The energy level differences from dog to dog contribute strongly to behavior. The dog with an excess of pent up energy is more likely to chew the trees in the yard than one that is content to live on the couch. The reactive or nervous dog may be easily traumatized by any event out of the ordinary, whereas the bold one finds the event a curious matter at most. Although basic temperament and energy levels are probably genetic in origin, and to some extent unchangeable, you can modify certain responses or behaviors. Planned exercise, obedience training, and

careful socialization can channel a dog's natural tendencies into behavior that befits a good companion.

Managing Excess Energy

The expected energy level of a breed is a very important consideration in deciding whether to live with that breed. Unfortunately, what you expect may not always be what you get. The St. Bernard that you expect to spend most of his life on the couch may have other ideas, and the exuberant Springer Spaniel that you think will bounce off the walls may find watching the paint peel off them the best way to pass time. Most of the time, however, dogs bred for activity, such as the Irish Setter or Boxer, will fulfill the owner's expectation. Although high activity or even reactivity may be a desired trait in some breeds, that activity level must be manageable for the family living with the dog. Activity in the field may be very appropriate, whereas pacing or charging through the house at all hours of the day and night is very annoying to most owners.

Your emotional state easily transfers to the dog. The excitable dog will become more reactive if you use a high-pitched, fast, excited voice and are also reactive, nervous, and excitable. You must handle the energetic or reactive dog with calm, firm, purposeful movements and speak to him in a normal, firm-toned voice. The deliberate, calm handling will help the dog stay calm. If you battle him to attach a lead to his collar, he will fidget and jump around even more fiercely. If the dog is hyperactive, take a firm grip on his handle and command him to sit in a slow, firm voice. If he doesn't sit, firmly and slowly grip the handle and place him into a sit. Hold him in place quietly, without anger or any unnecessary hand movements, until he ceases the battle and remains in position. When he settles down, quietly, calmly, verbally praise him. Praise an excited dog only verbally, because physical contact will tend to excite him even more. Try again to attach the lead. If he goes out of control again, repeat the forced sit, and when he relaxes, praise him. Repeat the process until the dog sits quietly. Do not attempt to put a lead on an excited dog.

Obedience training, with its one-on-one interaction between you and your dog, is an effective outlet for the energetic dog. Obedience not only teaches the dog to sit quietly but also requires him to concentrate, and thus, uses up brain power and energy. Obedience training will also permit you to control his activity in the house. The "settle" command is very effective and important for controlling excitement in the house. When the dog becomes overly excited or active in the house, place him in a settle. The settle should be at least ten minutes long, and he will usually fall asleep or at least relax by that time. When he gets up, he is usually calmer. If every time the dog gets overly excited you demand a settle of him, he will soon learn that the house is not the play yard. Unfortunately, you can't place the energetic or nervous dog in a settle for the rest of his life; therefore, he should have appropriate outlets to release energy.

Be conscientious in evaluating your own dog's energy level and adjust his lifestyle and routine exercise accordingly. If he is overly energetic the first recommendation a pet owner receives is to fence in a large backyard for the dog to use in running off energy. The pet owner, who may have had other ideas for the yard than making it a huge exercise run for the dog, creates a yard for the dog, only to realize he still exhibits an annoying overabundance of energy in the house. A large yard is useless if the dog does not use the area to run around. Few dogs that are past puppyhood will exercise themselves or get up several times a day for a jog around the yard just for the heck of running and using up energy. Dogs do not run around the yard unless something stimulates them, such as a passing mailperson, neighbor, or trash truck. When that happens, the dog is probably going to start running and barking, and the running ceases much earlier than the barking. Dogs in backyards spend most of their day, unless disturbed or stimulated by an event, sleeping, saving their resources for the time they are let into the house. A large backyard does not ensure that the dog is spending pent up energy.

Once the large backyard fails in its purpose, the next recommendation the pet owner receives is to acquire another animal for the dog to romp around with in the yard. Often this solution works out well; however, the play periods may be short, the two dogs may have compatibility problems or the new dog may have behavior problems. The only guaranteed assurance that a dog is exercising is to provide the dog with planned exercise.

EXERCISE

The type and duration of exercise you choose for your dog should be appropriate to his individual needs. The Mastiff may wilt after a half-mile run, while the Gordon Setter is not even breathing hard after a four-mile jog. A game of high flying Frisbee may be extremely hard on a Wolfhound's structure, whereas a Whippet may have no trouble

turning and twisting in the air to make a catch. Exercise that over taxes the dog's structure may have serious negative effects on his health, particularly if he is not gradually conditioned. When dogs or people become exhausted, more injuries occur. Too much or the wrong type of exercise for a young dog may strain his growing joints and bones. The dog that accompanies the marathon runner on a hot sunny day may not be able to stop running, even if he is exhausted and overheated. The motivation to stay with the owner is very high, and the dog will ignore pain, heat, and exhaustion until he collapses to remain with you. The motivation in a chasing game is also so high that a dog will not stop if injured or tired. A limping dog will ignore pain to chase a deer. Dogs do not always regulate their exercise with good health as a goal. Consequently, you must demonstrate good common sense in regulating your dog's physical activity. The same principles that apply to humans in their exercise programs also apply to dogs. Warm the dog up, and condition him slowly and methodically. Jumping and long forced jogs are not advisable until the dog is properly conditioned and at least 18 months old, when he has finished growing and is fully developed. Trotting a dog is better exercise and is easier on his structure than running him. If you do choose to run your dog, make sure he is on a lead or in a contained area such as a tennis court until he is trained so you can catch him when you decide he has had enough exercise.

The duration and type of exercise also depends on your schedule and commitment. The plan must be realistic so that you can follow through with the schedule on a long-term basis. The overzealous, well-meaning dog owner who begins a rigorous canine training plan may not be able to maintain the strenuous schedule. If the dog becomes accustomed to the exercise, he will suffer from the schedule change. The dog that is conditioned to a certain performance level will have built up endurance and energy to match the exercise program, and when the exercise is not available, he will have more energy to vent then when you started the program.

To avoid that kind of a fiasco, devise activities that can be maintained year-round. You can often set up indoor exercise that involves retrieving or fetching, tricks, hide-and-go-seek, or jumping over a stick and other obstacles in a small area or in the house. Frequently, city dwellers hesitate to get a dog, or feel guilty for owning one because of the lack of space for him to run. These owners can teach the dog to retrieve and jump obstacles as a way to exercise in a limited space. The city dweller who is creative in exercising his or her dog can offer the dog as good a quality of life as any country dweller could, regardless of the dog's size. If limited space is a disadvantage, it is also an advantage, in that the dog will always be a close companion. In the city, you cannot throw the dog out in the backyard for the entire day to sleep. The city dog, because of his environment, is able to constantly interact with family members, if only because he needs to be walked several times a day. Also, because of the close quarters, living with an ill-mannered, untrained, hyperactive dog is highly undesirable, so most city people are very conscientious about training their dogs. A good life for a dog does not necessarily have to include 100 acres or a large backyard for exercise. Quality of life is much more than just room to run.

DIET

Diet also contributes to energy levels. Feeding the excitable, nervous, or high-energy dog a high calorie food packed with extra nutrients devised for the performance or working dog will not help to calm him. The dog that already has too much energy to spare should be fed a high-quality diet designed for the companion pet. These foods have all the essential vitamins and minerals to keep a companion animal healthy without extra nutrients planned to maintain high energy.

A diet and exercise program customized to the dog's lifestyle to minimize excess energy levels makes controlling and directing behavior easier. But diet and exercise alone will not prevent the dog from becoming excited or control him in the face of events as exciting as the arrival of guests. That kind of control requires training along with the diet and exercise.

Excitement over Arriving Visitors

"Love me, love my dog" should not have to apply to all guests. Use the sit-stay at the door to prevent the excited dog from jumping up on visitors. You can practice the exercise at the door with a helper. The helper should ring the doorbell or sometimes knock to acquaint the dog with both sounds. When you and the dog get to the door, place the dog on a sit-stay. Hold the handle on the collar, and do not open the door until the dog is in position. If he moves, pop the collar by the handle to put him back in position. Open the door and if he moves, ignore the helper and concentrate on correcting the dog. Repeat the process several times with many different sessions until the dog sit-stays at the door. Always enforce the sit-stay at the door; otherwise, the dog will

Train the sit-stay and wait at the door
when people arrive.

learn that a sit-stay at the door is not always necessary. When the dog does stay, verbally, without excitement, praise him. When real visitors arrive, take the time to enforce the stay, even if the person has to wait at the door a moment. Waiting at the door is much more pleasant than being mauled by a 100-pound Bernese Mountain Dog, or any size dog. Do not release the dog from the sit-stay until the visitor has been in the house for a few moments, perhaps after the traditional greetings, and preferably when everyone is sitting down. Use a quiet, unexcited, "okay" release command. If the dog chooses to approach the visitor, the approach will be much more calm than it would have been after the initial knock or ring at the door. The dog's excitement will be defused by concentrating on sitting and staying, which gives him something else to think about besides jumping up. The exercise will also provide time for the dog to calm down from the stimulation of the doorbell or knock.

Visiting

You can use the "settle" command to discourage the dog from pestering guests once they are in the house. First practice with a helper. Command the dog to settle at your side. If you have trained the dog to settle in a specific spot, make sure he obediently goes to the designated area; near the area is not good enough. Letting the dog get away with only going close to the area teaches him that not going to the designated spot on command is acceptable. If necessary, take him to the designated spot. If he gets up, use the handle on his collar to pop him down again. If you get tired of taking the dog back to the designated spot time after time, you may want to attach a U bolt to a stationary object. You can attach the dog to the U bolt by a short chain that has swivel clasps at each end. Insist that the dog remain in the settle position while the guests are visiting. After some time has passed and the dog relaxes, he may move to another spot or calmly visit with the guests if visiting is acceptable to the guest and you. If the dog reverts to pestering the guests, command him to settle again. The dog will eventually learn that pestering is not acceptable and will give up trying if the settle command is enforced every time.

Socialization

Socialization is a process of systematic exposure to different stimuli presented in a non-threatening manner. You can't expect a dog that is afraid of active young children to remain calm if you put him in a small room with a rambunctious two-year-old. However, if the dog and child were each leashed to prevent any potentially threatening negative interactions and placed in a large room at first, after some time had passed, the dog would likely relax to some extent. Reward the dog for relaxed behavior, and the next time he and child come together, it can be in a smaller room, with the two of them closer. With enough repeated exposures in a non-threatening environment, the dog may learn not to fear children.

You must systematically socialize the young pup by taking him different places and watching closely for any fearful reactions. If the pup has an unrealistic or unjustified fearful reaction, continually expose him to the same and similar situations to desensitize him to them. A dog will become fearful and sensitized to other people, children, dogs, places, and noises if not exposed to these stimuli in a positive way on a regular basis. Even if he's socialized as a puppy, he can still become fearful if deliberate socialization is relaxed, particularly before he is 2-2 1/2 years of age. Dogs do not fully develop their adult bodies or personalities until somewhere around 2 years of age. The 6-month-old puppy that attended day care and puppy kindergarten, and was the

Photo by Deloris Reinke

outgoing star of the class, may withdraw and become fearful if you
don't continually expose him to diverse objects, people, and experiences. Therefore, socializing is a critical component to developing and
maintaining a stable temperament in a dog. The earlier you begin the
socialization process, the less fearful and more receptive the dog will
be to new situations.

Even the most socialized puppy will become startled or afraid at
one time or another without any apparent reason. Your reaction to the
incident may set a precedent for appropriate responses from the dog
in the future.

Soothing or removing a frightened dog from a perceived scary
situation reinforces fearful behavior. Talking to the dog in a sympa-

221

thetic manner rewards him for acting fearful. Socialization means exposure, not avoidance. If the dog is frightened, do not avoid the threatening situations. Purposefully expose him to uncomfortable situations and teach him to cope.

GROOMING

A gentle grooming can be as satisfying to the dog as being petted and can be very helpful in desensitizing him to handling. But the experience of being handled all over the body should not start at the groomer, veterinary office, or with a person the dog does not know. It should start with you, or better yet, the breeder.

To prepare the puppy or older dog to accept handling, touching, and brushing all over his body, offer him a bit of food to chew or nibble on during the handling or grooming to not only distract him from the process but to form a positive association between being touched and food. Don't just limit the handling to calm stroking. A gentle squeeze of the paw or a mild tug on the ear or tail can help desensitize the dog to children or special populations. Start off stroking or tugging gently and increase it in toughness. As you do, display a very jovial and playful demeanor so that the dog doesn't become threatened and associates play and pleasure with the rough handling. Inspect the dog's teeth and mouth often so that he becomes accustomed to having items removed or exams performed. As he becomes accustomed to your handling, ask other people to handle him. The more people who handle him positively, the less threatened he will be around people.

SOCIALIZING WITH PEOPLE

Dogs need to approach people at their own pace. When dogs approach people of their own volition on a loose lead, they generally do not feel threatened. If a dog is pushed, pulled, or forced to go up to a person, the experience will be negative and whatever fear or reservation he may have had will be affirmed. Most dogs become unsure and reserved about going up to people who are overly eager to pet them. Often people who love dogs the most get so excited they rush up to pet the dog without giving him the opportunity to sniff them and establish trust. Such an approach is interpreted by the dog as aggressive or threatening. If he draws back, these overzealous animal lovers can't stand the prospect that he might not like them, so they keep moving toward him, telling him "It's okay, I won't hurt you." The dog gets even more suspicious and backs up farther. Sometimes he'll even bite if the person's approach is persistent enough. Even the most socialized and

The Guard Dog and the Canine Welcome Wagon representatives.

bold dogs will draw back when people go toward them too quickly and aggressively.

Instead, intercept people and ask them to hold their ground and wait until the dog approaches them. Ask visitors to avoid staring at him, or making any fast movements toward him that could threaten him. The person should squat to the dog's level with a treat. The dog will either run up to the person or stretch cautiously to take the treat or sniff the air. Also keep a loose lead when people approach. Take care not to communicate apprehension by a tight lead. A lead that tightens when people approach, even if it's tightened to prevent the dog from jumping up, communicates tension to him. In addition, a tight lead is uncomfortable. The dog that experiences an uncomfortably tight lead and suspects apprehension from the owner every time a person approaches will naturally have a negative view of advancing humans. If the dog is a jumper, command him to sit and stay. Once you have enforced the command, even if it takes several corrections, and the dog is in the sitting position, the approaching person can offer a treat. If the dog jumps after receiving the treat, repeat the correction. When the dog is relaxed with the person close, release him to let him socialize.

Take every opportunity to expose the dog to people in a non-threatening manner by letting him approach them at will. When visitors come into the house, invite them to sit down and ask them to ignore the dog. As time passes with the visitor in the house, the dog that is unsure will gain confidence. The perceived threat decreases, and most dogs will become curious enough to sniff the visitor. After the dog has sniffed and feels more comfortable, have the visitor offer him a very tasty treat. Even if he doesn't take it, the visitor should keep offering it periodically. If the dog barks hysterically and backs up, place him on lead and keep him in a down position several feet from the visitor. Command the dog to be quiet, and if he does not respond, use the water bottle correction. The dog must learn to tolerate invited guests in the same room. When the guests get up to leave, maintain control of the lead without tightening it. Some dogs will attempt to nip people as they are on their way out of the house. If he does, deliver a snap on the lead, a cuff or a very strong shake correction. Repeat the entire situation by asking the guest to sit down and then leave again to provide an opportunity to correct the dog until he stops trying to nip.

If you are concerned about the dog biting, you can muzzle him. Place the muzzle on him fifteen minutes before guests arrive so that he doesn't associate the restraint with people arriving. If he associates negative emotions with guests arriving, he will view the entire experience as negative. Place the muzzle on the dog as naturally as attaching a lead. Give him a treat that he can lick through the muzzle, such as processed cheese spread. If the muzzle cues that a treat is forthcoming, having it put on will be a positive, or at the least, a neutral affair. The muzzle will not teach the dog not to bite, it is just a safety precaution, allowing him to be in the room with guests to learn that they are not a threat. If he growls, squirt him in the face and command, "Quiet." If he learns to respond without aggression, fit the muzzle a little looser with every session. Don't remove the muzzle until you are absolutely sure the dog has shown no indications of aggression. Be prepared to observe and act very quickly should he show any signs of reverting to aggressive behavior. Be prepared, as well, to take full responsibility for any poor judgments or injury to any persons involved no matter the circumstances.

SOCIALIZING WITH OTHER DOGS

Many of the social problems between dogs are the result of removing puppies from the litter too early. These dogs do not get adequate time during their most formative social period to learn proper canine etiquette. In the litter, dogs learn discipline and critical canine body language soon after weaning. As the puppies become more playful and annoying, the dam's corrections become stronger and more meaningful. At the same time, the littermates establish a hierarchy of power and body language to communicate social position. The puppies learn how to read body language through playing, fighting, eating together, and passing each other in a limited area. A submissive puppy learns not to approach the dominant puppy of the litter with a pounce because retaliation is sure to follow. When puppies miss these lessons, they never learn how to approach an older or dominant dog. Even the puppy who goes to a home with other dogs rarely gets experience equal to the interaction of littermates. These puppies will often lunge to play with another dog, regardless of the animal's size or its warning signals of irritation. The older dog that is annoyed or threatened may even snap at the puppy. The experience is usually very frightening to the puppy, and he can become apprehensive when greeting other dogs. He may even learn a defensive, growling approach to ward off other dogs. The growling causes fights, and each interaction intensifies the problem. Dogs must learn not to approach with a lunge or growl.

When two dogs are brought together, each should sit at his handler's side until he has had a minute to observe the other dog from a distance. Be very observant of any signs that indicate fear and/or ag-

Littermates establish a hierarchy through play, fighting,
and other social contact.

gression, such as raised hackles, staring, low growling, mounting, etc.
When no sign of aggression is evident, permit the dogs to sniff each
other on a loose lead. Be ready to pop back on the lead should either
of the dogs become tense, but keep the lead loose so as not to communicate your tension through it. Your tension may cue the dog to be
on guard for trouble. A chain reaction of tension will follow, often resulting in a fight. Once the dogs sniff each other and accept the close
contact without any evidence of an impending altercation, they will
usually relax and play or at least ignore each other.

Deal with aggressive gestures immediately. If the dog lunges,
growls, or mounts, command, "No" in a very firm, deep voice. Give him
a sharp collar correction and place him very close in a sit or down-stay.
If he moves, give him a collar correction that puts him back in the original stay position and spot. If the dog should continue to growl, give
him a harder snap on the collar, or if handy, a water correction with a
squirt bottle. Praise him when he is quiet. The dogs should not be
allowed to stare at each other because staring intensifies aggression.

Keep them a safe distance from each other, three to four feet apart, in a sit or down stay. Constant exposure to other dogs who are also under control, along with corrections to discourage aggressive behavior, will teach the dog to cope with being around others. I will never forget the first day Angel, a 120-pound Rottweiler bitch, dragged her owner into my class. The owner had called before class and asked if it was all right to bring Angel in on a pinch collar because she was very powerful and a little aggressive with other dogs. When the door opened and Angel saw the other dogs, she threw herself in the air with a full set of teeth exposed and the most vicious noise imaginable in spite of the pinch collar. My mouth dropped open as I stood there facing an image from a nightmare. The owner was a very sweet, soft-spoken lady who weighed about 98 pounds. My first words were, "I sure hope there is a very large and strong husband or boyfriend behind you." She said, "Yes, my husband is on his way in with our other Rottweiler." When he walked in, I just wanted to leave. The man weighed about 102 pounds. Luckily, Angel loved people, and we were able to muzzle her quickly. Angel worked in class for four weeks, receiving punishment for aggression and praise for tolerant behavior. The fifth week, a dog lunged at Angel and, with lightning speed, she turned away from the dog and toward her handler to avoid a correction. She must have decided that if she didn't look at the dog, it wasn't there. The sixth week we removed the muzzle after class when just a few trained dogs were present. Angel did sit-stays in the same room with them. We also allowed her to go up to crated dogs and sniff. The owner is still working with Angel around other dogs, but she can now walk Angel past dogs on leashes without eliciting aggressive behavior. Just recently, to my surprise and concern, the owner reported that Angel had struck up a relationship and even played with the dog next door, which she had an intense dislike for six months earlier. I cautioned her that Angel's sudden attitude change toward the dog next door does not mean that she will accept or play with all other dogs. The dog-aggressive animal may never be safe to let loose or play with other dogs. On the other hand, you can't teach the aggressive dog to accept the presence of others if he's isolated from them.

To avoid aggression between newly introduced dogs make arrangements to have them meet on neutral territory. The neutral ground will discourage the natural tendency each dog has to protect his own perceived territory. Using a Mikki muzzle is a good way to prevent injury while teaching a dog to tolerate the close proximity of others. Be sure to put the muzzle on him several minutes before the dogs are intro-

Introduce new dogs on neutral territory
and use a sit-stay to keep them
at a safe distance while you watch
for cues of aggression.

duced and offer him treats when the muzzle is in place. With patience, dogs can learn to practice constraint in the presence of each other.

INTRODUCING THE NEW DOG INTO THE HOME

Introducing another mature dog or even a puppy into your home can be a very delicate process. The initial meeting or first few days may not be eventful, and the original dog may even appear to welcome the new dog. But as time passes and the new dog becomes a fixture, they will begin to establish a social hierarchy, which can involve jealousy and fights. The first meeting of two dogs must be well supervised to prevent mishaps. In fact, newly acquainted dogs should not be left unsupervised for several weeks. Dogs may take three weeks or longer to adjust to a new or changed environment and adding another one to the household definitely changes the environment.

If possible, the first meeting between two mature dogs should be on neutral ground such as a park, or even down the street from home, to eliminate territorial behavior. Whether the meeting is on neutral territory or one dog's home turf, both dogs should be on loose leads, and controlled. One dog lunging or straining at his lead to get to the other could get the first time greeting off on the wrong foot. Allow the dogs to sniff each other on loose leads after they have sat for a few seconds to evaluate the situation. You can place one dog, usually the softer-tempered one, in a crate so that the other dog can sniff safely, and then you can proceed by having both dogs on a loose lead. If there are no signs of a forthcoming altercation, allow the dogs more lead to investigate each other. Pet each dog to communicate to them your acceptance of each animal. Initial playing should be permitted only on lead to limit unnecessary roughness, which might irritate one of the dogs and precipitate a fight. When the dogs appear accepting of each other, walk them into the house together so that one does not establish the house as territory during this meeting.

If the dogs show aggression, give them a harsh "no" command along with sharp collar corrections. Keep the dogs sitting until they calm down and relax. The first argument may indicate that they aren't compatible, and that a feud is in the offering. Some dogs never willingly accept newcomers, and you must spend much of your time on riot control. A good many dogs fight only when the owner is present because only then do they get excited enough to frenzy and jump around, bumping each other.

Obedience training is the key to keeping rival dogs under control. For instance, if when you come home you allow them to jump up and be out of control, there is a good risk of a fight. But if you make them

The dominant dog will often attack another dog
entering his territory.

sit and wait for you to greet them, they won't get in each other's way. When dealing with well-trained dogs, you can often curtail aggression by a timely verbal "no" correction. For example, if you catch the dogs staring at each other or stiff walking past each other, send a strong verbal "no" and defuse the aggression before a fight starts. Supervise all potentially tense situations, such as mealtime where the dogs may attempt to usurp each other's bowls. Don't permit either dog to eat from the bowl of the other.

You must also determine which dog is dominant or the aggressor, and always let the underdog into the yard or into the house first. The dominant dog is sure to attack the underdog that enters a territory the dominant dog has already claimed, but he will be very reluctant to attack the dog that already has possession of the territory. To prevent competition for toys, supply enough so that possession does not become a serious problem. Although dogs should be permitted to protect possessions in their own domain from other dogs only, not all dogs will respect the other's territory. Don't allow unreasonable confinement where one dog restricts the movement of the other around the house or intimidates the other when interacting with family members. Close supervision of two dogs who are not exactly best friends may be a long-term situation.

INTRODUCING A NEW PUPPY

To avoid overwhelming a new puppy when introducing him to an older dog, place him in a crate and let the older dog sniff through the openings. Occasionally, older dogs may appear frightened or very apprehensive about young puppies. The odor of the puppy may be so novel and strange that the dog does not comprehend that the new puppy is a canine. The dog may be so confused or threatened by the wiggly little creature that he may lash out with a snap. If the inexperienced puppy is very obnoxious and fearless, he may not heed the warnings of the older dog, and he can receive an angry bite. Conversely, the older dog may also relentlessly badger the puppy to play, making the puppy apprehensive or fearful. The older dog, that usually has more endurance, may expect the puppy to play unceasingly. Monitor the two dogs' play time or interactions until the puppy is understanding and responding to the older dog's language.

If the older dog snaps at the puppy out of annoyance or to ward him off, but with no intent to hurt him, do not correct the older dog. The older dog is communicating to the puppy, and the puppy must learn to heed such warnings. If the dog delivers an actual bite, the puppy probably did not pay attention to the warnings and the older dog stepped up the correction. These dogs must now be closely supervised, and the older dog must be corrected for the overly aggressive correction. If the puppy continues to ignore the meaning of the bite, the bites will get worse. These little altercations can easily turn into serious and frequent aggression when the puppy matures. Correct the older dog for the bite with a strong snap of the handle, and teach the puppy to stop annoying the older dog. When the older dog growls or snaps, or you suspect he is going to bite, a strong "No," or "Stop it" is in order. Both dogs should be commanded to "settle." Use "stop it" and "settle" whenever the puppy gets too wound up pestering the older dog.

Many socialization problems may be avoided if the puppy remains in the litter for the 9 1/2-to-10 weeks it takes to learn how to be a dog. Many breeders place their dogs with their new owners at 7 weeks because they are under the misconception that if they place the dog later, the bonding process to the new owner will not be as effective. The learned social behavior provided by the breeder through feeding and handling the pups will generalize to the new owner even after 7 weeks; therefore, the puppy does not have to be placed earlier to optimize bonding with the new owner. A puppy that is removed from the litter at 7 weeks may be robbed of crucial social litter experiences that could prevent many adjustment problems in a new home. Consequently, these puppies may have emotional difficulty socializing with other dogs. At 8 weeks of age the dog moves into the puppy fear or sensitive period. At this age, incidents in the puppy's environment can traumatize him relatively easily. The most ordinary events may frighten the puppy and have a profound and possibly lasting effect on his personality. A new home, no matter how wonderful, is a drastic change in the puppy's environment and is inherently stressful. The sensitive period is compounded for the 8-week-old that is placed in a new home and experiences anxiety associated with separation from the litter, new people, new rules, and maybe even a new, older, jealous dog to cope with on top of everything else. The puppy's immune system is further strained by a visit to the veterinarian for the customary health check and puppy shots. Housebreaking is stressful for a dog owner, and probably more stressful for the 8-week-old puppy, particularly if the new owner doesn't take the inevitable accidents on the carpet in the best possible frame of mind. Much stress can be eliminated for the pup if he remains in the familiar, stable environment of the litter for another week or two. Recently, the state where I live passed a law that makes the sale, transfer, release, or adoption of a canine under the age of 8 weeks old unlawful. This law was passed in recognition of the developmental immaturity of dogs under 8 weeks of age.

At 9 to 10 weeks old, the pup is generally past the sensitive period. The puppy steadily and gradually shows more confidence, curiosity, and willingness to learn. This older puppy will, generally, whine and cry less after being separated from the litter, be more prepared to learn than a younger, more stressed dog, and house train much easier than the younger pup because he has better control of his elimination system. Consequently, the owner's interactions with the puppy will be more positive and nurturing. In general, taking home the older pup will be less stressful to you, the pup, and your household, and he will be better able to learn how to socialize with other dogs.

Puppies should remain in the litters for 9-1/2 to 10 weeks
so they can learn socialization skills.

Photo by Deloris Reinke

Surviving Life with Multiple Dogs

Living with, and training more than one dog presents a whole new set of problems that don't exist in the single-dog home. Problem behaviors such as aggression, excitability, house soiling, etc., are compounded and multiplied by the number of dogs in the household. One dog may learn from another by joining him in a problem behavior. Unfortunately, very seldom do the dogs learn good behaviors; they usually learn all the behaviors you would rather they did not learn.

If you own two dogs, take the worse-behaved one to an obedience class and train the other one at home. Then switch; take the dog that you trained at home to obedience class to give him the experience of the class and other dogs. Work both dogs individually at home, and sometimes together. Many trainers adamantly discourage people from getting two puppies at the same time or from the same litter. While two puppies are double the trouble, trainers are also concerned that the dogs will bond with each other rather than the owner. But you can avoid that problem if you take the time to train both dogs separately. Obedience training provides quality one-on-one interaction time with each dog which facilitates bonding with the owner. And in any event, you must train each dog individually before attempting to train or work the unified pack. Once each dog has learned the basic exercises, train both at the same time, and enforce each command. If you command them to sit, both must sit. If one dog sits and the other doesn't, correct the dog that did not sit, and don't be surprised when the other one pops up and you have to reset him too. Two dogs take double the effort. Work the dogs in a small space so they cannot escape. The area should have few distractions and a low noise level at first. Add distractions later by practicing in different places and environments after the dogs obey the commands in the controlled training area. Training two dogs may be a time-consuming commitment initially, requiring ten-to-fifteen minutes a day with each dog and ten minutes of training together. After the dogs are trained, a ten-minute session a week, or using the exercises in the normal course of living, should maintain a well-trained pack.

Practice, patience, and unrelenting enforcement of the commands are the key to training. The reward for you is well-behaved dogs that contribute sanity to what might otherwise be a chaotic household.

Introducing the Dog to a New Baby

Many owners are rightfully concerned about introducing a new baby into a home where a dog has been the sole surrogate child for several years. Some people seek professional advice, while others get rid of the dog.

Careful supervision is paramount when the newcomer is brought into the house. The scent of the baby may be so foreign to the dog that he may not even realize the baby is a human. At first, most dogs are afraid of babies; in some cases, afraid enough to bite. The mere idea of such a disastrous interaction between a dog and child is a very strong incentive to gain maximum control of the dog's behavior. You should enroll the dog in an obedience school before the baby arrives.

Occasionally, dogs will exhibit strange and bizarre behavior toward the pregnant member of the household. This behavior may include urinating on the bed, or even aggression. The dog may sense an alteration in the woman's hormones or pheromones and react to these changes out of anxiety. If the pregnant woman can obedience train the dog, this may help the dog adjust to the changes.

Arrange for the dog to go out on a walk or stay with the neighbors when you bring the baby home to allow time to settle the baby into the house. The dog may be somewhat less protective of his territory if the baby is already in the house when he returns from the outing. Place him on lead, and observe him carefully for signs of fear or aggression. Let the dog sniff the baby in the other parent's arms. You can make a touching chain by holding the baby and touching the dog. Hold the baby's hand and offer a treat to the dog. Should the dog act fearful, command him to settle. If he becomes aggressive, correct the dog with a collar snap. Then command and enforce a down-stay. Carefully evaluate his actions and determine the liability of having an aggressive dog around a child. Should the aggression not subside immediately, for the child's protection, remove the dog from the home and consult with a knowledgeable professional.

When a new baby arrives, so do the visitors. Do not isolate the dog when visitors arrive or fuss over the baby, or he may learn to resent the new family structure. If you must contain the dog, crate him in the mainstream of activity so that he doesn't feel isolated and deprived of social contact.

The attention you give the new baby will inevitably result in a decrease of time and attention you give to the dog, and he'll surely feel it. This perceived neglect can manifest itself in problem behavior. An obedience course, even if the dog has previously attended one, can provide him with individual attention and enforce obedient behavior. But even the most obedient, loving animal should never be left unsupervised with the baby or any young child. No one can predict when the dog may become upset by the actions of an energetic, unsuspecting child, and the results can be devastating. For the child, the physical and emotional scars can be permanent; for the dog, an incident that could have been prevented with good management might mean the loss of his happy home, or even his life.

15

Spoiling and Games

Indulging a dog, or what some people term "spoiling" a dog does not cause behavior problems or the loss of dominance over him. You don't lose dominance status because you allow the dog certain comforts. Rather, you never established dominance in the first place if these comforts appear to alter the social structure between the two of you. If you allow your dog to lie on the couch and he becomes aggressive when you command him to get off he's not exhibiting dominance because of being allowed on the couch. This dog had a preconceived notion of dominance that was not resolved between you and the dog long before the couch incident. The aggression associated with the couch is just a display of the dog's dominant behavior. Keeping him off the couch doesn't resolve the dominant behavior; it will simply manifest at some other opportunity. Once the social and power status has been determined between you and your dog, you can only lose dominance or control if you cease to win challenges or enforce commands.

Janet L. Yosay

The dog that protests when you command him to get off the couch must be firmly taken off the couch and reprimanded with a collar snap or shake correction. Command him to get on and off the couch until he stops protesting. Handle letting him sleep in bed the same way. Snuff out any protests from him immediately when you command him to get off or move. He'll learn that these comforts are available only at your will.

Petting and touching the dog is an important aspect of the human-canine relationship. It is an extreme pleasure enjoyed immensely by both parties. To limit petting for fear of losing dominance to the dog is a horrible and unnecessary restriction, and is contrary to a close relationship between you and your dog. Imagine being instructed not to kiss your child, or worse yet, make the child earn the kiss by doing something. Loving relationships are built on touching and strong unrestricted displays of affection. The dog should not have to perform all the time to get a pat on the head or a stroke on the back. Neither should you allow him to pester you constantly for attention. The owner

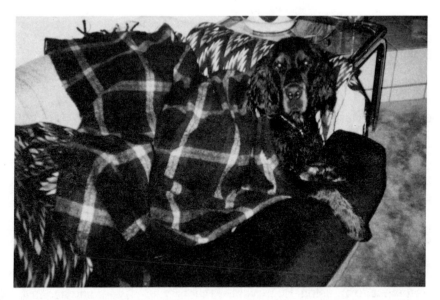

Allowing the dog human comforts does not weaken your authority unless you fail to enforce your authority when desired.

who has established a healthy relationship with his or her dog has the ability to control when petting is acceptable and unacceptable by simply teaching and enforcing a "stop it" or "settle" command.

Giving your dog people food doesn't have to turn him into a hardened table beggar. If he begs at the table, command and enforce a "settle" away from the table.

Spoiling your dog is a perfectly acceptable prerogative, as long as you maintain control by imposing and enforcing rules when necessary. As long as it is not confused with lack of discipline or allowing protests to go unchallenged and corrected, spoiling a dog does not produce behavior problems. Spoiling provides the opportunity for the owner to teach the dog when certain behaviors are permitted and not permitted.

Games

Dog games are an excellent and fun way to interact with the dog, as long as the game is played according to the owner's rules, not the dog's. Anytime during the game the dog gets out of hand and/or too aggressive, correct him. Take time out and command him to settle for a while before you resume the game. The one rule that holds for all games is that the dog is not allowed to plant teeth on any human body part. Even if he is soft-mouthed or never applies pressure, permitting mouthing risks injury. Consider the following scenario: A young child enters the house of a mouthy dog. The dog interprets the jerky or un-coordinated movements of the young child as play. He takes hold of the child's arm, and the child becomes frightened. The child attempts to pull away, and the dog applies a little more pressure to hold on to the arm. The child becomes more frightened, pulls harder, and may even use the other hand to hit the dog. The dog, intending only to play, could cause very serious injury to a fragile young arm, which will result in a very expensive lawsuit. I was once explaining to my class that a bite and ensuing scar could cost the owner $10,000 in damages, when a fellow started to laugh. Annoyed at the interruption of what I thought to be a very serious topic, I asked the gentleman why he found my statement so amusing. He explained that he was a lawyer and had just tried and won a case for a bite victim who was awarded $75,000, and there wasn't even a scar. Every game played with a dog can be played without permitting him to use teeth on body parts. Rags or toys can be tugged on instead of arms. If the dog nips or gets close to your body, give him a shake or cuff correction. Let him calm down and resume the game later. Even the gentlest dog can make a mistake or become rough as he gets more excited.

FETCH

Fetch with a ball, Frisbee, or stick spends a lot of the dog's energy. All dogs, even those not bred specifically for retrieving, have at some time during their puppyhood, retrieved something. It may have been an old shoe, a sock, or other item which may not have been intended for the dog's mouth. Dogs have a basic tendency to carry things in their mouths, and any dog can learn to retrieve on command. The best way to teach retrieving is by using a toy the dog loves. Place the dog on a lead and throw the toy a very short distance as you command "Fetch." Praise him for retrieving. For the first few throws, go after the object with him so that he gets the idea to run after the object and you don't accidentally pop him with the lead. Next, let the dog chase the object alone. Repeat the process throwing the toy a little farther each time he successfully retrieves the object. If the dog does not naturally chase and pick up inanimate objects, contact an obedience instructor to help

Most dogs love
to chase and
retrieve a ball,
stick, or Frisbee.

teach him. A knowledgeable trainer can teach any dog to retrieve. Even if a dog hates the game at first, he will eventually grow to love retrieving if it involves lots of motivation and reinforcement.

Most dogs will chase and retrieve a thrown object; the problem may be that the dog does not bring back the object. In that case, put him on a long line or retractable lead. When you play fetch, throw the object and command, "Fetch," or "Take." When the dog picks the object up, give a light snap on the lead and reel him in close. Command "Thank you," "Give," or "Drop it" and offer him a treat. Praise him and give him a treat for letting go of the object. If the dog does not let go for the treat, take the object out of his mouth and praise him. Continue to throw the object with the dog on a line until he is reliably bringing back the object. The first time you command him to retrieve without the line, do it in a small room or area so that the dog cannot get away or become distracted and run in another direction. If he does run off with the object, don't run after him. Running after him teaches him a new game: "keep away." Few people can catch a dog who is playing "keep away." The best tactic is to run away from the dog, who will naturally chase you; then the game becomes your game and you are in control. Praise the dog when he catches you. Be careful not to grab at him; that will also reinforce the "keep away" game. If you cannot get hold of him, run to a small enclosed area, drop to the ground, and act very silly. When the dog comes over to see what the problem is, you can take hold of the handle. This only works once or twice, so get the dog into an obedience class and teach him to return on command. If the dog doesn't run after you, stop playing. He will probably stand bewildered for a little while and then come over and drop the toy at your feet. Resume the game and stop again if he does not give up the toy.

SWIMMING

Retrieving is also a good motivator to teach the dog to swim. Most dogs will chase objects into the water. At the start, throw the object near the shoreline to get the dog used to the water, and increase distance when he doesn't seem reluctant about the water. The method I like best for teaching a dog to swim if they don't learn on their own by chasing objects into the water, is to carry the dog into the water just far enough so that he cannot touch bottom. I gently put him in the water and face him toward the shoreline. The first few times, I follow him as I lightly hold him around the sides while he swims to shore. Once he seems confident, I let him go the distance on his own. When he's confident about swimming and enjoys retrieving, I put the two together by throwing objects in the water. To encourage the novice swimmer, I always bring along an experienced canine swimmer to join in on the fun. Until I am sure the dog is physically conditioned to swim distance without exhaustion, I keep a floating line attached so that I can retrieve him if necessary. Swimming is great exercise and a lot of dogs love it as a game.

TUG-OF-WAR

Many pet professionals believe that dog owners should avoid playing tug-of-war with their dogs because the dogs may interpret the game as a battle for dominance. There is no evidence to suggest that the owner's control is diminished by playing tug-of-war. Dogs love playing it, and the game is a good release for pent up energy. The problem that does crop up in tug-of-war is hand nipping by the overzealous dog that grabs the rag closer and closer to your hand. Take even an accidental nip seriously, and correct the behavior with a shake or cuff.

A planned game of tug-of-war is very different from the game played by herding dogs when they pull on a person's pant leg. Correct this behavior with a squirt in the face from a water bottle containing very, very cold water. Pet owners often find this behavior amusing until the dog accidentally knocks down and hurts a child or rips an expensive pair of pants, and the legal bill comes in the mail.

TACKLE

Tackle is a full-body contact game in which the dog may become overly excited and place teeth on body parts. You can play tackle without permitting the dog to nip or bite appendages. A good, firm cuff or shake often deters nipping behavior. Tackle is probably more fun for the owner than the dog, because being tackled or restrained is usually not pleasant for any species. In fact, being restrained is so little fun for the dog, he may get aggressive. A dog feels very threatened by restraint, and his reaction may be to bite in defense. Correct the biting with a good cuff or shake, then consider playing another game. There are many other games that both parties can enjoy. However, a defensive bite may be a good reason to play the game again, to teach the dog that biting is unacceptable. A time may come when you will need to physically restrain the dog, and the game of tackle is a good way to desensitize him to it. Require that the dog submit, relax, or discontinue the struggle before you let him up from your grip and end the game. This is also a good opportunity to desensitize him to rough handling which he may encounter from children or special populations with coordination difficulties. Gentle squeezing of the paws, tugging of the ears, tail, and skin while playing or in a playful manner can help the dog accept unintentional rough handling. During petting, he can learn to enjoy hard pats in between gentle strokes.

HIDE-AND-SEEK

There are two ways to play hide-and-seek. You yourself may hide, or you may hide an object or piece of food for the dog to find. Start by making the hiding places very simple and in the dog's view, such as placing the biscuit under a paper or tissue or you hiding behind a chair. Initially, allow the dog to watch as you hide or hide the treat so that he'll catch on to the game faster. Tell him to "wait." Don't let him jump the gun. After you hide the object, command the dog to "find" or "fetch" as you let go of him. When he finds you or the object, give him lots of praise. Make the hiding places a little harder each time he succeeds in finding the prize. Dogs quickly learn to use their nose on the command "go find." The game could become so much fun, you might want to find a book on teaching him tracking and scent discrimination.

TRICKS

The easiest and most enjoyable way for a dog to earn praise is through tricks. You can quickly turn obedience training into entertainment for the dog, yourself, and many other people. Once the dog knows the basic obedience commands, you can modify these exercises into tricks. There are several books available on the subject. You can also easily turn behaviors into tricks by attaching a command to them and praising the dog. You can give a command such as "shake" whenever the dog naturally lifts his paw. Then praise him. When the dog finds a behavior that tickles a funny bone or elicits admiration, you can be assured he will repeat it. Tricks are a good break from the mundane and can relieve stress in a variety of circumstances. Tricks can endear the animal to the most hardened dog hater. Very importantly, tricks can be a good way for the dog to willingly earn praise, and a good reason to give him praise.

16
Formal Obedience Training

Through obedience training a dog can feel more secure and confident about how to behave and how his owner will react to him. Even the dog that does not exhibit problem behavior will benefit from obedience training by learning his owner's language. Obedience teaches the dog to associate certain events and behaviors with his owner's body and verbal language. This private communication line enriches the human-canine companion relationship.

Training should begin when you bring the dog home. Ideally, well before he is 6 months of age. If you acquire an older dog, you should also begin training the day he arrives. Old dogs *can* learn new tricks.

The first objective, no matter how old the dog is, is to teach him the rules of the house. Make sure he has all the appropriate inoculations before obedience classes start.

Puppies are fast learners. Training obedience before a dog has acquired bad habits, grown a full set of enamel weaponry, gained 120 pounds, and crowned himself leader is very sound practice. Training the young puppy must be a positive educational process rather than a series of harsh corrections. A competent professional trainer who has a good working knowledge about behavior can teach you to train the puppy with a buckle collar and positive motivation rather than through the use of aversive tactics. Aversive devices and tactics should only be used when there are no other choices, and the health and welfare of the owner, community, or dog are at risk. Such methods may damage the relationship between you and your dog. You should use them only under the guidance of a qualified professional.

The older dog may appear not to learn as quickly as the young puppy. The older dog has more life experience to draw on which may interfere with the new learning. Old habits will be more resistant to extinction. These habits may take longer to change than teaching new habits to a puppy that does not already have an established pattern of behavior. But you can teach the older dog, like the puppy, by motivational techniques rather than corrective methods.

The difference between motivational and corrective techniques is the manner in which the obedience exercises are taught. For example, teaching the "down" position with motivational methods might include either food and/or gentle physical placement of the dog and lots of praise, whereas the corrective technique may involve jerking him to the ground by the collar, often with no praise or very minimal positive reinforcement. A good training class teaches with motivational methods or positive reinforcement, and uses gentle punishment techniques only after the dog has learned the material, to enforce the commands as necessary.

Puppy Classes

The recent trend in various areas of the country is to distinguish between obedience classes for puppies and older dogs. Puppy classes are usually called kindergarten or socialization classes. These classes are for pups 16 weeks old and younger. Review the class content and exercise caution when contemplating entering a puppy in a kindergarten class. Many kindergarten classes set up a free-for-all play time with other puppies which might be fine if all breeds and temperaments were equal. The 16-week-old Rottweiler's style of play might not be a good match for the 16-week-old Toy Poodle. More than two dogs playing at the same time could be a serious free-for-all disaster. Recently, I read an article that discussed a puppy class that let twenty puppies play together at the same time with two staff members supervising. Chaos can only be the result if an altercation were to happen. Should the format of the class include free play time, keep a sharp eye on the reactions of the puppies. In my practice, I have seen several dogs that attended kindergarten classes where free-for-all play was part of the curriculum, and the effects on some of the puppies led to fear and aggression with other dogs as they got older.

Puppy preschool is generally structured for dogs 6 months of age and younger. The classes are formed for the sole purpose of socializing the puppies while the owners swap puppy stories, and the class outline consists mostly of games for puppies to play. Until the puppy is reliably trained, you may want to make sure the games are conducted on lead so that he doesn't learn that you have little control when the lead is off. The benefit for the puppy is positive social interactions with other people and puppies. The experiences the puppy has in preschool, both positive and negative, will have a strong influence on shaping the dog's adult personality. A good training school will assign only experienced assistants to supervise the preschool classes, because they are aware of the profound influence early experiences have on a young dog. Puppy play must be directed and supervised by a knowledgeable professional who is qualified to recognize situations that may have the potential to overwhelm or stress the ordinary puppy. A developing puppy personality must be nurtured in a confidence-building environment, not in an atmosphere where the puppy is the victim of another puppy bully. Puppy classes can be fun for the dog and owner, and are good supplements to a formal obedience course. However, these classes cannot substitute for formal obedience training which should start simultaneously to take advantage of the formative developmental learning phase the puppy goes through before he is 6 months old.

Puppy classes are often deficient on socializing the puppy with adult dogs and in providing basic formal obedience training. The puppy's most formative developmental period is the ideal time to be teaching the canine proper manners. Young puppies are attentive, prepared to learn, and, in the case of the larger breed puppies, still of a reasonable weight and size for even the most petite owner to control. Begin formal training during early puppyhood with the guidance of a professional adept in teaching positive motivational techniques. Because many trainers are under the misconception that formal obedience training needs to be done with choke and pinch collars, basic obedience is not emphasized in puppy classes to avoid harsh treatment and adverse effects on a youngster's personality. Puppies and older dogs can be taught very effectively without being choked or pinched with collars.

Obedience Classes

Classes for older dogs are called obedience classes. Class content and description will vary with each trainer. The ideal class is open to dogs of all ages and offers structured socialization with people and dogs, basic obedience, and problem solving. The class should also address canine behavior problems. Preventing behavior problems in puppies is critical, and for those who own older dogs, resolving behavior problems may be their primary reason for seeking training classes. The class should be based on gentle methods that can be used on dogs of all ages. There should be no difference between the methods used for

Obedience classes are open to dogs of all ages and offer basic obedience, problem solving, and structured socialization with other people and dogs.

training the puppy and those used to train the adult dog. If the class is not suitable for puppies, or if the class is just for puppies, it's not an all-around educational experience.

Finding Quality Canine Education

The demand for professional, quality education for dogs and their owners is increasing. Several organizations around the country are searching for a standard of excellence and a national accreditation program for dog training professionals. Currently, canine education in the United States differs in philosophy, content, and especially in quality from area to area. Not all canine education programs are equal. Local training schools or clubs may endorse different philosophies or programs simply because a particular trainer is a member of the club. Therefore, when looking for a trainer, research and observe classes at more than one training school to find the best class before enrolling.

Individuals who teach canine behavior and obedience classes must be more than dog trainers. The instructor must possess the qualities of an educator and be an expert on the topic of canine learning and behavior. Many problem behaviors start in puppyhood and are difficult for the novice eye to recognize. An expert on canine learning and behavior will be adept at recognizing problems and teaching the dog owner to modify behaviors before serious problems develop. A good educator possesses the ability to communicate ideas and information to others at different paces and levels and is masterful at problem solving and adapting to individual learning styles, human and canine. A competent, ethical professional will only teach material he or she has personally mastered.

REFERENCES

Recommendations from friends are a good start, however, friends may have only been exposed to one trainer and a limited variety of techniques which may not be the best trainer or technique. These people may not have had exposure to different trainers, and therefore, cannot make an equivocal comparison between one trainer and another. There may be several trainers or behavior consultants who specialize in different areas. Not all trainers are equal. Many people call themselves pet specialists and have very little understanding or experience with canine behavior. Some of these specialists may not even own a trained dog. An incompetent trainer can make the obedience experience very unpleasant, and the dog owner usually winds up blaming him/herself for not understanding the material, or even worse, blaming the dog. If the dog has a negative experience, he will hate obedience and his owner seldom follows through with training him. Request verification of a trainer's credentials. A good list of references would include character references, people who have attended his or her class, and other professionals and experts in the pet industry, such as veterinarians, groomers, and breeders.

EVALUATING THE SCHOOL

While most people are probably not willing to relocate their residence so their dog can attend the best obedience school in the country, don't decide to enroll your dog in a particular school solely because of location, cost, or the glamour of the facility. The quality of the staff and school has nothing to do with the price of the facility, the size of their ad in the local paper, or how close the facility is to home. As a general rule, competent professionals advertise their expertise and qualifications, not the beauty of the facility they rent or own. In fact be on alert for trainers who fill up the ad with information about the condition and location of their facilities. Prices vary as much as the experience and competency of the instructor, but they are not always representative of the instructor's ability. High prices do not insure competency; then again, when the price is low, you often get what you pay for.

Observe at least one of the instructor's classes before enrolling, and focus on watching the dog owners and the instructor. If you can observe more than one class, also track the progress of individual dogs. The behavior of the dogs during a one-time observation may not be a good gauge of the quality of the class. Some dogs may have previous training, or perhaps the dog that was pulling on the lead the third week of class could not walk on lead at all the previous week. The quality of the dog class is dependent upon the instructor's ability to obtain and maintain command of the class with good communication skills, easy-to-follow demonstrations, a well-planned course outline organized in a logical, progressive, sequential format, a professional attitude, and much knowledge of canine behavior and dog obedience. The class should encourage the participation and interaction of all its members. An adroit educator does not necessarily have all the answers, but he or she will have the resources to find the answers when called upon to do so.

Finding the best trainer and class may take some effort, but living with a dog is a ten-to-fifteen year emotional and financial investment, and his behavior may dictate whether you wake up in the morning or walk through the door at night after a long, hard day with a smile on your face.

QUALIFICATIONS FOR TRAINERS

Currently, trainers are not professionally licensed or certified, but there are a few organizations that offer endorsement such as the National Association of Dog Obedience Instructors, or the Animal Behavior Society. These organizations require that the trainer take an essay exam, and report books read, seminars and classes attended, and any other experiences that have enhanced their training expertise. One such experience is having earned obedience titles. In order to earn titles, the trainer and dog must perform a standard group of exercises according to a predetermined level of performance that is judged to be the measure of a well-trained dog. Utility, the highest level of obedience, can be very taxing on the dog and on the trainer's ability. A utility title may be a good qualification to consider when choosing between trainers.

A trainer who has lived with and trained a diversity of dogs—males, females, and several different breeds—will be more capable of understanding a wider variety of dog problems than the trainer who has only trained and lived with one single dog and one dog breed. Beyond gender and breed differences, the behavior problems in a multiple-dog home are very different from the problems in a single-dog home.

When looking for a trainer, it is appropriate to not only observe classes and ask for references and credentials, but to talk with the trainer to uncover any possible philosophical or personality conflicts as well.

QUALIFICATIONS FOR BEHAVIOR CONSULTANTS

Behaviorists, as trainers, are not yet required to be professionally licensed or certified. A behaviorist or behavior consultant should have the same qualifications as a trainer, with additional educational background in animal learning and behavior, and psychology. Theory has tremendous importance in furthering knowledge; however, when it comes to domestic dogs, practical experience is also imperative for the behavior consultant. A behavior consultant who can suggest solutions to problems must also be capable of implementing those solutions.

He or she needs to know practical, easy methods the dog owner can follow and maintain with regularity. The behavior consultant must not only determine a dog's problem areas and offer real-world solutions to them, he or she must also be capable of assessing the owner, the relationship, and the dog's environment.

The Dog's View of Obedience Class

At the start, the dog may well act like he hates obedience class and hide whenever he sees the leash. For dogs who have had their own way, being dethroned by having to obey is not a pleasant experience. A dog that is used to running the household will be resistant to change. Classes may also be unpleasant at first for the dog that has never been out of the backyard or around other dogs and people. The class environment can be frightening for the dog that has not been socialized. Fortunately, dogs are social animals that look for and happily accept leadership. Only if you don't supply leadership will your dog take control of your relationship or the household. Eventually, he'll not only accept gentle and firm guidance, he may even grow to enjoy obedience class. If the dog does not ever appear to enjoy the class, reevaluate the training methods you are using to determine if they are adequately motivating him.

Dogs who enter obedience classes are expected to be very unruly; if they were well-mannered, paying an instructor would be unnecessary. Therefore, be assured that you and your unruly dog are very welcomed to class. Often an owner is embarrassed about his or her dog's behavior and quits class to avoid disrupting the rest of the class. Many people who have overly rambunctious dogs run or work the dogs before class to tire them so that they won't be embarrassed. Unless you want to keep running the dog indefinitely to control his behavior, you should give your instructor the opportunity to see and work with him when he is fresh and energetic. If the dog does not exhibit the behavior in class that you are attempting to change, your instructor may not be able to help you work out the problems. Additionally, the exhausted dog is not going to learn very much from class if he is thinking more about sleeping than working. If your dog is truly disruptive or dangerous to the rest of the class, the trainer may choose to work with the two of you individually to achieve some control before you re-enter the class. However, if he or she asks you to permanently work off by yourself, find

Training fosters clear expectations and positive communication.

another school. If you are told not to come back because of your unruly dog, find a competent trainer next time. Don't give up. That is what obedience training is all about—changing the unruly dog's behavior—and a competent trainer can help you achieve that goal.

Dogs often become either very frightened or very excited during their first appearances at dog class. But this is to be expected, particularly if the dog has not been well socialized. A competent instructor will guide you in a positive approach to overcome your dog's fear and excitement. Avoiding class because the dog is unruly or frightened won't teach him to overcome his fear or contain his excitement.

Another phenomenon that frequently occurs in dog class, is canine amnesia. The dog that knew how to sit at home thinks "sit" is a meaningless sound in class. Many dogs are very obedient at home, but they do not generalize the training to other environments. A dog is not trained until he obeys the commands in all environments. The only way a dog will learn that "sit" means to sit, whether in obedience class, on the street, or in the veterinarian's office, is to practice the training in these situations. Obedience class will help the dog understand that obedient behavior applies to environments with other people and dogs.

One eight-to-ten week class is not enough to train a dog to respond under every circumstance or to ensure a lifetime harmonious human-canine relationship. Socialization and obedience are continuous processes. Dogs should attend socialization and obedience classes throughout their first two years of life until their adult personalities are permanently formed.

17

Euthanasia

The death of a dog means the ending of a long-term friendship. The pain felt by the devoted pet owner upon the death of a dog may be as intense and devastating as the pain of losing a human relative or friend. In the past, the intense grief of bereaved pet owners has not been understood by other people and/or professionals, and as a result, has been sadly minimized. Only recently have research projects and support groups emerged that understand and deal with the painful emotions resulting from the death of an animal companion. Bereavement specialists are available in many areas to help people work through these emotions.

Grief may be experienced in a variety of ways, from shock, anger, and denial that the animal is dead, to severe depression, guilt, and physical illness. Each person grieves in his or her own way. There is no wrong way to grieve unless the grief is so intense that the person is capable of self-harm or of harming someone else. The duration of the

255

Even the best friendships must someday reach an end.

grief depends on the individual and the circumstances. Some people may begin their grieving process when the animal has been diagnosed with a terminal disease, while others may not experience the grief for months after the demise of an animal. Commonly, individuals grieve for up to a year, and longer in some cases. The pain only subsides with the passage of time. No one can make the pain go away, other people can only help a person work through the anguish.

Well-meaning relatives and friends may attempt to replace the pet, only to find that the bereaved person is not ready to have another pet. New pets may distract the person from grief, but they can never replace the deceased animal. A new pet may even be bitterly rejected; therefore, the decision to get a new pet must be discussed at length with the grieving person. The best help relatives and family can give is to listen with unconditional acceptance to the individual's feelings about the pet and the person's loss. All too often, the pet owner's feelings are denied or minimized with statements like, "Get a grip, it's just a dog, you can always get another one," or "When are you going to get over this?

It's been two days." Although relatives, co-workers, and friends may be a good support system for the grieving person, they may not be able to understand the feelings associated with the loss of a close pet relationship. If the person needs more help psychologists and bereavement specialists are a good option.

The severity of the reaction to the death of a dog is also dependent upon the circumstances under which the dog dies and the part the owner played in his death. One of the most difficult decisions some dog owners have to make is whether to euthanize a pet for one reason or another. Euthanasia involves a lethal injection into the dog's bloodstream to help him humanely die. This decision can be one of the hardest decisions in a person's life.

A pet owner may be forced to look at the option of euthanasia in the case of the sick or aggressive animal. Neither circumstance will make the decision easier or lessen the guilt for the owner. In either situation, the main concern is the quality of life for the dog. The sick animal may be in pain and have to be subjected to so many uncomfortable medical procedures that he will probably have a very low quality of life. The very old senile dog that becomes blind, deaf, and incontinent probably doesn't have a high quality of life either. Incontinence can be very stressful on the owner, particularly an owner on a limited budget or a renter who may not be able to afford replacement furniture and flooring. The aggressive dog may have a poor quality of life as a result of always being on alert, or being isolated and corrected. These problems detract from a close relationship, and the negative memories may remain with the owner for a long time. Euthanasia permits the owner to help these sick or miserable animals die a gentle death, before their quality of life drops to unbearable levels and the good memories are overshadowed by the memory of the suffering animal.

Quality of life, unfortunately, is not a black-and-white condition that a veterinarian or other professional can determine. Most professionals will agree that if a dog has a terminal disease and is in extreme pain, euthanasia is a very humane act. Unfortunately, not all circumstances are so clear cut, and each individual must decide for him or herself when euthanasia is the correct option for the pet. The criteria that a person uses to determine when to euthanize a pet are personal. However, veterinarians are obligated to give the pet owner options and guidance when faced with making a decision about euthanasia. The American Veterinarian Medical Association and veterinary colleges across the country are working very hard to educate and train veterinarians to compassionately counsel pet owners about the option of euthanasia.

As difficult as the decision to euthanize the sick dog may be, the decision to lay an aggressive one to rest may be more so. The aggressive or mentally ill dog may be physically healthy, and the owner often feels an enormous amount of guilt for euthanizing an apparently sound dog. But the quality of life for this dog may be as poor as that of a sick animal. Both dog and owner are constantly stressed by the prospect of potential confrontations. Under these conditions the relationship suffers greatly. The owner may withdraw from interacting with the dog and tension can build up in the household. Still, owners of aggressive dogs experience the same intense grief when forced to euthanize their dogs as any owner does when a pet suddenly dies or is euthanized because of physical illness.

Arrangements for the euthanasia and disposal of the deceased pet are often a very important aspect of working out grief. The pet owner has several choices about the process of euthanasia and disposal of the animal. One important choice is whether he or she wants to be present during the euthanasia.

You have the freedom to choose whether to be present during the death of your pet, and any decision you make is personal and correct. Some pet owners would rather remember their dogs alive and may not want to be present during the death, while other owners have a strong need and desire to be present during the euthanasia. Euthanasia is generally a humane, pain-free death. Veterinarians are usually quite willing to schedule time to explain the process to pet owners. The veterinarian may even have the Animal Hospital Association video *The Loss of Your Pet*, which sensitively explains and enacts an actual euthanasia. The video may ease the pet owner's fear about the procedure.

The pet owner also has the right to choose to perform a funeral, memorial service, or other ritual that may be of comfort to him or her. The place of death can be the veterinarian's office, or another place the veterinarian is willing to perform the service such as in the comfort of your home or backyard, where the dog can be helped to die in a relaxed and familiar atmosphere. The atmosphere in which your dog dies must be acceptable to you. If one veterinarian is not willing to work with your wishes, consult another veterinarian.

Most veterinarians will ask whether you want to have your dog buried or cremated. Like a human, a dog can be buried in a public burial area or you can purchase a plot at a pet cemetery along with a casket. There are various options in the decoration and price. If you choose cremation, you can ask for the cremains and have them stored

Determining quality of life is a complex and personal issue.

in the container of your choice. You may just wish to spread the cremains in a favorite or meaningful place.

A few organizations have the technology to preserve the pet in a lifelike monument. The processes range from freeze-drying the body to mixing the cremains in a pottery substance and forming a statue in the likeness of your dog. The local pet cemetery may have information on companies that construct these memorials.

Likewise, just as in dealing with our own deaths, preparations for the death of a pet are best done well before the event, when emotions and stress do not get in the way. Pet bereavement counselors can be very helpful in making arrangements for a pet's death.

For some, the urge to get a new dog when another is dying or has died is very strong. A new dog can be a good distraction and comfort. But don't expect him to duplicate the deceased dog in personality. All dogs are individuals and come with their own personalities. You will always be disappointed when trying to replace the deceased dog because no other dog will ever be him. The new dog deserves to be treated as an individual and loved for his own idiosyncrasies and unique behavior.